Narrative Prosthesis

Corporealities: Discourses of Disability

David T. Mitchell and Sharon L. Snyder, editors

Books available in the series:

"Defects": Engendering the Modern Body
  edited by Helen Deutsch and Felicity Nussbaum

Revels in Madness: Insanity in Medicine and Literature
  by Allen Thiher

Points of Contact: Disability, Art, and Culture
  edited by Susan Crutchfield and Marcy Epstein

A History of Disability
  by Henri-Jacques Stiker

Disabled Veterans in History
  edited by David A. Gerber

Narrative Prosthesis: Disability and the Dependencies of Discourse
  by David T. Mitchell and Sharon L. Snyder

Backlash Against the ADA: Reinterpreting Disability Rights
  edited by Linda Hamilton Krieger

The Staff of Oedipus: Transforming Disability in Ancient Greece
  by Martha L. Rose

Fictions of Affliction: Physical Disability in Victorian Culture
  by Martha Stoddard Holmes

Foucault and the Government of Disability
  edited by Shelley Tremain

Bodies in Commotion: Disability and Performance
  edited by Carrie Sandahl and Philip Auslander

Moving Beyond Prozac, DSM, and the New Psychiatry:
  The Birth of Postpsychiatry
  by Bradley Lewis

Disability in Twentieth-Century German Culture
  by Carol Poore

Concerto for the Left Hand: Disability and the Defamiliar Body
  by Michael Davidson

Disability Theory
  by Tobin Siebers

Narrative Prosthesis

Disability and the Dependencies of Discourse

David T. Mitchell and Sharon L. Snyder

Ann Arbor

The University of Michigan Press

Copyright © by the University of Michigan 2000
All rights reserved
Published in the United States of America by
The University of Michigan Press
Printed and bound by CPI Group (UK) Ltd, Croydon, CR0 4YY

2011   2010   2009   2008   5   4   3   2

A CIP catalog record for this book is available from the British Library.

Library of Congress Cataloging-in-Publication Data applied for
ISBN 0-472-09748-2 (alk. paper)
ISBN 0-472-06748-6 (pbk. : alk. paper)

ISBN 978-0-472-09748-7 (alk. paper)
ISBN 978-0-472-06748-0 (pbk. : alk. paper)

To our children, Cameron and Emma,
for their beautiful differences

Contents

Preface   Mapping Identity: Disability and
              Other "Marked" Bodies   ix

Introduction Disability as Narrative Supplement   1

Chapter 1.   Representation and Its Discontents: The Uneasy
              Home of Disability in Literature and Film   15

Chapter 2.   Narrative Prosthesis and the
              Materiality of Metaphor   47

Chapter 3.   Montaigne's "Infinities of Formes" and
              Nietzsche's "Higher Men"   65

Chapter 4.   Performing Deformity: The Making and
              Unmaking of Richard III   95

Chapter 5.   The Language of Prosthesis in *Moby-Dick*   119

Chapter 6.   Modernist Freaks and Postmodern Geeks: Literary
              Contortions of the Disabled Body   141

Afterword   "The first child born into the world was
              born deformed": Disability Representations
              in These Times   163

              Notes   179

              Works Cited   197

              Index   207

Preface

Mapping Identity: Disability and Other "Marked" Bodies

In the early 1990s, when we first decided to pursue disability studies as an area of professional inquiry, we were both in the middle of our dissertations. We would spend days churning out pages on our respective topics while promising ourselves that once they were complete, we could research our "real" interest—those emergent "cripples of Constantinople" in Mark Twain and drifting communes of postmodern disabled children populating the literature we were reading (ostensibly for other purposes). One of Sharon's readers commented in her "defense" that he thought her writing had become more effective when she grew less interested in her original topic. That's one way to achieve scholarly distance! Michael Awkward, one of Dave's dissertation advisors, in hearing about our new interest in disability studies, immediately encouraged him to think about researching wounded masculinity in Hemingway. After all, a dissertation on multiperspectival novels by women of color was not the stepping stone to an academic position for a white male Ph.D. candidate.

Ross Chambers, another of Dave's dissertation directors, could also be counted upon to be intrigued. One day he presented us with a road map of "marked bodies" in culture that has continued to guide us in our scholarly journey. The chart, scribbled on a yellow piece of legal paper, was labeled "Marked Bodies" and bulleted an array of identities that "marked" human bodies as Other. Under "Gender" femininity would be marked. Under "Race" all categories outside of Whiteness marked a deviance. Under "Sexuality" heterosexuality remained neutral, while gay men and lesbians were bulleted as "different." In each case the designations proved multiple and varied—a gay white man was not as "marked" as a black lesbian female, who received three marks; a white, straight woman had only the strike of gender designated in her listing; a black gay male received two inflections on the grid. What intrigued us most of all was that Chambers had added on the category of "disability" at the end of the chart, followed by a large question mark. Beneath it he commented, "I don't know how disability fits in here, but it would be interesting to theorize the problem." Thus began our efforts to reach an understanding of the difference that disability makes. Where did disability fit on a map of marginality and identity?

Right away it seemed that disability was the only "mark" that could impinge upon each of the other categories. One could not become "female" if marked "male" (without radical surgery), one could not become "black" in a biological sense within a strictly Caucasian familial line, sexuality proved more ambiguous and slippery. But what made disability distinct was its unambiguous ability to impact every other identity category at any time. Even in the least-marked category—the "transparent" state of straight white male—disability clouded an otherwise unmarked social identity. At that time, as the beneficiaries of an earlier generation's activism for the Americans with Disabilities Act, we understood that while disability threatened to override other identifying marks, it continued to go unrecognized as a form of cultural alliance in academia and in public life. At this point, our interest in disability configurations still seemed largely intellectual. We silently negotiated physical obstacles while beginning to assess textual ones.

So we began by contemplating disability as an issue of representation and cultural stigma; every essay we read started to teem with disability references, metaphors, and implications. Disability proved ubiquitous and yet solicited little commentary. Even on a highly charged political campus such as the University of Michigan, disability seemed a far-off concern of the most committed "radicals." Meanwhile, disability continued to prove a stubborn "fact" of personal negotiation. Ironically, the day finally came when a handicap permit seemed a good alternative to the four hundred dollars' worth of parking tickets we had acquired. Was it the belief in "passing" that was lessening? Or was it that "ability" was lessening? Inside that found topic of disability, we were beginning to admit, was a life of hidden negotiations.

One could navigate a host of representational tropes about disability in books while simultaneously negotiating institutional and social narratives about one's own life. We would mull over Žižek's and Hegel's applications to disability subjectivity in the morning, and later find David being asked to walk across the room for a desk clerk at the local DMV. At night we would read Elaine Scarry's *The Body in Pain,* only to find ourselves encountering a neurologist's disbelief the next morning about the fact that David was "still walking." (Later on, we would continue to negotiate the responsibilities of each insurance hassle and medical venture after taking on the care of a disabled child.)

These parallel negotiations of institutions and texts brought us to inhabit an increasingly intertwined disability subjectivity. Ironically, the refusal of separate identities along the lines of "patient" and "caregiver" proved to be the monkey's wrench that brought the gears of many an institution to at least a temporary halt. We jointly plotted strategies of access, interpretation, and survival in the maze of what Gary Albrecht calls the "disability business." The experience of disability embedded itself in both of our habits and thoughts to such an extent that we no longer differentiated between who was and who was not disabled in our family. In other words, we became disability studies scholars out of a precipitous desire and need to unravel the Gordian knot of our own representational existence.

Early on, we discovered after a first round of job interviews at the Modern Language Association that our familial negotiation of disability was not going to be so easy to conceal to a hiring committee. While we might consider the daily circumnavigations of parking spaces, stairs, walking distances, and schedules as part of the "art" of disability living, we were growing concerned that deans might be thinking about insurance plans while potential colleagues worried over "special" favors. Requests for elevators during campus visits usually resulted in lengthy explanations about the key being lost and a walk up several flights of stairs as "good for the soul." Somehow, we had not even figured out how to schedule interview rooms at the MLA convention in a wintry Chicago within negotiable distance of one another. Committees were left waiting while we argued about getting onto the inaccessible shuttle bus.

We suppose that we began our own journey into disabled academic life like many others: with the hope that our colleagues would refrain from discussing the cane, brace, limp, stutter, lisp, bulge, tremor, aberration, or weakness. Disabled people can at least usually count on the fact that adults will refrain from speaking aloud any disability observations they do make. And what motivates our own reluctance? Mainly the expectation that to introduce one's disability into discourse (social or academic) is to suddenly have that single aspect subsume all others. Robert Murphy termed the phenomenon of having one's physical differences cancel out all other aspects of identity "disability creep." It is similar to the implicit undertones contained in referring to Michel Foucault's philosophical innovations as the work of a "gay" philosopher—suddenly the work sheds its more wide-ranging implications and threatens to become a political manifesto.

Ultimately one gains an identity whether chosen or not. Like our colleagues in race, sexuality, and gender studies, we sensed all the ways that disability could immediately be called upon to override the import of ideas. Like our colleagues in "queer" studies, we have found that the best solution involves an equivocal embrace of the "insult" that examines the power of this status bequeathed from the outside. To remark upon one's disability in academia is to unduly "mark" oneself. And openly remarking upon oneself as disabled cannot wholly mitigate against the perception of the category introducing a "freak show"–like atmosphere across the range of U.S. identity landscapes. This is the "threat" and promise that disability holds for our current theoretical work upon the representation of marginal identities in literature, film, and theory.

Just put a disabled character in a movie and watch reviewers comment upon the gratuitous nature of the exercise, the "unnecessary" sentiment or grotesque outrage, introduced by disability's mere inclusion. Audiences have all been schooled by tradition to assume that an artist must thereby be aiming for an Oscar or injecting a ready-made motive into a story. One finds this likewise to be the case in academic symposia, classrooms, and shopping malls. For disability entails a kind of immediate prefashioned notoriety—that of the one who overencumbers the visual scene. The one with the "slurred" voice, the thick glasses, the wheelchair, the pale skin, the unsightly protuberance, the birthmark, or the blemish. In order to *be* disabled, one must narrate one's disability for others in sweeping strokes or hushed private tones. And this narration must inevitably show how we conquer our disabilities or how they eventually conquer us. The lack of other options refuses us the pursuit of anonymity in ordinary involvements. These were the increasingly personal and political stakes of disability representation.

In the study that follows, each of our readings departs and arrives back to the solid facts of disability for us. Furthermore, the scenes of daily living, daily disability living, are bound up in our collaborative scholarship. While a focus of the "independent living movement," which we wholly endorse, has concentrated upon the goal of *autonomy* for disabled people, we would point out that the *interdependency* of disability living constitutes an important factor in achieved independence. Since this is likewise true for scholarly work, our own writing and publishing decisions help to emphasize the prosthetic nature of our collaborative projects. Just as feminism sought to expose the unacknowledged support of women who made public male endeavor possible, our own coauthored work has emphasized the intertwined nature of our research, insights, and writing. By working in tandem to develop our readings we have significantly increased the literary and historical scope that our work covers. Without this collaborative aspect of our relationship the current book could never have been completed. In our efforts to mutually supplement each other's materials, we have sought, on a more general level, to expose the prosthetic nature of all intellectual endeavor.

As disabled scholarly partners we have also witnessed the profound impact of disability upon our entire family. The continual navigation and intensive strategies that characterize life with a disability stretches far beyond the parameters of any single individual life; it reroutes the circuitry of partners and children, friends and family in ways that can be described as anything but individual. A quick example will suffice to make this point: during our stay at a Ronald McDonald House for one of our daughter's multiple surgeries, our son was "scolded" by a fellow resident for being too lazy to walk the stairs rather than taking the elevator. As a child in a family that includes a father with a mobility impairment, he had grown up knowing nothing different. We openly sought out elevators at every turn and would complain about their absence or inconvenient locations in public facilities. Our son had developed within a private family culture that hypervalued the necessity of elevators and never imagined the alternative validity of another mode of ascent or descent. Like most children he had unknowingly absorbed the values and rituals of his family without regard to the practices of a world largely landscaped to the needs of able-bodied individuals. As a culture, we have only begun to grapple with the myriad ways that disability shifts our expectations and creates alternatives to that which we regard as "natural" or, even worse, "normal."

Central in this project, then, are the many ways that a rhetorical identity chose us as much as we chose it. While many of us present ourselves as having come to our public disability roles as savvy disability advocates and politicos from the start, often we enter a representation that is waiting for us rather than the other way around. Disability is first thrust upon one from the outside as a deterministic identity rubric and then must be negotiated from the inside in order to create for oneself what Ross Chambers calls "room for maneuver." While many of us have fallen back onto our work and theory of other marginal identities to "explain" disability, we have also had to admit that disability could not be easily tacked onto the end of the marked identity chart. The question mark beneath the category persists because we have only begun to sort out the convergences and divergences of disability from other groupings of "marginality." Yet, since culture is consolidated within the space of shared social critique, disability studies scholarship in the humanities advances out of similar methodological beginnings as gender, race, and sexuality.

This book begins addressing the meanings of the question mark beneath the category of disability on the representational identity grid. In disability studies the notion of the "built" environment provides a common way to designate architectural and structural features devised as obstacles to people with disabilities. In this book we would like to theorize the ways in which the built environment also includes the mythologies, images, and characterizations about disability that comprise the majority of interactions in our imaginative lives. Our goal is to make narratives of disability a visceral language that significantly impacts our ability to imagine the lives of contemporary disabled populations. The negotiation of these historical coordinates of disability helps to create a more diverse array of options for thinking about disability as an intellectual category of inquiry and as an experientially based phenomenon. It is easy to fall prey to the self-congratulatory belief that we occupy the most progressive moment of disability awareness in history; however, these historical readings also intend to help readers situate their understanding of disability in a complex fashion.

This study could not have been undertaken without the work and help of numerous like-minded individuals met along the way. Over the past seven years, we have been privileged to work with colleagues in a newly emerging disability studies field. First, we would like to express our gratitude to other disability studies "partners": Carol Gill and Larry Voss; Karen and Jerry Hirsch; Brenda Jo Brueggemann and James Fredal; William Sayers and Lois Bragg; Anja Tervooren and Tüpfen; Nancy Mairs and George; Michael Berubé and Janet Lyons; Simi and David Linton; James Wilson and Cynthia Lewieki-Wilson. Our special thanks to our friend and mentor, David Wills, for his astute comments on our work during the writing of this manuscript. We also appreciate the many audiences who responded to earlier drafts from which the present chapters evolved: the Society for Disability Studies, the Smithsonian Museum of American History, the Modern Languages Association, the "Enabling the Humanities" symposium at The Ohio State University, and NIDRR's Conference on the New Disability Studies Paradigm.

Our work benefits from the insights of many disability studies scholars pursuing significant research in the field: Tobin Siebers, Paul Longmore, Carol Poore, Martha Stoddard Holmes, Mark Jeffreys, Felicity Nussbaum, Susan Crutchfield, Marcie Epstein, Helen Deutsch, Georgina Kleege, Martin Pernick, Henry Friedlander, Tammy Gravenhorst, Carrie Sandhal, Cindy La Com, Louise DeSalvo, David Wills, Johnson Cheu, Allen Thiher, David Gerber, Jennifer Sutton, Sander Gilman, Elizabeth Grosz, Susan Bordo, Tom Couser, Maria Frawley, Robert Garland, Martha Edwards, Dona Avery, Diane Herndl, David Hevey, Beth Haller, Wesley Smith, Ron Amundson, Anita Silvers, Doug Baynton, and Carolyn Tyjewski. We appreciate, as well, the many social scientists who go out of their way to make cross-disciplinary journeys, including Adrienne Asch, Phil Ferguson, Kay Schriner, Richard Scotch, Arthur Frank, David Pfeiffer, Henri-Jacques Stiker, Barbara Robertson, Nancy Mudrick, Susan Gabel, Gene Chelberg, Corinne Kirchner, Devva Kasnitz, Elaine Makas, Gary Albrecht, David Braddock, Glenn Fujira, David Gray, and Harlan Hahn. Please note that the present volume aims to attest that service on the Society for Disability Studies Board need not result in administrative burial! Commerce with British disability studies scholars keep us mindful of our "impairments"; thanks particularly to Mairian Corker, Petra Kuppers, Mike and Joy Oliver, Mark Priestly, Tom Shakespeare, and Majid Turmusani.

We particularly appreciate the latest generation of disability rights activists for keeping our communities strong, including Diane Coleman, Cal Montgomery, Stephen Drake, and the entire "Princeton 7" of *Not Dead Yet*. Cheryl Marie Wade goes in a class of her own—when we need a little strength we look to Gnarly Bones for poetry and politics. Thanks for helping us to say "gimp" and "crip" with flair! Our disabled artists also pursue terrific disability studies scholarship: Georgiana Kleege, Laurie Block, Anne Finger, Kenny Fries, Mary Duffy, Harilyn Rousso, Elizabeth Clare, Billy Golfus, Bob DeFelice, Jim Ferris, and Mike Irvin. Thanks also to Fanlight Distributors, particularly Ben Achtenburg, and Program Development Associates for promoting and supporting disabled film and video artists. We should acknowledge the disability community's vital cultural and political forums: "On a Roll" Radio and Greg Smith, *New Mobility* magazine and Barry Corbett, *The Ragged Edge* and Mary Johnson, *Mouth* magazine and Tom Olin, and *Disability Studies Quarterly* (founded by the late Irving K. Zola).

Rosemarie Garland-Thomson has willingly read everything we have written during the creation of this volume. She has provided her time, critiques, and suggestions in a supportive and insightful manner. Lennard Davis and his family have been overwhelmingly generous with time, useful pointers, and home space. Anja Tervooren not only ventured to the United States to explore U.S. disability studies, she helped us to proof, edit, and translate the material on Nietzsche for the present volume. Jim Porter's early and thoughtful responses to the Nietzsche sections also gave us helpful direction.

We are grateful to Dr. Katherine Seelman, director of the National Institute for Disability Rehabilitation and Research, for her financial support of the Society for Disability Studies over the years and for her vocal endorsements of humanities work in a field dominated by science and rehabilitation specialists. Her leadership has been invaluable in demanding that the medical and service industries recognize and incorporate new disability studies paradigms into their methodologies and research. Our friend and colleague, Jeanne Argoff, who heads up the Disability Funder's Network, puts endless energy into supporting disabled scholars and researchers. Judy Heumann, Assistant Secretary at the Department of Education, demonstrates an unflagging commitment to promoting inclusive educational policies. We thank Barb Trader and John Kemp for injecting disability culture into the programs of VSArts.

We would like to acknowledge all the friends who make life's negotiations worthwhile: Maria and Elora brought us home to Harlem and offered wonderful companionship. And in order to point out the many disability communities everywhere, we should acclaim the "Convaid Cruiser" brigade from the bleachers of Yankee Stadium. In the snowy North we thank friends and associates: Melissa Hearn, Toby Rose, Kay Payant, Miles Beckwith, Ray Ventre, Beverly Matherne, Tom Hyslop, Hugh and Maureen Andrews, Paul and Zhuang Lehmberg, Katie Hanson, Jim Livingston, Zach Thundy, and Carol and Don Bays. Penny, Bill, and Erin Olson are true friends. In particular we would like to thank Daryl Davis for the friendship and collegiality that help keep us motivated. Mike Strahan provided helpful research advice at Northern Michigan University's library. We thank the Department of English, the Faculty Grants Review Committee, and the Vice President of Academic Affairs for their support of our endeavors while we were at NMU. We would also like to extend our thanks to Michelle Jarman who followed us to Chicago and lent her expertise to the indexing.

We are grateful to Cheryl Emich and other teachers in the "Early-On" programs; Annie, Steve, and Peggy give old-fashioned meaning to school bus service. Effy and Brandon Smaby helped care for our daughter while we completed the manuscript, and Christy Greising helps with everything. Special thanks to the Poseys for their support and lessons in political commitment in the old leftist tradition. Thanks also to Shirley, Charlie, David, Dolores, Dale, Kathy, Zoe, Sharon, Mike, Cassie, and Garrick. William, Estel, Marianna Brown, Eugene, and Christine Hadley Snyder sustain the best family relations around. (Though we do not expect to fully pass grandmother's grammar test!)

Dr. Maureen Packard and Sharon Barnard at Cornell's New York Hospital provided for our family's participation in their innovative study on the effects of hyperbaric oxygen therapy on cerebral palsy.

Perhaps most of all we should recognize our graduate students at the University of Illinois who have devoted themselves to a future of research and scholarship in Disability Studies: Sarah Triano, Teresa Pacione, Yangling "Millie" Li, Joe Caldwell, Ann Aviles, Maureen O'Nell, Betty Erickson,

Sharon Lamp, Nefertiti Nowell, Sara Voght, Nina Robins-Byrns, Rebecca Masko, Susan Magasi, Sharon Smith, Dolores Kelly, Ann Cameron Williams, Gail Werblood, Mary Ann Solimine, Carlos Drazen, and others. We would also like to recognize the indefatigable efforts of the Disabled Students Union to change the physical and cultural climate of the academy.

Finally, hats off to LeAnn Fields, our editor extraordinaire at the University of Michigan Press. Disability studies could never have grown so far and so fast without her energy and commitment to its multiple domains.

As we complete this preface in Chicago, Illinois, we would like to thank the Department of Disability and Human Development for providing our new academic home in Disability Studies.

Introduction
Disability as Narrative Supplement

Narrative Stumbling Blocks

In *Narrative Prosthesis* we address the meanings assigned to disability as a representational identity in narrative art. While much of the early work on disability in the humanities has discussed popular media or single literary texts, this study analyzes an array of literary works produced at divergent moments in European and American history. The chapters that follow also pursue the subject of disability from multiple directions: as a character-making trope in the writer's and filmmaker's arsenal, as a social category of deviance, as a symbolic vehicle for meaning-making and cultural critique, and as an option in the narrative negotiation of disabled subjectivity. The centrality of these issues demonstrates that disability is a prevalent characteristic of narrative discourses.

Consequently, *Narrative Prosthesis* sets out its readings of disability within the domain of narrative theory. In this sense our book is not intended to provide a strictly historical study of disability—although each chapter is organized around the historical contexts for its literary and film sources. We do not organize our readings around a strict principle of literary tradition whereby each generation of artists responds to those who preceded them. However, the book does explain the ways in which authors, working from a variety of disability contexts, read and revise oppressive social rhetorics. We do not offer an overarching narrative of disability characterization, for one book cannot present an exhaustive account of disability "types" or characters. Instead we seek a finite series of strategies for theorizing the utility and appearance of disability in literary narratives, and we have chosen our texts as key moments in the rhetorical history of disability.

Finally, readers should not anticipate a work that theorizes the cultural situation of people with disabilities as mere reflection of literary and film representations. Instead, each of the chapters analyzes literary works as *commentaries* on the status of disability in other disciplines such as philosophy, medicine, and ethics. We argue that imaginative literature takes up its narrative project as a counter to scientific or truth-telling discourses. It is productively parasitic upon other disciplinary systems that define disability in more deterministic ways.[1] Rather than situate these imaginative writings as purely reactionary to, or uncomprehending of, these other disciplines' attitudes toward disability, we demonstrate that disability has been a forthright interest of literary narrative. While literature does not always take up disability in order to salvage its routinely denigrating social definitions, we argue that the socially "forbidden" nature of the topic has compelled many writers to deploy disability as an explicitly complicating feature of their representational universes. As a stumbling block to cultural definitions and artistic figurations, disability's representational challenge often becomes the direct topic of literature. The first order of business in this book, then, is to identify moments when disability becomes a primary preoccupation of narrative art.

Disability and Identity

In *Narrative Prosthesis* we mean to help locate disability's place on the map of multicultural studies. Our readings situate disability, like gender, sexuality, and race, as a constructed category of discursive investment. In fact, as we have argued elsewhere (*The Body and Physical Difference*, introduction), physical or cognitive inferiority has historically characterized the means by which bodies have been constructed as "deviant": the Victorian equation between femininity and hysteria; the biological racism that justified slavery and the social subordination of racial minorities; psychiatry's categorization of homosexuality as a pathological disorder; and so on. This socially imposed relationship between marginalized populations and "inferior" biology situates disability studies in proximity to other minority approaches. Like these other identity-based areas of inquiry, disability studies challenges the common ascription of inferior lives to persons with physical and cognitive differences.

Yet this relationship to multicultural studies is often a discomforting one. As feminist, race, and sexuality studies sought to unmoor their identities from debilitating physical and cognitive associations, they inevitably positioned disability as the "real" limitation from which they must escape.[2] This methodological distancing was necessary because identity studies resignified cultural beliefs grounded in material differences, real or imagined. Feminism delineates male fantasies of female alterity assigned to secondary sexual characteristics; race studies interrogates European binaries that subordinate people of color to an aesthetic of whiteness; queer studies confronts the deforming precepts of heterosexist conventions that moralize sexual behaviors as an outgrowth of cognitive maladjustment. In all of these cases, biological inferiority had to be exposed as a construction of discursive power. Formerly denigrated identities are "rescued" by understanding gendered, racial, and sexual differences as textually produced, distancing them from the "real" of physical or cognitive aberrancy projected onto their figures.

Even in disability communities a parallel phenomenon can be seen at work. In order to dissociate one's disability from stigmatizing associations, disabled people are encouraged to "pass" by disguising their disabilities. Prosthetic devices, mainstreaming, and overcompensation techniques, all provide means for people with disabilities to "fit in" or to "de-emphasize" their differences. There have also been hierarchies within our own communities where some disabilities are viewed as less assimilable than others. For instance, individuals with physical disabilities have historically disassociated themselves from those who have intellectual disabilities. From the segregation of special education classrooms to the systematic murder of people with cognitive disabilities in Nazi Germany, the fate of people with physical disabilities has often depended upon their ability to distance themselves from their cognitively disabled peers.[3] This internalized oppression has resulted from institutionally enforced hierarchies of disability.

For all populations physical and cognitive limitations constitute a baseline of cultural undesirability from which they must dissociate themselves in the quest for civil rights and for a lessening of stigmatization. Consequently, disability has undergone a dual negation—it has been attributed to all "deviant" biologies as a discrediting feature, while also serving as the material marker of inferiority itself. One might think of disability as the master trope of human disqualification. In *Narrative Prosthesis* we interrogate the historical repercussions of this dual negation from without and within disability communities, while importing many of the analytical techniques developed in studies of gender, race, and sexuality.

In tandem with other identity studies, one of our efforts is to exemplify the ways in which disability has been a sign of inferior life itself. Rather than pursue a discursive "solution" to these problems, however, the texts under discussion in this volume wrestle with the relationship between constructed and material identities. In this regard, disability occupies a unique identity that must navigate the terrain between physical/cognitive differences and social stigma. No purely constructivist reading can adequately traverse this political and experiential divide.[4] Out of this recognition, the question put to the representation of disability differs from that of other identity-based studies: can one possess a physical or cognitive anomaly that does not translate into a belief in one's social inferiority? This important query demonstrates one of the ways in which disability studies can make an important contribution to our current theoretical work on identity and difference.

Variations on Disability

Narrative prosthesis, the controlling theme throughout this book, refers to both the prevalence of disability representation and the myriad meanings ascribed to it. The importance of disabled figures to artistic portrayal can be illustrated in the drawing of "cripples and beggars" (1550–55) attributed to Pieter Brueghel and reproduced on the cover of this book. The assembly of disabled subjects in Breugel's illustration serve as prototypes for figures that would later emerge in his most renowned works: *Mad Meg* (1562), *The Blind Leading the Blind* (1568), *The Peasant Woman* (1568), *The Cripples* (1568), and other works art historians find suggestive of the grotesque landscapes of Hieronymous Bosch.[5] Brueghel spent much of his career illustrating the lives of the peasantry in a mode less romanticized than did such later painters as Manet. He rejected the classical aesthetic of such Italian masters as Raphael by turning to subjects who distorted the ideals of bodily symmetry in painting.[6] His figures of cripples are evidence for what many critics have seen as an unflinching devotion to detailing the "misery of the human condition." Brueghel's works (particularly his masterworks composed in the year before his death) rely upon the representational power of deformity and disability to expose the bodily life repressed within classicism. As one of his admirers would argue about paintings that teemed with corporeal and cognitive aberrancy, "Here Nature, interpreted in painted images / And viewed through her cripples, is stupefied by finding that Bruegel is her equal" (Stechow 150).

In the drawings of various "cripples," replete with each one's individuated mobility emphasized by various prosthetics, Brueghel saturates his landscapes with displays of human deviance. As Stechow's comment suggests, much was gained through the graphic portrayal of disability. First, if one could view such "perversions" with an attentive eye, then one could gather together the variety of human life that nature puts before us. Second, the portrayal of cripples would often be claimed as proof that an artist remained committed to recording even the most disturbing products of humankind and God. Third, Brueghel's paintings of cripples could rival nature's own blemishes by "rehabilitating" them within the aesthetic sweep of his own portrayals. Fourth, Brueghel sits at the beginning of a representational tradition that would come to mark the life of the peasantry through disability. In the latter sense, disabled figures would provide a contrast to the graceful aesthetic conventions that governed depictions of royalty and the upper echelons of Renaissance society.

In this brief analysis we can begin to understand that disability served as a primary weapon in the artistic repertoire which sought to establish the "common people" as an appropriate subject. Brueghel's reputation depends to a great degree upon his depiction of deviance, and consequently his work emblematizes the power which lies behind representational art's perennial fascination with disability. This engagement with the myriad differences characterizing the life of cripples and the underclasses situates Brueghel and the painterly tradition in a moment of transition. To defy classicism's imperative to depict only unblemished bodies, Brueghel seized upon disability's power to disrupt and variegate the visual encounter with unblemished bodies. This innovation allowed the artist to deviate (in both a literal and an aesthetic sense) from a tradition that was increasingly static in its obsession with symmetrical physical forms.

Yet, while cripples provide productive value for Bruegel, his attendant association of them with a debased humanity did little to challenge public perceptions of their figures. Brueghel's work on cripples emblematizes the contradictory aspect of our conceptualization of narrative prosthesis: he detailed "crippled" differences faithfully while simultaneously metamorphosing those differences into social satires. The beautifully rendered figures in *The Blind Leading the Blind,* for example, dramatize a biblical allegory that equated a lack of sight with wayward leadership. On the back of the wood panel upon which *The Cripples* was created, Brueghel sardonically scribbled, "Cripples go and be prosperous!" This contrasting deployment of disability—as a device of artistic innovation that entrenched disability's associations with corruption—serves as a parable for many of the representations of disability traced in this book.

Subsequent chapters analyze specific aspects of the discursive dependency upon disability as narrative prosthesis, and our discussions of disability as a device of characterization identify how various historical periods influenced literature's appropriation of disability. Most basic to the identification of character through disability is the way in which physical and cognitive differences have been narrated as alien to the normal course of human affairs. To represent disability is to engage oneself in an encounter with that which is believed to be off the map of "recognizable" human experiences. Making comprehensible that which appears to be inherently unknowable situates narrative in the powerful position of mediator between two separate worlds. As we discuss at length in chapter 2, it is the narrative of disability's very unknowability that consolidates the need to tell a story about it. Thus, in stories about characters with disabilities, an underlying issue is always whether their disability is the foundation of character itself. The question is not whether disability is cause or symptom of, or distraction from, a disturbing behavioral trait, but whether its mystery can be pierced by the storyteller.

Thus, one of the theories undergirding the chapters ahead is that disability inaugurates the act of interpretation. In a manner parallel to Foucault's analysis in *The Birth of the Clinic,* we argue that literary efforts to illuminate the dark recesses of disability produce a form of discursive subjugation. The effort to narrate disability's myriad deviations is an attempt to bring the body's unruliness under control. As we will demonstrate, disability's representational "fate" is not so much dependent upon a tradition of negative portrayals as it is tethered to inciting the act of meaning-making itself. The importance of this textual convention cannot be underestimated. While other identities such as race, sexuality, and ethnicity have pointed to the dearth of images produced about them in the dominant literature, disability has experienced a plethora of representations in visual and discursive works. Consequently, disabled people's marginalization has occurred in the midst of a perpetual circulation of their images. Curiously, a social erasure has been performed even as a representational repertoire has evolved. We take up the reasons for this paradox in the chapters that follow.

Narrative Prosthesis

The controlling concept of this volume, narrative prosthesis, situates the experience and representational life of disability upon the ironic grounding of an unsteady rhetorical stance. In a literal sense a prosthesis seeks to accomplish an illusion. A body deemed lacking, unfunctional, or inappropriately functional needs compensation, and prosthesis helps to effect this end. Yet the prosthesizing of a body or a rhetorical figure carries with it ideological assumptions about what is aberrant. The judgment that a mechanism is faulty is always already profoundly social. The need to restore a disabled body to some semblance of an originary wholeness is the key to a false recognition: that disabilities extract one from a social norm or average of bodies and their corresponding (social) expectations. To prostheticize, in this sense, is to institute a notion of the body within a regime of tolerable deviance. If disability falls too far from an acceptable norm, a prosthetic intervention seeks to accomplish an erasure of difference all together; yet, failing that, as is always the case with prosthesis, the minimal goal is to return one to an acceptable degree of difference.

It is important to state at the outset that this argument does not deny the reality of physical incapacity or cognitive difference. Rather, we set out the coordinates of the social reception and literary representation of those labeled deviant on ideological as well as physical planes. David Wills defines *prosthesis* as a term that mediates between the realm of the literary and the realm of the body. In relation to the latter, Wills argues that, far from signifying a deficiency, the prostheticized body is the rule, not the exception. All bodies are deficient in that materiality proves variable, vulnerable, and inscribable. The body is first and foremost a linguistic relation which cannot be natural or average. The textual nature of language, be it oral or print, lacks the very physicality that it seeks to control or represent. A normal body, as Lennard Davis has demonstrated, is a theoretical premise from which all bodies must, by definition, fall short. The body is up against an abstraction with which it cannot compete because the norm is an idealized quantitative and qualitative measure that is divorced from (rather than derived from) the observation of bodies, which are inherently variable. This false model of an ideal body also fails to consider the contingencies of bodies functioning within specific social and historical contexts. It is, in other words, a body divorced of time and space—a thoroughly artificial affair.

Consequently, to return to Wills's fluid notion of prosthesis, the deficient body, by virtue of its insufficiency, serves as baseline for the articulation of the normal body: "the prosthetic body will not be an exception but the paradigm for the body itself. If you will, it is by means of prosthesis that I wish to insist on the non-originary status of the body" (137). The relation between a body and the language used to describe it is unstable, an alien alliance: materiality is not language, and language cannot be material, although each strives to conform to the terms of the other. We engage our bodies in efforts to make their stubborn materiality "fit" ideals. Likewise, words give us the illusion of a fix upon the material world that they cannot deliver.

For Wills this relation between body and word can take on at least four separate poses (137–41).

The word that issues from a body is often believed to glean a corporeal aura from its material host.

The word always augments a prosthetic relation to an exterior material that it cannot possess or embody.

> A word returns to the body a sense of possession of the external world that it cannot possess.

> The body's need to comprehend a materiality external to it is answered via the ruse of language—that is, the word provides the body with the necessary illusion of its successful entrance into the space of the Other.

This inability of the body to possess, via the word, that which is external to it grounds Wills's (and thus our own) more varied and less singular idea of prosthesis.

While an actual prosthesis is always somewhat discomforting, a textual prosthesis alleviates discomfort by removing the unsightly from view. As we discuss in chapter 2, the erasure of disability via a "quick fix" of an impaired physicality or intellect removes an audiences' need for concern or continuing vigilance.[7] Rather than closet the marred body, the chapters that follow reinstitute its discomforting presence. *Narrative Prosthesis* is first and foremost about the ways in which the ruse of prosthesis fails in its primary objective: to return the incomplete body to the invisible status of a normative essence. The works under scrutiny here tend to leave the wound of disability undressed so to speak. Its presence is enunciated as transgressive in that literary works often leave the disabled body as a troubled and troubling position within culture.

The prosthetic function in most of the works that follow, then, is to undo the quick repair of disability in mainstream representations and beliefs. In part, this book is about the literary *accomplishment* of a faulty, or at least imperfect, prosthetic function. *The effort is to make the prosthesis show, to flaunt its imperfect supplementation as an illusion.* The prosthetic relation of body to word is exposed as an artificial contrivance. Disability services an unsettling objective in these literary works by refusing its desired cultural return to the land of the normative. Ironically, the accomplishment of the works under scrutiny here is to expose, rather than conceal, the prosthetic relation.

Beyond this elucidation of disability as transgressive of social ideals, this literary strategy also has a visceral effect on the lives of disabled people. While disability's troubling presence provides literary works with the potency of an unsettling cultural commentary, disabled people have been historically refused a parallel power within their social institutions. In other words, while literature often relies on disability's transgressive potential, disabled people have been sequestered, excluded, exploited, and obliterated on the very basis of which their literary representation so often rests. Literature serves up disability as a repressed deviation from cultural imperatives of normativity, while disabled populations suffer the consequences of representational association with deviance and recalcitrant corporeal difference.

The paradox of these two deployments, artistic versus historical, cannot be reconciled. Nor can art, in its dependency upon disability, be simply castigated for linking disability and abject deviance. Literary forms—like disabled ones—are discordant in their unwillingness to replicate a more normative appearance. That which breaks with the conventions of desirability at any historical moment garners an unseemly attention for itself as the very product of its deviance. Disability, like the designation of artistic innovation, derives value from its noncompliance with social expectations about valid physical and cognitive lives. To address this recalcitrant deviance as strategic in one register (the literary) does not suggest that it has the same effect in the other (the embodied lives of disabled people). Yet both must cope with the repercussions of misreadings and their social aftermaths. And thus, as we discuss in chapter 3, a Nietzschean philosophy that designates that which is normative as ironically most sick could justify the Holocaust first practiced and perfected upon the bodies of disabled people.

Narrative prosthesis, then, is our way of situating a discussion about disability within a literary domain while keeping watch on its social context. The phrase tries to capture the myriad relations between the literary and the historical. First, narrative prosthesis refers to the pervasiveness of disability as a device of characterization in narrative art. Second, it enables a contrast between the prosthetic leanings of mainstream discourses that would disguise or obliterate the evidence of physical and cognitive differences, and literary efforts that expose prosthesis as an artificial, and thus, resignifiable relation. Third, it refers to the problematic nature of the literary's transgressive ideal in relation to social violence that often issues from the repetition of a representational formula (or antiformula). This third approach draws out the often discomforting "fit" between literary disability and the "real" of disabled peoples' historical experiences. Finally, it acknowledges that literary representation bears on the production and realization of disabled subjectivities. While these relationships are inevitably prosthetic in nature—that is, narrative offers an illusive grasp of the exterior world upon which it signifies—disabled people's options are inevitably tethered to the options that history offers.

Thus, rather than condemn the literary as bankrupt with regard to disability, we attend to the nuanced relations of literary and social responses to disability. The humanities component of disability studies offers scholars and students the ability to return to a history of representations to reassess our understanding of disability and thus of ourselves. As Meaghan Morris argues in *The Pirate's Fiancé*, one productive response to a bankrupt, but dominant, image is to formulate subjectivities in contradistinction to that which is supplied by the dominant culture (2–6). Thus, our emphasis upon a narrative theory of disability rides upon the necessity of reclaiming histories of disability. We do so to help seize a more variegated and politicized disabled subjectivity for our own era. That is ultimately the pragmatics of the literary study of disability and its promise.

Overview of the Book

The first chapter, "Representation and Its Discontents: The Uneasy Home of Disability in Literature and Film," discusses the myriad intersections of race, gender, sexuality, nationality, and class in an emergent disability studies in the humanities. Studies of disability in the archives provide a multifaceted base upon which to build our own period's investigation of disability. Explaining the ways that disability scholars have complicated our understanding of negative representations without surrendering a usable politics, we offer *representational discontent* as a governing logic for the humanities within the evolution of disability studies. To this end, our first chapter theorizes the development of five methodological components within disability studies: negative imagery, social realism, new historicism, biographical studies, and transgressive resignification. Throughout the chapter we assess both the *pervasive* and the *hypersymbolic* nature of disability.

Central to the second chapter, "Narrative Prosthesis and the Materiality of Metaphor," are two predominant tropes of disability characterization. Disability provides a common formula for differentiating a character's uniqueness through the identifying features of physical and behavioral "quirks" or idiosyncrasies. Yet, while disability often marks a protagonist's difference and is the impetus to narrate a story in the first place, a complex disability subjectivity is not developed in the ensuing narrative. In Sophocles' *Oedipus the King*, disability is a metaphor of personal and social ruin. Through Oedipus' lameness and blinding, the play provides Sophocles' more abstract social commentary on hubris with a "tangible body" of evidence. This metaphorization of disability supplies the myth with a solid hold in corporeality. These examples show that disability supplies a multiple utility to literary characterizations, even while literature abandons a serious contemplation of the difference that disability makes as a socially negotiated identity.

Whereas chapter 2 analyzes limiting narrative conventions of disability in popular literature and myth, the remainder of our study is occupied with literary investments in disability tropes. The third chapter, "Montaigne's 'Infinities of Formes' and Nietzsche's 'Higher' Men," is a bridge to the more concentrated readings of literary art that follow. It outlines two antithetical approaches to the function of disability in systems of representation. At opposing ends of a philosophical tradition, the early Enlightenment writings of Montaigne and the post-Enlightenment thought of Nietzsche provide linchpins for opposing representations of disabled lives in a philosophical tradition. Both move their interpretations of "cripples" toward a disruption of philosophical discourses, and both interrogate the normative expectations that surround disabled figures. First, Montaigne stresses the disabled body as an expression of the diversity of God's works that he calls "infinities of formes." Thus he critiques the premodern penchant for interpreting disability as a sign of divine disfavor and superstitious revelation. Montaigne's pragmatic approach to disability prefaces Enlightenment science and a refusal to interpret bodies as vehicles for religious meanings.

In stark contrast, Nietzsche ironically champions disability as extreme devalued difference. His segregated community of cripples, inoculated against the insipidities of mainstream German culture by virtue of their exile, interrogates the ambitions of Rationalist philosophy. Nietzsche's cripples also emerge as central haunting figures in his critique of Christianity's curative propositions. Chapter 3 establishes the contrary impulses of disability figuration in Montaigne's efforts at assimilation as opposed to Nietzsche's ironical celebration of the socially unassimilable and explores their possibilities for narrating disabled lives.

The fourth chapter, "Performing Deformity: The Making and Unmaking of Richard III," continues our concern with influential disability figurations that circulate across high and low cultural arenas. We read Richard III as confounding prototype more than stereotype. While the malevolent "hunch-back'd toad" has been decried as bad publicity, he has also been embraced and resignified by disabled artists across centuries. Richard as disabled avenger is a key figure in film art's grounding in physiognomy as a visual interpretive practice. We argue that this prototypical visual display of physical disability provided dramatists and silent-era filmmakers with the dual intrigue of a "high" art characterization and a "low" popular convention. Shakespeare's depiction of a disabled individual as singular heroic protagonist—as the first "modern subject"—makes possible the study of cultural investments in revived performances of disability across continents and over the course of four centuries.

In chapter 5, "The Language of Prosthesis in *Moby-Dick*," we return to physiognomy within a nineteenth-century context. For Melville, who fictionalizes an ever-shifting universe of meanings, empirical discourses that attempt to stabilize definitions once and for all provoke a dangerous inelasticity in human thought. While critiquing many of the predominating intellectual trends in Victorian America, Ishmael upends the fashionable pseudosciences of physiognomy and phrenology—two ideologies that have proven devastating to the bearers of physical differences in history. In spite of his laughing rejection of these false sciences of the human surface, Ishmael interprets Ahab's "monomaniacal" personality as the sole product of his amputation by Moby-Dick. The novel represents Ahab's resourcefulness in making an accessible ship out of the *Pequod* but eventually condemns the one-legged captain to a deterministic fate. Ahab believes that language grasps the essence of a tangible reality, but the "language of prosthesis" exposes a simulation at work in the linguistic apprehension of the universe. "Reality" is merely an effect of the duplicity of language, a false leg that cannot quite replace the lost original. In this way, Ahab's prosthetic leg serves doubly as both the organizing trope of the novel's myriad substitutions and the mechanism of the obsessive captain's own undoing.

Chapter 6, "Modernist Freaks and Postmodern Geeks: Literary Contortions of the Disabled Body," compares the treatment of disability in the symbolic experiments of modernism with the hyperreal landscapes of postmodernism. Our analysis of Sherwood Anderson's grotesque novel of the rural Midwest, *Winesburg, Ohio,* and Katherine Dunn's dystopic postmodern fantasy, *Geek Love,* consolidates a tradition of disability representation as social critique. Anderson's novel makes possible a literal theory of narrative prosthesis, we argue, by recognizing a bona fide story in the encounter with external differences. His small-town characters, stultified by provincial middle America, mirror internal psychological distortions with physical irregularities: nervous twitches, immobility, inappropriate gesticulations, and so on. In each case the outward manifestation prefigures the impact of restrictive mores upon the lives of its small-town residents.

Taking Anderson's novel as a predecessor, Dunn's cult classic *Geek Love* self-reflexively interrogates the pervasive reliance upon disability as a device of literary characterization. Proffering a family of self-induced physical and cognitive aberrations, she creates a macabre comedy that satirizes the sensationalism of fetishistic capitalism and literary spectacle. Dunn situates disability as a mundane occurrence of human mutability that is to be distinguished from its more spectacular and performative freak-show cousin. Anderson and Dunn identify the centrality of disability to literary characterization and the "deforming" precepts of a tradition that has sacrificed the humanity of its characters in the evolution of the body as a saleable commodity.

In the afterword, "'The first child born into the world was born deformed': Disability Representation in These Times," we look at the future of disability representation in a discussion of key contemporary authors.

Taking Leslie Fiedler's cue that disability "remains the last outpost" of exploratory fiction, we catalog American works that situate disability as a critical component of their narrative interests. Rather than signify disability as a symbol of cultural ruin, these works narrate the experience of disability as a social and lived phenomenon. In the wake of the systematic murder of disabled people (and particularly children) during the Holocaust, recent works come to terms with the American intellectual origins of euthanasia and eugenics. A palpable urgency characterizes this writing that interrogates the country's responsibility for many of the rationales used in catastrophic Nazi practices.

Specifically, our readings focus upon four key novels: William Faulkner's *The Sound and the Fury,* J. D. Salinger's *The Catcher in the Rye,* Harper Lee's *To Kill a Mockingbird,* and Ken Kesey's *One Flew Over the Cuckoo's Nest.* Taken together, these works comprise a substantial portion of the works taught in U.S. secondary and postsecondary educational curricula. Our point here is to advance ways in which important arguments about disability can be addressed with materials already at hand. Yet, without a developed disability studies methodology in place, these interpretations have been at best obscured, and, at worst, ignored in criticism and pedagogy.

Finally, we end with a discussion of Richard Powers's recent disability novel, *Operation Wandering Soul,* and Atom Egoyan's film adaptation of Russell Banks's *The Sweet Hereafter,* in order to suggest that future representational modes of disability may mine the archives for the identification of a more complex disability subjectivity, one that has been both historically bequeathed and directly tied to the material basis of disability experiences themselves. Thus, the future of disability begins with an informed turn to the past. It also involves the risk of a developed intimacy with the material basis of subjectivity itself.

Chapter 1

Representation and Its Discontents: The Uneasy Home of Disability in Literature and Film

Introduction: The Uneasy Home of Representation

This chapter surveys disability studies in the humanities. As will become evident, scholars have unearthed an impressive array of works that take disability as a significant feature of characterization. This dependency upon disability as a distinguishing facet of literary and filmic depictions establishes the pervasiveness of narrative prosthesis. Disability scholars in the humanities, particularly since the 1990s, have provided a large and varied criticism for the interpretation of images of disability. We divide this scholarship into five methodologies: studies of negative imagery, social realism, new historicism, biographical criticism, and transgressive reappropriation. Collectively, they demonstrate the array of critical tools already at work in disability studies, as well as the potential for significant revisions to current methodologies.

Disability's prominence in narrative discourses and the relative absence of critical commentary upon this fact prior to the advent of disability studies in the humanities suggest that disability is, for the critical enterprise, both promising and discomforting—as proves true of all prosthetic interventions. In this sense, disability studies in the humanities shares an approach with our readings of the literature, which is to expose rather than disguise the prosthetic relation of disability and characterization as a contrivance. This inverse ideal grounds our concept of narrative prosthesis throughout this volume.

Beginning nearly thirty years ago, a resurgence of concern over the consequences of dehumanizing representations (monster, freak, madman, suffering innocent, hysteric, beggar) resulted in suspicion over the ultimate utility of representational studies about disability. Truly, literary and historical texts have rarely appeared to offer disabled characters in developed, "positive" portraits.[1] Does literary/cultural studies have anything to offer our apprehension of disability other than demeaning portraits of disabled people in history and the archive? Can findings in this inquiry be connected to the contemporary situation of disabled people? The idea that literary study has little to offer our politicized understandings of disability experience rests uncomfortably with us. Yet how do humanities scholars justify their work in an area historically dominated by medical and scientific concerns?

Previously, proponents of the universality in art sought to salvage disabled literary characterizations as evidence for inherent frailties in "the human condition." For example, Herbert Blau defends literary portraits of disability by explaining that they cause us to "concede that we are all, at some warped level of the essentially human, impaired" (10). A catalogue of representations in literature include some of the most influential figurations of "suffering humanity" across periods and cultures: the crippled Greek god Hephaestus; Montaigne's sexually potent limping women; Shakespeare's hunchback'd king, Richard III; Frankenstein's deformed monster; Bronte's madwoman in the attic; Melville's one-legged, monomaniacal Captain Ahab; Nietzsche's philosophical grotesques; Hemingway's wounded war veterans; Morrison's truncated and scarred ex-slaves; Borges's blind librarians; Oë's brain-damaged son. Astonishingly, this catalog of "warped" humanity proves as international as it does biologically varied. Why does characterization of disability so often result in indelible, albeit overwrought, literary portraits?

We suggest that the problem disability studies scholars perceive in the representational study of disability is the result of two predominating modes of historical address: overheated symbolic imagery and disability as a pervasive tool of artistic characterization. Yet while scholars in literary and cultural studies have produced important readings of individual disabled characters and the centrality of disabled types to specific genres, we have largely neglected to theorize the utility of humanities work for disability studies in particular, and disabled populations in general. This chapter surveys developments in the study of disability across the humanities in an effort to provide a governing logic for the necessity of the humanities to the evolution of disability studies in general.

We also seek to explain the myriad ways that scholars have complicated the question of "negativity" without surrendering a usable politics. Recent studies of disability in the archives provide a manifestly multifaceted base upon which to build our own period's address of disability representations. Consistent throughout will be our own efforts to assess both the pervasive and the hypersymbolic nature of disability as a grounding for our later theorizations of narrative prosthesis. Somewhere between these difficulties, humanities scholars make their uneasy home in disability studies.

Negative Imagery

From the outset the majority of critical approaches to disability representation sought to theorize negative imagery. As with many investigations by scholars in the humanities into the social construction of identity, disability scholars first interrogated common stereotypes that pervaded the literary and filmic archives. Disability was viewed as a restrictive pattern of characterization that usually sacrificed the humanity of protagonists and villains alike. A few characters continually surfaced as evidence: Shakespeare's murderous, hunchbacked king, Richard III; Melville's obsessive, one-legged captain, Ahab; and Dickens's sentimental, hobbling urchin, Tiny Tim. The repeated citation of these three figures as central to disability characterization initially demonstrated, at the most basic level, that disability existed in canonical literary works. Literary scholars promoted the idea that disabled characters, unlike racial minorities and homosexuals, for example, played a visible role in several of the most important works in European and American literature.[2] While the recourse to these three examples gave the impression that this presence was hardly overwhelming, interpretations of negative disability images nonetheless secured the argument that disability had been neglected in the critical tradition. The early scholarship also demonstrated literature's complicity in the historical devaluation of people with disabilities.

One of the first collections to devote space to literary and media images—Gartner and Joe's *Images of the Disabled, Disabling Images*—emphasized the pernicious nature of stereotypes. In it such writers and scholars as Leonard Kriegel, Deborah Kent, and Paul Longmore exposed representation as a devious device of mainstream and artistic mediums. Kriegel's essay, "Disability as Metaphor in Literature," took on the entire literary tradition, boldly declaring that depictions of disability fell far short of realistic portrayals of human complexity. In his analysis of a performance of the coronation scene in *Richard III,* he located what he believed to be the two most pervasive and insidious images in the literary tradition:

> In the ascent, the red-caped figure crawls up the steps [to the throne], like some gigantic insect, to take that which he has cheated others of. Imposing its limitations to rob legitimacy, the broken body begs for compassion. In the history of Western literature, both before and after Shakespeare, there is

little to be added to these two images, although there are a significant number of variations upon them. The cripple is threat and recipient of compassion, both to be damned and to be pitied—and frequently to be damned as he is pitied. (7)

Importantly, Kriegel's sense of outrage is paralleled by many disability critics who see the metaphoric opportunism of literature as a form of public slander. In establishing the two poles of disability characterization—threat and pity—Kriegel provided a shorthand method for disability scholars to gain control of a limiting literary archive. *Richard III* represents an early example of stigmatizing cultural dictates to which even Shakespeare capitulates. The writer's world, according to Kriegel, evidenced the "vantage point of the normals" (7), and characters with disabilities could be expected to evidence a scapegoating attitude rife in culture and history writ large. As Shari Thurber pointed out, "The disabled have a bad literary press" (12). Even so, the literary archive would at least serve as a repository for documenting demeaning attitudes toward people with disabilities.

Kriegel's commentary proved emblematic of the negative-image school of criticism, which diagnosed literature as another social repository of stereotypical depictions. Unlike other minority (such as race and sexuality) studies of literary representation that found a desired counter to demeaning cultural attitudes in their own literary traditions, literary scholars of disability found little refuge in creative discourses. The negative-image school found literary depictions to be, at best, wanting, and, at worst, humiliating: "While metaphoric use of disability may seem innocuous enough, it is in fact a most blatant and pernicious form of stereotyping" (Thurber 12). The core of this argument centered upon disabled characters as one and the same with disabled people. There was a direct correlation, argued these scholars, between debasing character portraits and demeaning cultural attitudes toward people with disabilities.

In this way, the negative-imagery school set out to establish a continuum between limiting literary depictions and dehumanizing social attitudes toward disabled people. In his seminal essay "Screening Stereotypes: Images of Disabled People in Television and Motion Pictures," Paul Longmore diagnosed film and television as influential reinforcers of cultural prejudice against disabled people. Rather than Kriegel's two predominant images in literature, Longmore found three stereotypes commonly perpetuated by electronic media: "disability is a punishment for evil; disabled people are embittered by their 'fate'; disabled people resent the nondisabled and would, if they could, destroy them" (67). Longmore's analysis of popular media paralleled Kriegel's arguments in that both saw contemporary attitudes about people with disabilities as informed by repeated paradigms and plots.

The restrictive elements of stories about disability helped create an uncompromising public belief in the limited options for people with disabilities: "Disabled characters abound, but the ways in which they are portrayed and the development of narrative around them is relentlessly negative" (Pointon and Davies 1). From the outside, the meager nature of these disabled characters' lives were depicted as inevitably leading toward bitterness and anger that made them objects of suspicion. In fact, Kriegel and Longmore argued in tandem that disability portrayals could be understood as a cathartic revenge by the stigmatizers, who punish the stigmatized to alleviate their own worries about bodily vulnerability and inhumane social conditions.

What stands out in the analyses of the negative-image school is the importance of plots that emphasize individual isolation as the overriding component of a disabled life. The angst surrounding the status of people with disabilities surfaced in expressive discourses as a desire to seclude the offending party within a drama of his or her own making. Longmore first identified this element as the most pervasive and debilitating aspect of disability representation. By depicting disability as an isolated and individual affair, storytellers artificially extracted the experience of disability from its necessary social contexts. The portraiture of disability in literature and electronic media "psychologized" the cultural understanding of disability. Disabled characters were either extolled or defeated according to their ability to adjust to or overcome their tragic situation. Longmore and others pointed out that "[social] prejudice and discrimination rarely enter into either fictional or nonfictional stories, and then only as a secondary issue" (74). Because representations of disability tend to reflect the medicalized view that restricts disability to a static impairment entombed within an individual, the social navigation of debilitating attitudes fails to attain the status of a worthy element of plot or literary contemplation.

The failure of a politicized interest to show itself in the disability plot could be evidenced in any number of ways within a variety of genres. Hafferty and Foster, for example, argue that the defining feature of disabled experience is "an awareness that issues when disabilities and handicaps are created through interactions between people with physical impairments and an unyielding and antagonistic environment" (189). Yet their analysis of disabled detectives in crime novels discovers that the reading public is encouraged to "view matters that are rightly located within social settings as residing in individual achievements and/or failures" (189). Literary techniques such as passive dialogue and readerly identifications with individual protagonists serve as stylistic conventions in the detective genre that help "shape the messages being delivered" (193). Hafferty and Foster's focus upon negative representations was humanities-based "proof" that discrimination against disabled people not only existed but was fostered by the images consumed by readers and viewers.

While the analysis of the negative image was carefully supported by a largely structuralist model that slotted disability types into generic classifications and representational modes, the unearthing of discriminatory images tended to collapse all representations into a sterile model of false consciousness. In *The Cinema of Isolation,* Martin Norden extended Longmore's argument about isolating media portraits by drawing up all of film history into a net of conspiracy. The Hollywood filmmaker, according to Norden, participates in an exploitative scheme that capitalizes upon the visual spectacle that disabilities offer to the camera eye. Film has taken the place of the nineteenth-century freak show "in the name of maintaining patriarchal order" (6). In spite of the historical prevalence of disabled people in film, Norden condemned nearly every image as the product of filmic castration anxiety and discriminatory beliefs. As Pointon and Davies point out, "It is too simplistic to talk about 'negative' compared with 'positive' images because although disabled people are in general fairly clear about what might constitute the former, the identification of 'positive' is fraught with difficulty" (1). Scholarship on the negative image strained beneath the weight of such wholesale condemnations of representational portraits.

In spite of research that saw most artistic and popular representations of disability as debilitating to the social advance of disabled people the analysis of negative images helped to support the idea that disability was socially produced. Identifying common characterizations that reinforced audiences' sense of alienation and distance from disability began an important process of scholarly attempts to rehabilitate public beliefs. Literature and film provided a needed archive of historical attitudes from which to assess ideologies pertaining to people with disabilities. While social scientists sought to understand contemporary beliefs about disabled populations, humanities scholars began to sift through expansive representational preserves. These materials solidified arguments in disability studies about disabled peoples' position as historical scapegoats. In many ways this impulse still undergirds a humanities-based politics of critiquing the trite and superficial portraits churned out on a daily basis by the mainstream media. To change negative portrayals, a powerful commentary was needed to make authors more self-conscious of the conventions at work in their own media.

In addition, humanities scholars of the negative image looked for the opportunity to identify against the grain of disability's presumed malignancy or excessive fragility. For example, Leonard Kriegel declared an identification with Richard III's antipathy toward the incomprehension of an able-ist world, even as he condemned Shakespeare's too easy bid for dramatic pathos. If Kriegel's affectation seemed perverse, he nonetheless anticipated later efforts to embrace disabled characters' definitive humanity (or alien-ness) as a move of transgressive identification. In this manner, scholars in the humanities began to seek out the lines of convergence and divergence from their own experiences in literature and film.

Social Realism

One important insight that consistently surfaced in the scholarship on negative imagery was that the majority of disability portraits were inaccurate and misleading. A new social realism[3] was needed to counter misguided attitudes about people with disabilities. As Deborah Kent argued in "Disabled Women: Portraits in Fiction and Drama," one could posit a direct correlation between the lives of fictional disabled females and social attitudes toward women with disabilities in general: "An assessment of the disabled woman's place in literature may serve as a barometer to measure how she is perceived by society. Conversely, the literary image of the disabled woman may influence the way disabled women are seen and judged in real life" (48). The equation between fictional images and the distorted images one faced as a disabled person was from the social realist perspective a way of elevating the analysis of literature to a pragmatic necessity.

Like many persons in materialist literary movements before—Georges Lukács for Marxism, Virginia Woolf for feminism, W. E. B. Du Bois for African American studies—disability critics demonstrate the inadequacy of historical images by identifying that which was left out of the picture or distorted for the sake of a dramatic portrayal. Social realism calls for more realistic representations. The social realists' primary criterion centers upon whether literary depictions serve as correctives to social misapprehensions about the specifics of experiences of disability. We can sum up this line of approach in the humorous point made by Irv Zola in his survey of popular detective fiction. Out of hundreds of novels that forward disabled detective "heroes," never once did Zola find a wheelchair user commenting, "God dammit, how I hate stairs" (505). Realism promotes a more direct depiction of the reality of disabled characters—from architecture to attitudes. Realistic depictions, argues social realism, will offer familiarity with an experience that has been understood as thoroughly alien.

Social realist scholarship seeks to decrease the kinds of alienation that pervade social views of disabled people. If the negative image results from associations of disability with personal failure, tragic loss, and excessive dependency, then social realists search for more accurate images that could effectively counterbalance this detrimental history. One positive exception to the cinema of isolation is found in *Waterdance,* a 1980s film drama that documents the medical, romantic, and social life of a recently paralyzed man. The realism of *Waterdance* can be located, for some, in its depiction of the punishing technology of modern medicine or by the camaraderie that develops between disabled men on a hospital ward. The call for social realism also helps to boost critical interest in autobiography as a representational reality that counters artistic metaphors and opportunistic spectacle. G. Thomas Couser's *Recovering Bodies* analyzes the restorative properties of recent disability memoirs not only to the writers but to the literary tradition itself. In each of these examples, humanities scholars seek reparation in a more adequate representation, to be found in films, autobiographies, or fictions that attend directly to the embodied experience of disabled characters. To offset a negative portrait, realist images offer up a more substantive, fleshy substitute.

Following Zola's lead, several commentators stress inaccurate portraiture by striking at the level of representation itself—disabled characters, they argue, fail to measure up to the "reality" of disabled lives. The paraplegic writer Andre Dubus amusingly explains the limitations of Hollywood films about disability in his discussion of the award-winning *Passion Fish:* "I remember one scene in Louisiana, they're (the paraplegic protagonist and her aide) on a wharf and there's this little skiff, and she tells the nurse, 'Get me in the boat.' Now these are things I live with all the time. Next scene, she's in the boat, and I said, 'How the fuck did she lower this woman from the chair into the boat in the water?' Show me that and you've got some story" (5). Others such as Hafferty and Foster's discussion of Deaf detectives in crime novels argue that despite the characteristic feature of "deafness," the protagonist rarely experiences the dilemmas of life as a hearing-impaired person negotiating a hearing world. Deaf or hearing-impaired detectives are rarely depicted as having to supply themselves with "a steady stream of sign language interpreters to facilitate [their] daily communication with others," nor are they subject to the routine or disastrous misinterpretations of daily life. Their summation of this lack of fictional realism evidences that fictional detectives "may be deaf, but [their] lack of hearing seems to have no impact on, or even relationship to, [their] work as . . . detectives" (195).

In identifying examples of inaccurate characterization, social realism does not call for "positive images" that would celebrate the lives of people with disabilities in a romanticized light. Rather, scholars approach even self-styled "positive" portraits with skepticism and save some of their most severe critiques for notions of disabled "heroism." Paul Darke admonishes his readers that David Lynch's *Elephant Man* "is not the liberal, tolerant, and pro-difference film it, and its supporters, suppose it to be. . . . often the positive image of disability is really very negative, so, beware of bearers of positive images!" (341). For Darke, not only does the film of Merrick's life distort the facts of his experience within an incarcerating medicalized view of monstrous oddity, but the production objectifies his image in a freak show–like spectacle of difference for the titillation of its viewers.

Within the social realist perspective, inadequate representation is attributed to two predominating factors: either the paucity of "positive" examples in narrative traditions, or the undertheorized nature of what constitutes a negative image. In other words, the call for more realistic depictions of disability proves another side of the negative-imagery coin because to critique inadequate, dehumanizing, or false representations is to simultaneously call for more acceptable representations. Yet the distinction between negative and positive proves a difficult one to define. As Darke points out, that which parades itself as "fixing" the historical record often ends up in the pathos of an individual life or in the falsely superhuman portrait of the overcompensating crip.

Most importantly, the social realist perspective develops arguments that demonstrate the narrative penchant for extracting the social conditions of disability from the act of characterization itself. British scholars such as Tom Shakespeare argue this point most succinctly, noting that fictional portraits often ignore "the way in which disability is a relationship between people with impairment and a disabling society" (287). Unlike other identity movements that called for a politics based upon more individualized representations of their lives, social realism argues that depictions of disability have suffered from a history of excessive individuation. Isolation and excessive idiosyncrasy were the bane of disabled people's representational lives, and social realism pushes for the necessity of a relational or social model.

As David Hevey argues in *The Creatures That Time Forgot*, "The reformation of oppressive imagery is only important (or, at least, more than superficially) if it is linked to wider social issues, such as access" (102).

"Positive images" would be determined not by their ability to portray disabled people in a good light; rather, Hevey argues, acceptable portrayals entail the refusal to disavow or suppress the site of struggle and oppression that characterizes a contemporary experience of disability. Hevey and other social realists insist upon politicizing disability by portraying it as the result of the interaction between impairment and physical and attitudinal environments. Limitation needs to be represented in a visceral way, but it should not be relegated to the level of an individual predicament or a purely embodied phenomenon.

The call for action in social realism centers upon a belief that disability will continue to be misconstrued and relegated to the "dustbins" of history if the able-bodied are left to construct images from their own prejudices (Shakespeare 283). The issue comes down to controlling the means of production. If disabled people take responsibility for the production of their own images, the social realists reason, images will evolve into more acceptable forms. A literal representation of disability would capture the myriad negotiations of a fraught social environment, obstacles would prove themselves of societal making rather than individual limitation, and technology previously hidden in the corners of homes and institutions would take center stage in the drama of disability as a lived experience. In this view, the recent remake of Alfred Hitchcock's 1955 film *Rear Window* with Christopher Reeves was revolutionary in its tracking shots of respirator tubing and high-tech sets sporting gurneys and elevators.

Thus, the social realist perspective would supply an openly politicized image of disability. As Hevey again puts it, the issue of positive representation is "tied to the general movement for rights . . . whereby image-politics become a part of the struggle for access, not an excuse for it" (103). The acceptable image legislated by the social realists would be based first and foremost upon a representational advocacy wherein images function as a weapon of political action and as redress to social incomprehension.

New Historicism

The social realist model has dominated recent theories of disability in the humanities. The political objectives that inform this perspective fueled some of the innovations of recent work in a nuanced historical revisionism. While the influence of social realism continues, however, recent investigations have diverged from some of the social realists' foundational assumptions. Critiques or revisions of social realism have been based upon four key principles relating to aesthetics and historical retrieval: (1) social realism assumed that disability tended to be concealed rather than pervasive in literary and film traditions; (2) the practitioners created a largely ahistorical paradigm that overlooked the specificity of disability representation as an ideological effect of particular periods; (3) social realism presumed that no disability perspective informed the "inaccurate" images that pervaded the social realist's critique; and (4) social realism projected its own contemporary desires onto the images it sought to rehabilitate.

Both the scholarship on negative images and social realism adopted a relatively static structuralist methodology. Interpreters channeled all images into a few representational possibilities, and the results became monolithic. There was the passively suffering angel of the house, the overcompensating supercrip, the tragically innocent disabled child, the malignant disabled avenger, and the angry war veteran. While these shorthand categorizations indeed showed up in popular texts and genre formulas, they preempted a more engaged historical scholarship. The generic classification of disabled types produces an ahistorical interpretation that tends to see disability representations as slanderously consistent across cultures and periods.

How could disability scholars complicate the issue of negative representation by placing disability within a more specific historical context? Could disability scholars develop a theory capable of explaining the seeming paradox that dehumanizing portraits of disabled characters could also buttress a previous generation's critique of debilitating institutions such as medicine? Would disability studies in the humanities rest its contribution on the depreciation of its own archival material in the name of stereotypical creations and suspect politics?

To begin with, a new historicism of disability representations in the humanities sought to perform an anthropological unearthing of images that could help to reconstruct a period's point of view on human variation. Stories provided more than cultural escapism: as explanatory paradigms, they revealed the supernatural and social origins of disability's appearance in the world. An early example came in Susan Schoon Eberly's discussion of the figure of the changeling in European folklore. Eberly argued that cultural uncertainty about the origins of physical disabilities such as dwarfism, cretinism, cerebral palsy, Down's syndrome, and so on, often engendered tales of fantastical children: "Specific examples of changelings, solitary fairies— both domesticated and reclusive—and the offspring of fairy-human matings . . . seem to offer identifiable portraits of children who were born, or who became, different as a result of identifiable congenital disorders" (58). The "special nature" of changelings, who often did not walk, talk, or run unless they were not being watched, suggests a literary effort to explain a mysterious physical phenomenon. The changeling tales sat on the cusp of a historical shift between medieval superstition and medical diagnoses of congenital disabilities.

In a vein parallel to Eberly's arguments about disability as an explanatory mystery of literary interest, Davidson, Woodill, and Bredberg contend that the rampant representations of disability in nineteenth-century children's literature serve a similar function. Borrowing from a primarily religious discourse of social instruction for the middle classes, Victorian tracts on disability forward physical variation as a divine mystery that cannot be comprehended by empirical discourses: "Disability cannot be understood in human terms. Like all forms of human suffering, it needs to be placed within God's mysterious scheme of things" (43). As instructional tales, Victorian children's literature evidence a penchant for discussing disability in terms of individual responsibility and the need for charity toward the infirm. Nineteenth-century authors sought to mitigate social readings of malignancy by enfolding disabled children within a paternalistic cultural logic of financial and moral benevolence.

Unlike social realist methodology, historical revisionists focus the majority of their attention upon the function of disability in "high art." The importance of efforts to historicize disability representations demonstrates that artistic narratives play a key role in forwarding a logic or system of explanation for birth anomalies and environmental accidents. Even after the professionalization of modern medicine, literature continues to serve an important explanatory function in the cultural understanding of disability. The changeling figure offered up by Eberly and by Davidson, Woodill, and Bredberg proffered disability as a product of mainstream beliefs, and literature participated in the process of trying to pierce its mystery by offering up tales of otherworldly creatures or social "unfortunates." The historical analysis of disability helps to identify the shifting investments of cultures when confronted with the variability of human biology and psychology.

Within the studies developed by new historicism, disability is recognized as a product of specific cultural ideologies that do not simply reveal reductive or stigmatizing attitudes. As Diane Price Herndl theorizes in her work on the female invalid in Victorian literature, the disabled subject should be interpreted neither as an "entirely passive construct nor as an entirely active agent" (12). Instead the writer and disability as the representational object of the writer's discourse situate themselves more dynamically with respect to the culture within which they are produced. "Neither the woman experiencing an illness nor the author writing a story about a woman's illness is free of the ways that illness has been represented before, but neither one is entirely constrained either" (12). Herndl's turn complicated the terrain of previous approaches by arguing that disability portraits provide a window onto a more dynamic interchange between culture, author, text, and audience. Disability is a product of an interaction between all of these positions that create and re-create the disabled body as a potent product of literary investment.

Thus, while the prototypical image of the leisurely Victorian woman may fit comfortably with the image of suffering femininity because each is stripped of her agency within a patriarchal and able-ist order, nineteenth-century women writers also sought to challenge that image. Consequently, while Charlotte Perkins-Gilman's portrait of a woman's descent into madness in *The Yellow Wallpaper* could be interpreted as an unflattering portrait of cognitive disability, the storyteller's strategy upends the controlling medical model of femininity's excessive frailty and emotional instability. While the infamous hunchbacked doctor, Chillingworth, in *The Scarlet Letter* grows increasingly decrepit as his immoral motivations deepen, Hawthorne's characterization strategy evolved out of nineteenth-century literary efforts to condemn medical practitioners to the deterministic dictates of their own pathologizing discourse on the body. Both of these stories evidence a "negative" outcome with respect to the disabled character, but their object of critique parallels the political objectives of the contemporary disability movement.

The resistance to dismissing disability images as merely detrimental proved evident in an array of essays included in our anthology *The Body and Physical Difference*. Historical revisionist efforts produced interpretations that situated disability as both a perpetual societal obsession in the West and as the object of complex cultural beliefs. Many of these efforts unearthed examples of cultures that in surprising ways integrated, rather than scapegoated, people with disabilities. Martha Edwards argues that rather than holding a static, denigrating belief about disability, as had been previously maintained, ancient Greek texts evidence that disabled people were often integrated into the fold of ancient communal life. Felicity Nussbaum locates a utopian political alliance between marginalized disabled and feminist communities depicted in Sarah Scott's eighteenth-century novel *Millenium Hall*. Maria Frawley analyzes Harriet Martineau's Victorian autobiographical explorations of invalid subjectivity that revised the traditionally passive medical patient into an active negotiator of her own corporeal experience. Cindy LaCom argues that nineteenth-century women writers countered the monstrous sexuality of female disability in male novels with more empowering images of disabled women who escaped the patriar-chal discourse of feminine objectification. In her discussion of twentieth-century German literary representations of disability, Elizabeth Hamilton documents a movement from the grotesque to the political in the works of disability autobiographers. Rosemarie Garland Thomson argues that dis-ability in the works of African American women writers serves to destabi-lize the dominant binary codes of abnormal/normal, male/female, desired/undesired, by openly exploring marginal identities in political, rather than stigmatizing, terms. Finally, Caroline Molina's reading of the film *The Piano,* argues that the female protagonist's "disabling" muteness is resignified by the end of the story into a sign of female refusal to participate in masculinist discourses.

What connects these alternative interpretations of disability is a twofold interest in using an expansive literary archive to solidify the variability of human physiology and reactions to biological mutability. Disability had begun to be recognized as a potent vehicle of political critique at various moments in the literary tradition. By and large these alternative representa-tional modes had been ignored by literary and disability critics alike because of insufficient paradigms for analyzing disability as a site of literary invest-ment. What changes in these analyses is not the disabled object of represen-tation itself, but rather the goals of the methodology brought to bear on it. This archival resurrection demonstrates that disability, like all representa-tional objects, can be mobilized in a variety of directions. In demonstrating the existence of alternative disability discourses within literature and film, scholars challenge the assumption that our moment occupies the only "for-ward-looking" cultural perspective on disability in history.

Other scholars in *The Body and Physical Difference* interpret historical reactions to disability as the site of conflictual ideological agendas. Scholars applying this approach deflect attention away from disability representation and toward a critique of social institutions that authored disability as Other. Lennard Davis assesses the paradox of the art historian's ability to interpret the armless body of the Venus de Milo as a vision of aesthetic perfection, while cultures continued to devalue human "armless" figures as less than ideal. Following the American Civil War, David Yuan finds that the rise of a modern prosthetics industry sought to "rehabilitate" not only wounded war veterans but also a national wound that had disrupted North-South relations. Jan Gordon interprets the potent symbolism of male disability in D. H. Lawrence's *Lady Chatterley's Lover* and other modernist works, as an effort to symbolize the decline of privilege and power in the British aris-tocracy. Martin Pernick demonstrates that eugenics, as exemplified in propaganda films that rationalize the medical murder of disabled infants, ultimately premise the determination of expendability upon an aesthetic criterion. David Gerber compares competing ideological interests of the political Right and Left in the patriotic "repair" of war hero Al Schmid's blindness in *The Pride of the Marines* and in his relation to the Blind Veterans Association. Paul Longmore reads the telethon industry's sentimental display of childhood disability as a product of nineteenth-century American discourses on paternalistic philanthropy. In a critical look at contemporary U.S. disability autobiography, Madonna Miner contrasts the stories of disabled men and women in order to assess their purchase upon traditional narrative schemas of male emasculation and female victimization.

At work in these approaches has been a developing conception of what Lennard Davis set out to define in *Enforcing Normalcy* as the "construction of the normal world" (22). Within this schema Davis and the essayists mentioned above invert the historical imperative to designate, define, and diagnose disabilities, by turning the "normal" into the producer of pathology. Rather than authorize cultural institutions as the arbiters of deviance, the study of normalcy would expose disability as "not a discrete object but a set of social relations" (11). The production of disability as human oddity or exceptional limitation in science, as in art, would be founded upon the norm's ability to disguise itself as transparently average. In this way the corporeal norm poses as universally desirable—the barometer against which all biologies are assessed and compared. Normalcy studies debunk the norm as an ideological abstraction that is based upon a faulty empiricism.

The medical anthropologist George Canguilhem argues that medicine's decision in the nineteenth century to use a bodily ideal to assess an inherently dynamic and adaptive biology effectively surrendered any claim to scientific objectivity (155). Much recent literary criticism rests upon this inversion: rather than simply deviating from widely expressed biological traits, disabilities demonstrate that the ideal cannot exist without its "deviant" contrast. Using literary and filmic archives to demonstrate that norms shift through history and across cultures, normalcy scholars theorize concepts of the norm as not only flawed and artificial, but feeding a eugenicist mind-set. In so theorizing, the humanities continue to wage a pivotal battle against the objectification of disability in medical science and its popular offshoots.

All of these studies speak to the primacy of disability as narrative prosthesis in representational discourses. While disability is a common feature of narrative characterization, however, disabled characters have been consistently received by readers and viewers as isolated cases. Building upon the narrative theories of Susan Stewart, we have argued that "[d]isability studies seeks to understand the ways in which we produce the 'private room' of disability in our most public discourses" (*Physical Difference* 17). The historical revisionist turn in the humanistic study of disability sought to dismantle this "private room," consolidating a body of scholarship that disability is not only *integrable* but *integral* to human communities and biologies across time (Stiker). In other words, the historical revisionists argued that physical and cognitive difference was the rule rather the exception of historical experience.

Biographical Criticism

One result of this historical revisionism has been to seek out authors and artists in history who were themselves disabled—or who were involved with disabled people. With disability saturating narrative discourses in the literary and filmic archives, one may also presume that some of the works themselves had been produced by disabled people or writers with disability-identified perspectives. Within biographical criticism's approach to the contexts of authorship three tendencies have predominated: (1) analyses of critical readings of disability by able-bodied and disabled scholars alike; (2) the analysis of the relationship between literature and medicine; and (3) interpretations by disabled writers of other disability characterizations in history.

Biographical archival work on notoriously "deformed" storytellers, such as Aesop and Socrates, and disabled and chronically ill authors such as John Milton, Alexander Pope, Lord Byron, Samuel Johnson, John Keats, Stephen Crane, Katherine Mansfield, Virginia Woolf, and Marcel Proust (among many others) have sought to discern a "disability logic" informing their individual artistic works and personas. This undertaking has resulted in serious corrections and complications of the literary historical record while also challenging the idea that disability images have been exclusively the product of able-ist authors. Since disability offers up its own routing of an author's experience in the world, biographical scholarship on disabled authorship properly assumes that revisiting texts from this orientation will yield important insights into the influence of disability identities upon creative efforts. Whereas, as Lennard Davis points out, "successful disabled people . . . have their disability erased by their success" (*Normalcy* 9), this scholarly work seeks out the inevitable impact of disability upon the creator's worldview.

In "Infinities of Formes" we claim for disability studies scholarly works such as Eleanor Gertrude Brown's *Milton's Blindness*. Originally published in 1934 and recently reissued by Columbia University Press as a landmark in Milton studies, Brown's book grounds its interpretation of Milton's poetry upon her own experience as a blind person. Taking on an openly essentialist claim to her understanding of Milton's verse, Brown acknowledges the power that disabled experience can lend to interpretations of disability: "To the interpretation of Milton's life and writing after the loss of sight, I add my knowledge of blindness. And on account of this bond of union, I bring to the task an interest such as Milton must have given to the writing of *Samson Agonistes*. Thus, by similarity of experience alone, I am rendered a more able critic" (preface). From a disability vantage, with a decidedly "contemporary" inversion of "able" rhetoric, Brown asks disability questions of Milton's poetics—a method that results in fresh and compelling interpretations.

The importance of the critic's commitment to locating the contexts of the experience of disability cannot be overstated. Whereas Alexander Pope's influential standard biographer, Maynard Mack, placed Pope's scoliosis in a sphere separate from his poetics—a move that results in fairly abstract pronouncements about Pope's off-quoted line, "This long disease my life"— disability scholar Helen Deutsch overlaps Pope's "deformed" body and his classical poetics to insightful results. Deutsch contends that "deformity enables Pope's particular brand of imitation to go originality one better: his poetry marks itself not as original but as impossible to duplicate" (*Resemblance* 27). In recent work Deutsch also explores the implications of disabled authorship for eighteenth-century poetics: her research "considers the history of the authorial body in eighteenth-century Britain, beginning with the visible deformity of Alexander Pope's curved spine and closing with the indecipherable inwardness figured by Samuel Johnson's unruly body . . . Disability has in fact distinguished the English literary canon—itself a product of the eighteenth century—as a catalog of authorial monsters and paradoxically representative oddities" ("Dr. Johnson," forthcoming).

The discovery and "outing" of disabled authors in literary history has followed upon archival work undertaken by practitioners in the field of literature and medicine. As is borne out by its name, the field of literature and medicine partakes of an affinity with the disposition of medical practice. Hence, scholars have undertaken research in order to label authors in history with contemporary medical diagnoses and assess their attitudes toward their doctors (never very good)! One finds in this branch of literary studies primarily a focus upon literary depictions of doctors and their treatment of diseased patients.[4] This allows literature-and-medicine critics, for example, to focus upon a birth scene in Toni Morrison's *The Bluest Eye* in order to critique Polly's insulting treatment from white doctors while overlooking the fact of her "crippled gait" as a key component of her character and her relationship to her husband.

Pivotal in the literature-and-medicine arena, Philip Sandblom's *Creativity and Disease* usefully discerns examples throughout history of artists and writers who have found creative potential in the experience of a physical or cognitive impairment. His research serves as a useful casebook of disabled writers; Sandblom even claims an identification with disabled people by recalling his own victimization at the hands of medical error. At the same time, like those of many medical professionals, his assessments psychologize disabled artists, with all the distance, prejudice, and misconstrual engendered by an objective posture. Indeed, he rehabilitates the good intentions of literary history's doctors against the insults of their writer-patients. Among many examples of ill-founded literary diagnosis, Sandblom quotes Sir Francis Bacon's equation between deformity and vengeful personality as a means for understanding the psyches of Lord Byron and Daniel Defoe: "These unfortunates [people with congenital malformations], then, sometimes react with quiet resignation but more often with revolt and extreme efforts to compensate, now and then with artistic creation" (Sandblom 199). In Bacon's words, "Whosoever hath anything fixed in his person that doth induce contempt, hath also a perpetual spur in himself to rescue and deliver himself from scorn, therefore all deformed persons are extreme bold" (Sandblom 107).

Whereas Sandblom interprets Byron's work as an overwrought revenge upon the universe, biographical criticism would reread Byron's poetics with an eye toward his artistic vantage upon social attitudes. In other words, just as sociological disability studies assesses the social, as opposed to the personal, origination of disability issues, so does the new literary study of disability look to the social and aesthetic grounds for the artist's revisionary efforts. In disability studies, biographical critics are likely to argue that Byron's embrace of Shakespeare's villainous hunchback Richard III, and his refiguring of the play in his drama *The Deformed Transformed,* follow Pope's own penchant for claiming as personal monikers all the slings and arrows ("bottlenecked spider," "hunchback'd toad") tossed in the direction of "monstrous" humans. This transformative impulse in literary work, undertaken by disabled literary artists, figures prominently in our own moment's effort to find evidence of disability perspectives—even disability as a social role and subjectivity—in history.

This biographical line of interpretation of disability has led scholars to analyses of the disability involvements of able-bodied writers in history as well. Scholarship is immersed in interpreting the effects of disability households and experiences upon writers such as Walt Whitman, Mark Twain, and Mary Austin. How does Whitman's nursing of wounded and disabled Civil War veterans inform his poetical claims about fostering perfect national health? How do Twain's significant relationships with deaf friends affect his depictions of deaf characters and American Sign Language? Does Austin's institutional incarceration of her cognitively disabled daughter find expression in her art and writing?

Many literary scholars have assessed Virginia Woolf's sickbed seclusion with bouts of illness as key to her creative life. How might we interpret her squabbles over the invalid pronouncements of men with disabilities on women's writing? While one might expect Woolf to show a natural sympathy toward disabled communities and other socially marginalized identities, often the opposite is true. Throughout *A Room of One's Own,* Woolf complains that society rates women's abilities even below those of crippled men in the great ladder of existence. While critiquing the superfluous nature of male discourse upon female mystery, she asserts that "whether they were old or young, married or unmarried, red-nosed or humpbacked—anyhow, it was flattering, vaguely, to feel oneself the object of such attention, provided that it was not entirely bestowed by the crippled and the infirm" (28).

Similar examples abound in the tradition, for minority commentators tend to situate disability as a social grouping from which they must escape to assert the positivity of their own culturally devalued identity. Film scholar Judith Halberstam has argued that imposing stigmatized physical traits upon minority bodies evidences an ideological devaluation of the dominant culture toward sexual and racial minorities. In other words the "real" stigma of a disability deforms the otherwise evident value of gender and race as cultural differences.

As a counter to the participation of authors in the historical devaluation of disability identity, many writers have sought out alternative models in the archives to balance against their own experience as disabled people. The Japanese writer Kenzaburo Oë, who fathered an autistic son, reclaims the work of Flannery O'Connor as an example of a disabled author who wrote eloquently out of her own experience of lupus. In rereading O'Connor's posthumously published letters, Oë argues that the very basis of her originality sprang from her navigation of a debilitating condition: "I am sure it is the same accumulated practice that comes into play when the obstacles encountered by all those who labor in the fields of art are somehow—by trial and error—cleared to reveal a landscape no one has seen before" (57).

The nineteenth-century German philosopher Friedrich Nietzsche, whose work we discuss in chapter 3, can be interpreted in a parallel way. Nietzsche, who suffered severe migraines, stomach ulcers, and later in his life underwent a stroke and became aphasic, spent much of his life's work ironically championing such social outsiders as "cripples" and "grotesques." Because the physically unsightly are cordoned off from a stultifying mainstream culture, Nietzsche reasoned, their value would "reside" in "the very terms of their social ouster." *Twilight of the Idols,* his work on Socrates' well-known deformities, claims that the philosopher's body disrupted the Athenian faith in the correlation between bodily beauty and moral goodness. Yet, despite Socrates' physical nonconformity, Nietzsche critiques him for championing the supremacy of rationality and ignoring the power of his own aberrant corporeality. According to Nietzsche, much of the Greek philosopher's appeal for the ancient Athenians was based upon the freak show–like spectacle of a thinker who championed rationality as beauty in spite of the physical evidence to the contrary. Arguing that Socrates' visible presence introduced the destabilizing power of physical difference into philosophical discourse, Nietzsche berates Socrates and his followers for sacrificing the power of "the ugliest man" to the more banal superiority of abstract reason (*Twilight* 40).

Just as disability scholars in the humanities now search the archive for evidence of a countertradition of disability representations, so have researchers and writers before them searched. This championing or critique of one disabled writer by another demonstrates that a consciousness of disability has been available during prior ages. If one is cut off or isolated from a community of like-minded individuals, the archive can operate, not as a repository of dehumanizing values, but as an imaginative refuge for alternative ways of seeing. Disability, like other devalued social groupings, is first imposed from the outside as a source of stigma and then navigated from the inside as a mode of social redress. The inversionary tactics in Nietzsche and Oë involve an open embrace—even a stalwart declaration—of those who are most debased by cultures of the normal.

Future work will continue to review literary archives to counterpose artistic lives and the literary corpus. These textual studies will inevitably complicate a socially progressive model of disability history if only because many disabled people have made names for themselves as literary artists. This notoriety has often occurred in spite of an open grappling with the meaning of disability. Rather than a negativity, disability has provided the spur that allowed writers to unveil new landscapes of contemplation. Much work is currently under way in this new and fruitful line of inquiry—one that dovetails with efforts to show disability as a foundation for social and aesthetic work.

Transgressive Reappropriation

Whereas much work in the humanities has focused on interpretations of disability as a social process or a minority experience, Nietzsche's embrace of the value of outsiderness (those whom he ironically termed "the higher men"), discussed at length in chapter 3, points to the possibility of a transgressive narrative space for disability. Rather than rail against the unjust social exclusion of cripples, scholars have begun to attend to the subversive potential of the hyperbolic meanings invested in disabled figures. Much of the early work in disability studies centered upon the extreme emotions such as fascination/repulsion that disability conjures up in the cultural imaginary. The potency of these visceral reactions suggests that there is something significant at stake in the screening of disability from public view. We have argued elsewhere that while other minority identities have been allowed a space in liberal discourse for reclaiming their cultural meanings as a form of empowerment, disability has been viewed as revealing the ludicrous extremes of identity politics ("Foundations" 245). Whereas "Black Is Beautiful" or "Gay Pride" redresses the derision heaped upon a minority community by a dominant culture, disabilities have been blocked from access to a similar political status (245). The category of disability, according to many of the most "liberal" advocates, represents an undesirable state of being that no political triage can repair. Disability has been portrayed within many circles as the straw that breaks the camel's back of identity politics.

Yet, like other social movements, advocates for disability rights, artists, and scholars have recognized the power available in resignifying terms such as *cripple* and *gimp*. As opposed to substituting more palatable terms, the ironic embrace of derogatory terminology has provided the leverage that belongs to openly transgressive displays. The power of transgression always originates at the moment when the derided object embraces its deviance as value. Perversely championing the terms of their own stigmatization, marginal peoples alarm the dominant culture with a canniness about their own subjugation. The embrace of denigrating terminology forces the dominant culture to face its own violence head-on because the authority of devaluation has been claimed openly and ironically. Thus, the minority culture deflects the stigmatizing definition back on to the offenders by openly advertising them in public discourse. The effect shames the dominant culture into a recognition of its own dehumanizing precepts. What was most devalued is now righted by a self-naming that detracts from the original power of the condescending terms.

In a parallel fashion, disability scholars have also attempted to identify and reclaim the power of formerly stigmatized representations in literature. The influential critic Leslie Fiedler's early essay "Pity and Fear: Images of the Disabled in Literature and the Popular Arts" explains the potential power of literary transgression most pointedly: "we will have to exorcize our ambivalences toward the afflicted . . . by turning not to ersatz paeans of the heroism of the crippled, but to disturbing mythic literature; including *Richard III*, over which (let me confess in closing) I still shudder, and *A Christmas Carol*, over which I have wept more than once—and will, I suspect, weep again" (13). For Fiedler the literature of disability poses the problem of feeling drawn to that which seems most reprehensible (fear) or sentimental (pity). Yet he neither bemoans nor celebrates literary portraits but situates them within human psychology. For Fiedler, literary representations of disability do not resolve so much as tap into visceral emotions.

Fiedler complicates the idea of unsatisfactory imagery by placing literary representation within a psychoanalytical framework. The ambivalence readers sense in literary presentations of disabled characters is a vicarious experience of a previous culture's uncertainty about its disabled populations. While literature does not provide an antidote to this ambivalence, it does provide a window onto the complex nature of attitudes and their origins. Rather than explain away the visceral nature of responses to physical and cognitive differences, Fiedler seizes upon ambivalence as a universal response to the mystery of human variation. The upshot is not that negative imagery reveals dehumanizing attitudes, but rather that disability representation explicitly evokes powerful sentiments within the safe space of textual interactions. These "powerful sentiments" emanate from the transgressive power signified by physical and cognitive difference. Readers are seduced into an encounter with their most extreme reactions as a way of facing up to the imagined threat that they pose.

It is this visceral potential in the disruption caused by the disabled body that makes it both a primary tool for writers and an important vein for scholarly investigation. In Fiedler's book-length study *Freaks*, he explains that the viewer of the freak show spectacle experiences an encounter between self and other.

> The true Freak, however, stirs both supernatural terror and natural sympathy, since, unlike the fabulous monsters, he is one of us, the human child of human parents, however altered by forces we do not quite understand into

something mythic and mysterious, as no mere cripple ever is. . . . Only the true Freak challenges the conventional boundaries between male and female, sexed and sexless, animal and human, large and small, self and other, and consequently between reality and illusion, experience and fantasy, fact and myth. (*Freaks* 24)

Two issues are of importance in Fiedler's effort to define the power of the freak's physical spectacle. First, the terror of the challenge to the self's boundaries, which are believed to be more or less absolute, suggests that the spectacle of extraordinary bodily difference upsets the viewer's faith in his/her own biological integrity. The viewer of the freakish spectacle does not experience a feeling of superiority in his or her closer proximity to the normal ideal, but rather senses his or her own body to be at risk. The power is in the challenge of the self's stability rather than in its security.

Second, the division between the ordinary "cripple" and the spectacular freak is less absolute than Fiedler claims. While freak shows artificially exaggerated physical differences to enhance the encounter with difference (Bogdan), encounters with the freak and with routine disability fall on a continuum. The display of disability discomforts the viewer's identification with bodily ability or normalcy by destabilizing (albeit in a less spectacular manner) that which he or she takes to be biologically typical. The freak show enhances rather than singularly produces a reaction that already exists within the viewer.

Whereas Fielder would argue for a disjunction between the freak and the disabled person, disability scholars such as Rosemarie Garland Thomson have argued for the identification of a continuum between the two con-structed social positions. Thomson designates the arrival of freak shows in the United States as anything but a fleeting historical anomaly. Tethered to a period of rapid industrialization in America's "golden age" that "put bod-ies on arbitrary schedules instead of allowing natural rhythms to govern activity" (*Freakery* 11), the freak show promised the spectacle of a glimpse into the taboo underworld of human oddity. Such an amusement was to "assuage viewers' uneasiness either by functioning as a touchstone of anx-ious identification or as an assurance of their [own] regularized normalcy" (11). This approach to the "distasteful" freak of negative imagery or social realism helps to investigate not only the overwrought symbolism of physical differences, but also identifies the transgressive power invested in the social encounter with aberrancy.

Rather than view the freak as a rarified deviation, the essays in *Freakery* supply portraits of a widespread cultural phenomenon that speaks to the cul-tural fascination with spectacles of difference. As Thomson argues, the turn-of-the-century phenomenon of the freak show did not end, but rather dispersed into the "entertainment discourses of vaudeville, circuses, beauty pageants, zoos, horror films, rock celebrity culture, and Epcot Center" (13). In charting this proliferation of discourses around figures of human difference, *Freakery* identifies the political undercurrents of disability as a centerpiece of contemporary American popular culture. These studies also demonstrate a model of political power available to those who tap into the transgressive reservoirs of fascination and repulsion. Even the scholarship of its discomforting borders breaks down the assumed distance between spectator and object by violating the cultural dictum of silence that surrounds bodily deviation.

As a corollary to Thomson's overall critical project, which explores "a critical gap between disabled figures as fashioned corporeal others whose bodies carry social meaning and actual people with atypical bodies in real-world social relations" (*Extraordinary Bodies* 15), Helen Deutsch and Felicity Nussbaum pursue a related project. Tracing out the implications of a host of objectifying social and medical categories, from "monstrosity" to "aesthetic ugliness" to the "exotic deformed," the essays in "*Defects*" focuses upon the dovetailing of physical differences with categories of Otherness such as femininity and impoverishment. As many of the essayists in the collection demonstrate, in the eighteenth century open public discussions were conducted about what "marks the boundaries between the increasingly significant categories of the typical and atypical human being, the 'normal' and the 'abnormal'" (5). In the process of conversing about these issues, nonetheless, many eighteenth-century writers (including some with disabilities) seized the opportunity to harness the transgressive power of physical otherness and shake the foundations of aesthetic and cultural value:

> Swift's Lemuel Gulliver in his giant incarnation and as a pigmy exhibited for money is among the most obvious examples [of the physical and mentally "defective"] from literature. The lesser-known *Memoirs of Martin Scriblerus* includes discussions of conjoined, or "Siamese," twins joined at the back, the little Black Prince, and the "Man-mimicking Manteger." Alexander Pope's own diminished height, humpback, and general frailty made him a curiosity, and his *Dunciad* (1728) teems with monstrosities. . . . In addition, the deaf-mute Duncan Campbell attracted Eliza Haywood's attention and that of several other commentators during the early decades of the eighteenth century because of his second sight and his ability to use sign language. Sarah Scott's colony of the maimed served the women of *Millenium Hall* (1762), and she linked ugliness to virtue in her midcentury translation of a French novel, *Agreeable Ugliness: Or, the Triumph of the Graces* (1754). . . . Damaged literary heroines include Henry Fielding's *Amelia* (1751), who met with an accident that injured her nose, and the learned but lame and pockmarked Eugenia in Frances Burney's *Camilla* (1796). (Deutsch and Nussbaum 4–5)

Importantly, these examples evidence not only the centrality of disability to the period, but also an emerging recognition of ways in which difference can be harnessed to the alternative ends of minority and literary cultures. The critical connection between disability and femininity as monstrous deviances allows the editors to create a representational continuum between two surveyed and devalued biologies. Each emphasizes, not the other category's alien qualities, but the body's contest of restrictive social ideals and controls. As both Fiedler and Thomson point out, the literary encounter with deviance at first heightens alienation and then ultimately collapses the distance between disability and the inherently social processes that mark bodies as falling outside acceptable norms.

While most of the work in the humanities to date has centered upon physical disability as its grounding object of study, one of the major new areas of research in disability studies will need to be that of cognitive disabilities. Although cognitive disabilities have surfaced in the current research, only a few studies take the representation of psychological difference as their primary concern. For instance, Otto F. Wahl's *Media Madness: Public Images of Mental Illness* points out that images of madness pervade popular discourses such as mainstream television and film. While Wahl pursues the negative connotations of these images with a social realist methodology, arguing that "harmful images" exert a divisive pull upon audiences, other scholarship has begun to show an interest in the transgressive potential of "madness" as a shared fascination for literature and medicine alike. Allen Thiher's monumental study *Revels in Madness: Insanity in Medicine and Literature,* analyzes a surprising history of concordance between these two seemingly disparate (even antithetical) fields of study. According to Thiher, literature has historically provided the "applied" basis for "articulating the ways that madness can be experienced, lived as it were, in its alterity. . . . Both medicine and literature have had constant recourse to theater and to theatrical metaphors to describe, in various ways, the dynamics of madness" (24). This approach has made literature and medicine (particularly psychology and psychiatry) more intimate bedfellows than has been previously recognized.

Beginning with ancient Greece, Thiher's study demonstrates that literary stories of mental discordance have provided the foundation for scientific explanations of cognitive deviance. Rather than view this historical material as superficial and primitive, Thiher argues for a historical vision of madness as that which could productively give voice to the existence of disparate, and even antithetical, "realities." For instance, the autobiographies of the French Romantic Rousseau sought to validate "madness" as essential to the acquisition of insight, for "the power of madness to effect disclosure and bring about vision" brought writers "beyond the collectivity to an unmediated relation with the Word" (216–17). This exclusive access of those designated "mad" in their own time to a direct encounter with Truth was in keeping with the long-standing association of madness with divine revelation and was also an example of the transgressive possibilities offered by an individual's claim to various kinds of insanity. For Thiher, the power to claim the transgressive alterity of madness proved so alluring that even when people with mental disabilities were threatened with eradication, as during the Salem witch trials, individuals donned the mantle of insanity to articulate their experience of an alternative cognitive reality. Within this perspective individuals (artistic and otherwise) have openly claimed psychological difference rather than dissimulate its power over their own lives.

This disruption of a reader's identification with fictional ideals of normalcy through encounters with "transgressive disabilities" provides an unusual opportunity to rechart a period's fashioning of the meaning of disability. Interrogation of received beliefs and values situates the power of stigmatized bodies and minds as profoundly disconcerting rejoinders to biological absolutism. Since literature so often imagines its project as one of social questioning and radical critique, an important continuity can be formulated between contemporary disability politics and artistic production. While disability scholars in the humanities have been careful to avoid romanticizing the possibilities implicit in disability's transgressive "outings" of a culturally closeted phenomenon, they have revised simplistic assumptions about the characterization of disability. If the display of radical physical and cognitive deviance in narrative proves ultimately ambiguous to the values of our own disability movement, it nonetheless reveals that even the most "derisive" portrait harbors within it an antithesis, its own disruptive potential. At the least, disability scholars have provided a means for contemplating the ways in which earlier periods recognized and deployed the transgressive possibilities that aberrancy proffered.

Conclusion: The Necessity of Representation (and Its Discontents)

Representation inevitably spawns discontent. All portrayal (artistic or documentary) proves potentially allegorical in the sense that the act of characterization encourages readers or viewers to search for a larger concept, experience, or population. Thus, the effort to represent is inevitably fraught with politics. The question of disability's service to "negative" portrayals is profoundly complex and central to our thinking about narrative prosthesis. Any response is riddled with difficulty because the question is, first and foremost, social in its making. What one generation of interpreters views as "humane" can be challenged by the next, and so on and so forth. This is particularly true of the representation of disability because even well-meaning representations often result in violent justifications.

Let us provide just a brief example to underscore this point. The other day we were contacted by a journalist who wanted to write a piece about a new wave of children's books that feature characters with disabilities as protagonists. His hypothesis was that these were new identity-affirming portraits (this was spoken with a tinge of sarcasm for political correctness) that sought to instruct readers that "people with disabilities were just like everyone else." He wanted to know if previous stories about children with disabilities usually represented disability as a cautionary tale about bad things that can happen to you. We offered up examples of research, such as Eberly's argument that medieval stories presenting children with disabilities as visitors from fairy kingdoms sought to explain the appearance of congenital disabilities to premedical cultures. We mentioned early-twentieth-century children's stories that used disabilities as evidence that one had entered a fantastical world of imagination where the impossible could come true. Our point was that prior generations had produced ways of thinking about disability that were not solely cautionary. We added that, of course, such stories also provided a rationale for many parents who left their disabled children to die on beaches because the fairies would be returning them to their fantastical place of origin.

The issue of representation and what it produces in readers proves exceedingly complex. In chapter 3 we discuss how Nietzsche's ironic championing of the segregation of disabled people was used by the Nazis as an ideological manual to support the murder of disabled people, Gypsies, and Jews during the Holocaust. In the afterword we discuss Richard Powers's rendition of the Shinto myth that records the birth of a first "deformed" child to First Man and First Woman. The parents promptly ship their offspring out into the ocean in a makeshift boat to erase the evidence of their failure. Our arguments in *Narrative Prosthesis* situate disability as both origin and end—its desired eradication in each generation is countered only with the ferocity of an ultimate recalcitrance to such violent "utopian" programs.

This is the very real and dangerous terrain of representation that scholarship in the humanities and our conception of narrative prosthesis attempt to navigate. It is the heart of our own politics, which cannot be channeled into "acceptable" or "unacceptable" representation. Since the seemingly abstract and textual world affects the psychology of individuals (and, thus, the cultural imaginary), the interpretation of these figures and their reception proves paramount to the contribution of the humanities to disability studies. One cannot assess the merits or demerits of a literary portrait, for example, without understanding the historical context within which it was constructed and imbibed. Nor can one ignore the often disastrous consequences of even the most inspired tales.

What has proven most striking in the humanities' investigations of disability and in the construction of this study is the overview of disability throughout history and across cultures that literary and filmic archives provide. While one can charge discrimination and the lack of civil rights for people with disabilities in our own moment, the contention cannot be adequately demonstrated as systemic until a historical record of treatment has been reconstructed. In addition, disabled people inevitably navigate the representational types of an era—the narrated prosthetic couplings between difference and its social meanings—as coordinates operative in their own psyches. Imaginative works are integral to the alternatives produced for imagining disability by those "contained" within the rubric itself. Readers and viewers find their own personal interpretations of disability inevitably influenced by their imaginative encounters with disabled people in fictional works. For instance, Martha Stoddard Holmes's *Fictions of Affliction* analyzes Victorian culture's production of two predominating definitions of disability—the innocent afflicted child and the disabled beggar as enemy of the state. Writers with disabilities and authors who wrote about disability necessarily navigated these polar oppositions. In turn, the repetitious referencing of these discursive tropes provided a field of options for interpreting disability in the Victorian period that profoundly influenced the subjective experience of disability and the evolution of disabled subjectivity. Because literary archives provide a repository for historical reactions along these lines, the humanities have begun the important task of bequeathing a more sophisticated history of disability to disability studies and people with disabilities as a whole.

Whereas the survey of policies, incarcerating institutions, legislation, and so forth, provides an overview of state-authored responses to quandaries posed by disabled populations, fictive representations provide access to less legalistic or "official" contexts for understanding disability. Whereas the ancient Athenians' belief in the perfectability of the physical body produced a mythology that proffered only one disabled God (Hephaestus), Lois Bragg has argued that the pantheon of Gods with disabilities in ancient Norse myths demonstrates a popular emphasis upon the value of personal sacrifice for one's community. In this sense, the analysis of imaginative works allow scholars in the humanities to record a history of people with disabilities that comes closer to recapturing the "popular" values of everyday lives. If disability is the product of an interaction between individual differences and social environments (architectural, legislative, familial, attitudinal, etc.), then the contrast between discourses of disability situates art and literature as necessary to reconstructing the dynamics of this historical interaction.

This history is by no means complete, but the readings that follow demonstrate that attitudes and programs toward disabled people prove less static or exclusively detrimental than most scholars originally anticipated. The history of disability, like the history of any socially produced constituency, proves surprisingly uneven and multifaceted. Our work is to understand this multiplicity in its richness. After all, how do we adequately assess our own era's reactions and representations without a thoroughgoing knowledge of other cultures and generations? What does it say about our own culture's penchant for designating disability if previous cultures did not see the need for doing so? How do we address the significant differences between disability and other minority studies without the linguistic and identity-based interpretative methodologies that have been largely pioneered in the humanities?

As a linguistic "signifier" disability also incites discontent, for the rubric proves as slippery as any minority category imposed from without. Singular designations attempting to contain a diverse people with widely variable histories represented by categories such as "demoniacs," "the halt and lame," "cripples," "the handicapped," or even our own contemporary rubric of "disabled people," inevitably result in those who are labeled chafing against the imprecision and the monolithic representational characteristics assigned to the category. This discomforting effect is the product of the uneasy fit of narrative prosthesis itself.

Yet, importantly, this inevitable discontent that representation incites serves as one of the primary catalysts to culture formation. Many of us have wondered if disability cultures exist and, if so, in what forms. Since cultural groupings always occur in reaction to prior exclusionary definitions that obscure the human multiplicity of the designated population, the critique of representation consolidates a process of identification itself among those who forward the critique. In our video *Vital Signs: Crip Culture Talks Back*, and our essay "Talking about *Talking Back*," we bring to the platform the political critiques of artists and academics with disabilities in order to establish that disability culture exists within the space of shared critique. This does not suggest that the critique is monolithically formulated across the community, but rather that the necessity of talking back to an uncomprehending and able-ist parent culture suffuses a bona fide, even impudent, minority culture. As one identifies the voices that seek to redress the inadequacy of dominant representations of experiences, one also delineates the contours of a rapidly consolidating cultural perspective.

Thus, the productivity of discontent is more than purely academic or negative in nature. The study of disability by scholars in the humanities, even through its repudiations of representational models, constructs a formidable disability "identity." This identity proves to be most resilient because it does not consist of a "positive" content. It does not simply replace a less acceptable representation with another equally fictive but alluring one. Rather, disability culture remains largely "reactionary" because no adequate representational antidote exists. As John Frow has argued, "the diversity of language games is a prerequisite for the openness of the social system; conversely, the achievement of a 'consensus'—and therefore of an end to discussion—would represent a form of violence (or 'terror') done to the dynamic of social argument" (139). Instead, disability culture continues to levy its critiques of contemporary and historical representations while playing the trickster's game of being everywhere and nowhere at once.

However, even a communal identity cannot spring up wholesale and unprecedented without being accompanied by the work of historical retrieval. If one of the main projects of disability studies is to assert, once and for all, that disability is an integral part of the human condition, then there is great advantage in demonstrating the persistence of disabled people and their contributions in history. Henri-Jacques Stiker makes a similar point in *The History of Disability,* arguing that integration will prove inadequate if it must be on the terms of the dominant culture's "normalizing" criteria. Instead, one must argue for the integral nature of disability as a category of human difference that cannot be absorbed into a homogenizing scheme of a people's shared attributes. If one argues that the current predicament of, and social attitudes toward, people with disabilities are inadequate, then demonstrating the kaleidoscopic nature of historical responses to disability is an important tool for interrogating the "naturalized" ideology hiding behind current beliefs.

How do we make visible the historical presence of disabled people, so often erased from the human record? One answer is the analysis of preserved discursive and visual mediums such as literature, art, and film. We do not privilege the representational modes of texts that come under the purview of humanities scholars; rather, our scholarship recognizes a more complex constellation of relationships made available in these domains. Writers, painters, historians, filmmakers, like all of us, are subject to the limiting beliefs of their own historical moments, but whereas people with disabilities are often peripheral to domains outside of medicine, art persists in returning to portrayals of disability as a sustained preoccupation. Demonstrating and interpreting the reasons for this perpetual return comprises the bulk of the work in the chapters that follow. Thus, while the representational portraits we investigate often prove unsatisfactory, they allow us viscerally to encounter disability in a way that we could not otherwise. The very discontent produced by the prosthetic relation that is representation provides a fulcrum for identifying the culture that *might be* rather than that which *is*.

Chapter 2
Narrative Prosthesis and the Materiality of Metaphor

Literature and the Undisciplined Body of Disability

This chapter prefaces the close readings to come by deepening our theory of narrative prosthesis as shared characteristics in the literary representation of disability. We demonstrate one of a variety of approaches in disability studies to the "problem" that disability and disabled populations pose to all cultures. Nearly every culture views disability as a problem in need of a solution, and this belief establishes one of the major modes of historical address directed toward people with disabilities. The necessity for developing various kinds of cultural accommodations to handle the "problem" of corporeal difference (through charitable organizations, modifications of physical architecture, welfare doles, quarantine, genocide, euthanasia programs, etc.) situates people with disabilities in a profoundly ambivalent relationship to the cultures and stories they inhabit. The perception of a "crisis" or a "special situation" has made disabled people the subject of not only governmental policies and social programs but also a primary object of literary representation.

Our thesis centers not simply upon the fact that people with disabilities have been the object of representational treatments, but rather that their function in literary discourse is primarily twofold: disability pervades literary narrative, first, as a stock feature of characterization and, second, as an opportunistic metaphorical device. We term this perpetual discursive dependency upon disability *narrative prosthesis*. Disability lends a distinctive idiosyncrasy to any character that differentiates the character from the anonymous background of the "norm." To exemplify this phenomenon, the opening half of this chapter analyzes the Victorian children's story *The Steadfast Tin Soldier* in order to demonstrate that disability serves as a primary impetus of the storyteller's efforts. In the second instance, disability also serves as a metaphorical signifier of social and individual collapse. Physical and cognitive anomalies promise to lend a "tangible" body to textual abstractions; we term this metaphorical use of disability the *materiality of metaphor* and analyze its workings as narrative prosthesis in our concluding discussion of Sophocles' drama *Oedipus the King*. We contend that disability's centrality to these two principle representational strategies establishes a conundrum: while stories rely upon the potency of disability as a symbolic figure, they rarely take up disability as an experience of social or political dimensions.

While each of the chapters that follow set out some of the key cultural components and specific historical contexts that inform this history of disabled representations, our main objective addresses the development of a representational or "literary" history. By "literary" we mean to suggest a form of writing that explicitly values the production of what narrative theorists such as Barthes, Blanchot, and Chambers have referred to as "open-ended" narrative.[1] The identification of the open-ended narrative differentiates a distinctively "literary" component of particular kinds of storytelling: those texts that not only deploy but explicitly foreground the "play" of multiple meanings as a facet of their discursive production. While this definition does not overlook the fact that all texts are inherently "open" to a multiplicity of interpretations, our notion of literary narrative identifies works that *stage* the arbitrariness of linguistic sign systems as a characterizing feature of their plots and commentaries. Not only do the artistic and philosophical works under discussion here present themselves as available to a multiplicity of readings, they openly perform their textual *inexhaustibility*. Each shares a literary objective of destabilizing sedimented cultural meanings that accrue around ideas of bodily "deviance." Thus, we approach the writings of Montaigne, Nietzsche, Shakespeare, Melville, Anderson, Dunn, and an array of post-1945 American authors as writers who interrogate the objectives of narrative in general and the corporeal body in particular as discursive products. Their narratives all share a self-reflexive mode of address about their own textual production of disabled bodies.

This textual performance of ever-shifting and unstable meanings is critical in our interpretive approach to the representation of disability. The close readings that follow hinge upon the identification of disability as an ambivalent and mutable category of cultural and literary investment. Within literary narratives, disability serves as an interruptive force that confronts cultural truisms. The inherent vulnerability and variability of bodies serves literary narratives as a metonym for that which refuses to conform to the mind's desire for order and rationality. Within this schema, disability acts as a metaphor and fleshly example of the body's unruly resistance to the cultural desire to "enforce normalcy."[2] The literary narratives we discuss all deploy the mutable or "deviant" body as an "unbearable weight" (to use Susan Bordo's phrase) in order to counterbalance the "meaning-laden" and ethereal projections of the mind. The body's weighty materiality functions as a textual and cultural other—an object with its own undisciplined language that exceeds the text's ability to control it.

As many theorists have pointed out, this representational split between body and mind/text has been inherited from Descartes (although we demonstrate that disability has been entrenched in these assumptions throughout history). Keeping in mind that the perception of disability shifts from one epoch to another, and sometimes within decades and years, we want to argue that the disabled body has consistently held down a "privileged" position with respect to thematic variations on the mind/body split. Whether a culture approaches the body's materiality as a denigrated symbol of earthly contamination (such as in early Christian cultures), or as a perfectible *technē* of the self (as in ancient Athenian culture), or as an object of medical interpretation (as in Victorian culture), or as specular commodity in the age of electronic media (as is the case in postmodernism), disability perpetually serves as the symbolical symptom to be interpreted by discourses on the body. Whereas the "able" body has no definitional core (it poses as transparently "average" or "normal"), the disabled body surfaces as any body capable of being narrated as "outside the norm." Within such a representational schema, literary narratives revisit disabled bodies as a reminder of the "real" physical limits that "weigh down" transcendent ideals of the mind and knowledge-producing disciplines. In this sense, disability serves as the *hard kernel* or recalcitrant corporeal matter that cannot be deconstructed away by the textual operations of even the most canny narratives or philosophical idealisms.[3]

For our purposes in this book, the representation of disability has both allowed an interrogation of static beliefs about the body and also erupted as the unseemly *matter* of narrative that cannot be textually undone. We therefore forward readings of disability as a narrative device upon which the literary writer of "open-ended" narratives depends for his or her disruptive punch. Our phrase *narrative prosthesis* is meant to indicate that disability has been used throughout history as a crutch upon which literary narratives lean for their representational power, disruptive potentiality, and analytical insight. Bodies show up in stories as dynamic entities that resist or refuse the cultural scripts assigned to them. While we do not simply extol these literary approaches to the representation of the body (particularly in relation to recurring tropes of disability), we want to demonstrate that the disabled body represents a potent symbolic site of literary investment.

The reasons for this dependency upon disability as a device of characterization and interrogation are many, and our concept of narrative prosthesis establishes a variety of motivations that ground the narrative deployment of the "deviant" body. However, what surfaces as a theme throughout these chapters is the paradoxical impetus that makes disability into both a destabilizing sign of cultural prescriptions about the body *and* a deterministic vehicle of characterization for characters constructed as disabled. Thus, in works as artistically varied and culturally distinct as Shakespeare's *Richard III*, Montaigne's "Of Cripples," Melville's *Moby-Dick*, Nietzsche's *Thus Spoke Zarathustra*, Anderson's *Winesburg, Ohio*, Faulkner's *The Sound and the Fury*, Salinger's *The Catcher in the Rye*, Lee's *To Kill a Mockingbird*, Kesey's *One Flew Over the Cuckoo's Nest*, Dunn's *Geek Love*, Powers's *Operation Wandering Soul*, and Egoyan's *The Sweet Hereafter*, the meaning of the relationship between having a physical disability and the nature of a character's identity come under scrutiny. Disability recurs in these works as a potent force that challenges cultural ideals of the "normal" or "whole" body. *At the same time, disability also operates as the textual obstacle that causes the literary operation of open-endedness to close down or stumble.*

This "closing down" of an otherwise permeable and dynamic narrative form demonstrates the historical conundrum of disability. Characters such as Montaigne's "les boiteaux," Shakespeare's "hunchback'd king," Melville's "crippled" captain, Nietzsche's interlocutory "throng of cripples," Anderson's storied "grotesques," Faulkner's "tale told by an idiot," Salinger's fantasized commune of deaf-mutes, Lee's racial and cognitive outsiders, Kesey's ward of acutes and chronics, Dunn's chemically altered freaks, and Powers's postapocalyptic wandering children provide powerful counterpoints to their respective cultures' normalizing Truths about the construction of deviance in particular, and the fixity of knowledge systems in general. Yet each of these characterizations also evidences that the artifice of disability binds disabled characters to a programmatic (even deterministic) identity. Disability may provide an explanation for the origins of a character's identity, but its deployment usually proves either too programmatic or unerringly "deep" and mysterious. In each work analyzed in this book, disability is used to underscore, in the words of Richard Powers, adapting the theories of Lacan, that the body functions "like a language" as a dynamic network of misfirings and arbitrary adaptations (*Goldbug* 545). Yet, this defining corporeal unruliness consistently produces characters who are indentured to their biological programming in the most essentializing manner. Their disabilities surface to explain everything or nothing with respect to their portraits as embodied beings.

All of the above examples help to demonstrate one of the central assumptions undergirding this book: *disability is foundational to both cultural definition and to the literary narratives that challenge normalizing prescriptive ideals.* By contrasting and comparing the depiction of disability across cultures and histories, one realizes that disability provides an important barometer by which to assess shifting values and norms imposed upon the body. Our approach in the chapters that follow is to treat disability as a narrative device—an artistic prosthesis—that reveals the pervasive dependency of artistic, cultural, and philosophical discourses upon the powerful alterity assigned to people with disabilities. In short, disability characterization can be understood as a prosthetic contrivance upon which so many of our cultural and literary narratives rely.

The (In)visibility of Prosthesis

The hypothesis of this *discursive dependency* upon disability strikes most scholars and readers at first glance as relatively insubstantial. During a recent conference of the Herman Melville Society in Völös, Greece, we met a scholar from Japan interested in representations of disability in American literature. When asked if Japanese literature made use of disabled characters to the same extent as American and European literatures, he honestly replied that he had never encountered any. Upon further reflection, he listed several examples and laughingly added that of course the Nobel Prize winner Kenzaburo Oë wrote almost exclusively about the subject. This "surprise" about the pervasive nature of disabled images in national literatures catches even the most knowledgeable scholars unaware. Without developed models for analyzing the purpose and function of representational strategies of disability, readers tend to filter a multitude of disability figures absently through their imaginations.

For film scholarship, Paul Longmore has perceptively formulated this paradox, asking why we screen so many images of disability and simultaneously screen them out of our minds. In television and film portraits of disability, Longmore argues, this screening out occurs because we are trained to compartmentalize impairment as an isolated and individual condition of existence. Consequently, we rarely connect together stories of people with disabilities as evidence of a wider systemic predicament. This same phenomenon can be applied to other representational discourses.

As we discussed in our introduction to *The Body and Physical Difference,* our current models of minority representations tend to formulate this problem of literary/critical neglect in the obverse manner (5). One might expect to find the argument in the pages to come that disability is an ignored, overlooked, or marginal experience in literary narrative, that its absence marks an ominous silence in the literary repertoire of human experiences. In pursuing such an argument one could rightly redress, castigate, or bemoan the neglect of this essential life experience within discourses that might have seen fit to take up the important task of exploring disability in serious terms. Within such an approach, disability would prove to be an unarticulated subject whose real-life counterparts could then charge that their own social marginality was the result of an attendant representational erasure outside of medical discourses. Such a methodology would theorize that disability's absence proves evidence of a profound cultural repression to escape the reality of biological and cognitive differences.

However, what we hope to demonstrate in this book is that disability has an unusual literary history. Between the social marginality of people with disabilities and their corresponding representational milieus, disability undergoes a different representational fate. While racial, sexual, and ethnic criticisms have often founded their critiques upon a pervasive absence of their images in the dominant culture's literature, this book argues that images of disabled people abound in history.[4] Even if we disregard the fact that entire fields of study have been devoted to the assessment, cataloging, taxonomization, pathologization, objectification, and rehabilitation of disabled people, one is struck by disability's prevalence in discourses outside of medicine and the hard sciences. Once a reader begins to seek out representations of disability in our literatures, it is difficult to avoid their proliferation in texts with which one believed oneself to be utterly familiar. Consequently, as in the discussion of images of disability in Japanese literature mentioned above, the representational prevalence of people with disabilities is far from absent or tangential. As we discussed in the previous chapter, scholarship in the humanities study of disability has sought to pursue previously unexplored questions of the utility of disability to numerous discursive modes, including literature. Our hypothesis in *Narrative Prosthesis* is a paradoxical one: disabled peoples' social invisibility has occurred in the wake of their perpetual circulation throughout print history. This question is not simply a matter of stereotypes or "bad objects," to borrow Naomi Schor's phrase.[5] Rather, the interpretation of representations of disability strikes at the very core of cultural definitions and values. What is the significance of the fact that the earliest known cuneiform tablets catalog 120 omens interpreted from the "deformities" of Sumerian fetuses and irregularly shaped sheep's and calf's livers? How does one explain the disabled gods, such as the blind Hod, the one-eyed Odin, the one-armed Tyr, who are central to Norse myths, or Hephaestus, the "crook-footed god," in Greek literature? What do these modes of representation reveal about cultures as they forward or suppress physical differences? Why does the "visual" spectacle of so many disabilities become a predominating trope in the nonvisual textual mediums of literary narratives?

Supplementing the Void

What calls stories into being, and what does disability have to do with this most basic preoccupation of narrative? Narrative prosthesis (or the dependency of literary narratives upon disability) forwards the notion that all narratives operate out of a desire to compensate for a limitation or to reign in excess. This narrative approach to difference identifies the literary object par excellence as that which has become extraordinary—a deviation from a widely accepted norm. Literary narratives begin a process of explanatory compensation wherein perceived "aberrancies" can be rescued from ignorance, neglect, or misunderstanding for their readerships. As Michel de Certeau explains in his well-known essay "The Savage 'I,'" the new world travel narrative in the fifteenth and sixteenth centuries provides a model for thinking about the movement of all narrative. A narrative is inaugurated "by the search for the strange, which is presumed different from the place assigned it in the beginning by the discourse of the culture" from which it originates (69). The very need for a story is called into being when something has gone amiss with the known world, and, thus, the language of a tale seeks to comprehend that which has stepped out of line. In this sense, stories compensate for an unknown or unnatural deviance that begs an explanation.

Our notion of narrative prosthesis evolves out of this specific recognition: a narrative issues to resolve or correct—to "prostheticize" in David Wills's sense of the term—a deviance marked as improper to a social context. A simple schematic of narrative structure might run thus: first, a deviance or marked difference is exposed to a reader; second, a narrative consolidates the need for its own existence by calling for an explanation of the deviation's origins and formative consequences; third, the deviance is brought from the periphery of concerns to the center of the story to come; and fourth, the remainder of the story rehabilitates or fixes the deviance in some manner. This fourth step of the repair of deviance may involve an obliteration of the difference through a "cure," the rescue of the despised object from social censure, the extermination of the deviant as a purification of the social body, or the revaluation of an alternative mode of being. Since what we now call disability has been historically narrated as that which characterizes a body as deviant from shared norms of bodily appearance and ability, disability has functioned throughout history as one of the most marked and remarked upon differences that originates the act of storytelling. Narratives turn signs of cultural deviance into textually marked bodies.

In one of our six-year-old son's books entitled *The Steadfast Tin Soldier,* this prosthetic relation of narrative to physical difference is exemplified. The story opens with a child receiving a box of tin soldiers as a birthday gift. The twenty-five soldiers stand erect and uniform in every way, for they "had all been made from the same tin spoon" (Campbell 1). Each of the soldiers comes equipped with a rifle and bayonet, a blue and red outfit signifying membership in the same regiment, black boots, and a stern military visage. The limited omniscient narrator inaugurates the conflict that will propel the story by pointing out a lack in one soldier that mars the uniformity of the gift: "All of the soldiers were exactly alike, with the exception of one, who differed from the rest in having only one leg" (2). This unfortunate blemish, which mars the otherwise flawless ideal of the soldiers standing in unison, becomes the springboard for the story that ensues. The incomplete leg becomes a locus for attention, and from this imperfection a story issues forth. The twenty-four perfect soldiers are quickly left behind in the box for the reason of their very perfection and uniformity—the "ideal" or "intended" soldier's form promises no story. As Barbara Maria Stafford points out, "there [is] only a single way of being healthy and lovely, but an infinity of ways of being sick and wretched" (284). This infinity of ways helps to explain the pervasive dependency of literary narratives upon the trope of disability. Narrative interest solidifies only in the identification and pursuit of an anomaly that inaugurates the exceptional tale or the tale of exception.

The story of *The Steadfast Tin Soldier* stands in a prosthetic relation to the missing leg of the titular protagonist. The narrative in question (and narrative in a general sense) rehabilitates or compensates for its "lesser" subject by demonstrating that the outward flaw "attracts" the storyteller's—and by extension the reader's—interest. The act of characterization is such that narrative must establish the exceptionality of its subject matter to justify the telling of a story. A subject demands a story only in relation to the degree that it can establish its own extra-ordinary circumstances.[6] The normal, routine, average, and familiar (by definition) fail to mobilize the storytelling effort because they fall short of the litmus test of exceptionality. The anonymity of normalcy is no story at all. Deviance serves as the basis and common denominator of all narrative. In this sense, the missing leg presents the aberrant soldier as the story's focus, for his physical difference exiles him from the rank and file of the uniform and physically undifferentiated troop. Whereas a sociality might reject, isolate, institutionalize, reprimand, or obliterate this liability of a single leg, narrative embraces the opportunity that such a "lack" provides—in fact, wills it into existence—as the impetus that calls a story into being. Such a paradox underscores the ironic promise of disability to all narrative.

As we point out in chapter 4, on the performance history of disabled avengers descended from Shakespeare's *Richard III:* Difference demands display. Display demands difference. The arrival of a narrative must be attended by the "unsightly" eruption of the anomalous (often physical in nature) within the social field of vision. The (re)mark upon disability begins with a stare, a gesture of disgust, a slander or derisive comment upon bodily ignominy, a note of gossip about a rare or unsightly presence, a comment upon the unsuitability of deformity for the appetites of polite society, or a sentiment about the unfortunate circumstances that bring disabilities into being. This ruling out-of-bounds of the socially anomalous subject engenders an act of violence that stories seek to 'rescue" or "reclaim" as worthy of narrative attention. Stories always perform a compensatory function in their efforts to renew interest in a previously denigrated object. While there exist myriad inroads to the identification of the anomalous—femininity, race, class, sexuality—disability services this narrative appetite for difference as often as any other constructed category of deviance.

The politics of this recourse to disability as a device of narrative characterization demonstrates the importance of disability to storytelling itself. Literary narratives support our appetites for the exotic by posing disability as an "alien" terrain that promises the revelation of a previously uncomprehended experience. Literature borrows the potency of the lure of difference that a socially stigmatized condition provides. Yet the reliance upon disability in narrative rarely develops into a means of identifying people with disabilities as a disenfranchised cultural constituency. The ascription of absolute singularity to disability performs a contradictory operation: a character "stands out" as a result of an attributed blemish, but this exceptionality divorces him or her from a shared social identity. As in the story of *The Steadfast Tin Soldier,* a narrative disability establishes the uniqueness of an individual character and is quickly left behind as a purely biological fact. Disability marks a character as "unlike" the rest of a fiction's cast, and once singled out, the character becomes a case of special interest who retains originality to the detriment of all other characteristics. Disability cannot be accommodated within the ranks of the norm(als), and, thus, the options for dealing with the difference that drives the story's plot is twofold: a disability is either left behind or punished for its lack of conformity.

In the story of *The Steadfast Tin Soldier* we witness the exercise of both operations on the visible difference that the protagonist's disability poses. Once the soldier's incomplete leg is identified, its difference is quickly nullified. Nowhere in the story does the narrator call attention to a difficult negotiation that must be attempted as a result of the missing appendage. In fact, like the adventurer of de Certeau's paradigmatic travel narrative, the tin figure undergoes a series of epic encounters without further reference to his limitation: after he falls out of a window, his bayonet gets stuck in a crack; a storm rages over him later that night; two boys find the figure, place him into a newspaper boat, and sail him down the gutter into a street drain; he is accosted by a street rat who poses as gatekeeper to the underworld; the newspaper boat sinks in a canal where the soldier is swallowed by a large fish; and finally he is returned to his home of origin when the family purchases the fish for dinner and discovers the one-legged figure in the belly. The series of dangerous encounters recalls the epic adventure of the physically able Odysseus on his way home from Troy; likewise, the tin soldier endures the physically taxing experience without further remark upon the incomplete leg in the course of the tale. The journey and ultimate return home embody the cyclical nature of all narrative (and the story of disability in particular)—the deficiency inaugurates the need for a story but is quickly forgotten once the difference is established.

However, a marred appearance cannot ultimately be allowed to return home unscathed. Near the end of the story the significance of the missing leg returns when the tin soldier is reintroduced to his love—the paper maiden who pirouettes upon one leg. Because the soldier mistakes the dancer as possessing only one leg like himself, the story's conclusion hinges upon the irony of an argument about human attraction based upon shared likeness. If the maiden shares the fate of one-leggedness, then, the soldier reasons, she must be meant for him. However, in a narrative twist of deus ex machina the blemished soldier is inexplicably thrown into the fire by a boy right at the moment of his imagined reconciliation with the "one-legged" maiden. One can read this ending as a punishment for his willingness to desire someone physically perfect and therefore unlike himself. Shelley's story of Frankenstein (discussed in chapter 5) ends in the monster's anticipated obliteration on his own funeral pyre in the wake of his misinterpretation as monstrous, and the tin soldier's fable reaches its conclusion in a similar manner. Disability inaugurates narrative, but narrative inevitably punishes its own prurient interests by overseeing the extermination of the object of its fascination.

In the remainder of this chapter we discuss the ramifications of this narrative recourse to disability as a device of characterization and narrative "rehabilitation." Specifically, we analyze the centrality of the disability's "deviant" physiognomy to literary strategies of representation, and discuss disability as that which provides writers with a means of moving between the micro and macro levels of textual meaning that we phrase the materiality of metaphor.

The Physiognomy of Disability

What is the significance of disability as a pervasive category of narrative interest? Why do the convolutions, distortions, and ruptures that mark the disabled body's surface prove seductive to literary representation? What is the relationship of the external evidence of disability's perceived deviances and the core of the disabled subject's being? The disabled body occupies a crossroads in the age-old literary debate about the relationship of form to content. Whereas the "unmarred" surface enjoys its cultural anonymity and promises little more than a confirmation of the adage of a "healthy" mind in a "healthy" body, disability signifies a more variegated and sordid series of assumptions and experiences. Its unruliness must be tamed by multiple mappings of the surface. If form leads to content or "embodies" meaning, then disability's disruption of acculturated bodily norms also suggests a corresponding misalignment of subjectivity itself.

In *Volatile Bodies* Elizabeth Grosz argues that philosophy has often reduced the body to a "fundamental continuity with brute, inorganic matter" (8). Instead of this reductive tendency, Grosz calls for a more complex engagement with our theorizations of the body: "the body provides a point of mediation between what is perceived as purely internal and accessible only to the subject and what is external and publicly observable, a point from which to rethink the opposition between the inside and the outside" (20). Approaching the body as a mediating force between the outside world and internal subjectivity would allow a more thoroughgoing theory of subjectivity's relationship to materiality. In this way, Grosz argues that the body should not be understood as a receptacle or package for the contents of subjectivity, but rather plays an important role in the formation of psychic identity itself.

Disability will play a crucial role in the reformulation of the opposition between interior and exterior because physical differences have so often served as an example of bodily form following function or vice versa. The mutability of bodies causes them to change over time (both individually and historically), and yet the disabled body is sedimented within an ongoing narrative of breakdown and abnormality. However, while we situate our argument in opposition to reading physical disability as a one-to-one correspondence with subjecthood, we do not deny its role as a foundational aspect of identity. The disabled subject's navigation of social attitudes toward people with disabilities, medical pathologies, the management of embodiment itself, and daily encounters with "perfected" physicalities in the media demonstrates that the disabled body has a substantial impact upon subjectivity as a whole. The study of disability must understand the impact of the experience of disability upon subjectivity *without simultaneously situating the internal and external body within a strict mirroring relationship to one another.*

In literature this mediating role of the external body with respect to internal subjectivity is often represented as a relation of strict correspondence. Either the "deviant" body deforms subjectivity, or "deviant" subjectivity violently erupts upon the surface of its bodily container. In either instance the corporeal body of disability is represented as manifesting its own internal symptoms. Such an approach places the body in an automatic physiognomic relation to the subjectivity it harbors. As Barbara Maria Stafford has demonstrated, practices of interpreting the significance of bodily appearances since the eighteenth century have depended upon variations of the physiognomic method.

> Physiognomics was body criticism. As corporeal connoisseurship, it diagnosed unseen spiritual qualities by scrutinizing visible traits. Since its adherents claimed privileged powers of detection, it was a somewhat sinister capability. . . . The master eighteenth-century physiognomist, Lavater, noted that men formed conjectures "by reasoning from the exterior to the interior." He continued: "What is universal nature but physiognomy. Is not everything surface and contents? Body and soul? External effect and internal faculty? Invisible principle and visible end?" (84)

For cultures that operated upon models of bodily interpretation prior to the development of internal imaging techniques, the corporeal surface was freighted with significance. Physiognomy became a paradigm of access to the ephemeral and intangible workings of the interior body. Speculative qualities such as moral integrity, honesty, trustworthiness, criminality, fortitude, cynicism, sanity, and so forth, suddenly became available for scrutiny by virtue of the "irregularities" of the body that enveloped them.

For the physiognomist, the body allowed meaning to be inferred from the outside in; such a speculative practice resulted in the ability to anticipate intangible qualities of one's personhood without having to await the "proof" of actions or the intimacy of a relationship developed over time. By "reasoning from the exterior to the interior," the trained physiognomist extracted the meaning of the soul without the permission or participation of the interpreted.

If the "external effect" led directly to a knowledge of the "internal faculty," then those who inhabited bodies deemed "outside the norm" proved most ripe for a scrutiny of their moral or intellectual content. Since disabled people by definition embodied a form that was identified as "outside" the normal or permissible, their visages and bodily outlines became the physiognomist's (and later the pathologist's) object par excellence. Yet, the "sinister capability" of physiognomy proves more complex than just the exclusivity of interpretive authority that Stafford suggests. If the body would offer a surface manifestation of internal symptomatology, then disability and deformity automatically preface an equally irregular subjectivity. Physiognomy proves a deadly practice to a population already existing on the fringes of social interaction and "humanity." While the "authorized" physiognomist was officially sanctioned to interpret the symbology of the bodily surface, the disabled person became every person's Rorschach test. While physiognomists discerned the nuances of facial countenances and phrenologists surveyed protuberances of the skull, the extreme examples offered by those with physical disabilities and deformities invited the armchair psychology of the literary practitioner to participate in the symbolic manipulation of bodily exteriors.

Novelists, dramatists, philosophers, poets, essayists, painters, and moralists all flocked to the site of a physiognomic circus from the eighteenth century on. "Irregular" bodies became a fertile field for symbolists of all stripes. Disability and deformity retained their fascination for would-be interpreters because their "despoiled" visages commanded a rationale that narrative (textual or visual) promised to decipher. Because disability represents that which goes awry in the normalizing bodily schema, narratives sought to unravel the riddle of anomaly's origins. Such a riddle was inherently social in its making. The physiognomic corollary seemed to provide a way in to the secrets of identity itself. The chapters that follow demonstrate that the problem of the representation of disability is not the search for a more "positive" story of disability, as it has often been formulated in disability studies, *but rather a thoroughgoing challenge to the undergirding authorization to interpret that disability invites.* There is a politics at stake in the fact that disability inaugurates an explanatory need that the unmarked body eludes by virtue of its physical anonymity. To participate in an ideological system of bodily norms that promotes some kinds of bodies while devaluing others is to ignore the malleability of bodies and their definitively mutant natures.

Stafford's argument notwithstanding, the body's manipulation by physiognomic practices did not develop as an exclusively eighteenth-century phenomenon. Our own research demonstrates that while physiognomics came to be consolidated as a scientific ideology in the eighteenth and nineteenth centuries, people with disabilities and deformities have always been subject to varieties of this interpretive practice. Elizabeth Cornelia Evans argues that physiognomic beliefs can be traced back as far as ancient Greece. She cites Aristotle as promoting physiognomic reasoning when he proclaims, "It is possible to infer character from physique, if it is granted that body and soul change together in all natural affections . . . For if a peculiar affection applies to any individual class, e.g., courage to lions, there must be some corresponding sign for it; for it has been assumed that body and soul are affected together" (7). In fact, one might argue that physiognomics came to be consolidated out of a general historical practice applied to the bodies of disabled peoples. If the extreme evidence of marked physical differences provided a catalog of reliable signs, then perhaps more minute bodily differentiations could also be cataloged and interpreted. In this sense, people with disabilities ironically served as the historical locus for the invention of physiognomy.

As we pointed out earlier, the oldest surviving tablets found along the Tigris River in Mesopotamia and dated from 3000 to 2000 B.C. deployed a physiognomic method to prognosticate from deformed fetuses and irregular animal livers. The evidence of bodily anomalies allowed royalty and high priests to forecast harvest cycles, geographic conditions, the outcomes of impending wars, and the future of city-states. The symbolic prediction of larger cultural conditions from physical differences suggests one of the primary differences between the ancient and modern periods: physical anomalies metamorphosed from a symbolic interpretation of worldly meanings to a primarily individualized locus of information. The movement of disability from a macro to a micro level of prediction underscores our point that disability has served as a foundational category of cultural interpretation. The long-standing practice of physiognomic readings demonstrates that disability and deformity serve as the impetus to analyze an otherwise obscured meaning or pattern at the individual level. In either case the overdetermined symbolism ascribed to disabled bodies obscured the more complex and banal reality of those who inhabited them.

The readings to come demonstrate that while on a historical level the meaning of disability shifted from a supernatural and cultural to an individual and medical symbology, literary narratives persisted in integrating both interpretive possibilities into their story lines. The final section of this chapter analyzes this dual appeal of disability to literary metaphorics. Here we want to end by pointing out that the knee-jerk impulse to interpretation that disability has historically instigated hyperbolically determines its symbolic utility. This subsequent overdetermination of disability's meanings turns disabled populations into the vehicle of an insatiable cultural fascination. Literature has dipped into the well of disability's meaning-laden depths throughout the development of the print record. In doing so, literary narratives bolstered the cultural desire to pursue disability's bottomless interpretive possibilities. The inexhaustibility of this pursuit has led to the reification of disabled people as fathomless mysteries who simultaneously provoke and elude cultural capture.

The Materiality of Metaphor

Like Oedipus (another renowned disabled fictional creation), cultures thrive upon solving the riddle of disability's rhyme and reason. When the limping Greek protagonist overcomes the Sphinx by answering "man who walks with a cane" as the concluding answer to her three-part query, we must assume that his own disability served as an experiential source for this insight. The master riddle solver in effect trumps the Sphinx's feminine otherness with knowledge gleaned from his own experience of inhabiting an alien body. In doing so, Oedipus taps into the cultural reservoir of disability's myriad symbolic associations as an interpretive source for his own riddle-solving methodology. Whereas disability usually provides the riddle in need of a narrative solution, in this instance the experience of disability momentarily serves as the source of Oedipus's interpretive mastery. Yet, Sophocles' willingness to represent disability as a mode of experience-based knowledge proves a rare literary occasion and a fleeting moment in the play's dramatic structure.

While Oedipus solves the Sphinx's riddle in the wake of his own physical experience as a lame interpreter and an interpreter of lameness, his disability remains inconsequential to the myth's plot. Oedipus's disability—the result of Laius's pinning of his infant son's ankles as he sends him off to die of exposure—"marks" his character as distinctive and worthy of the exceptional tale. Beyond this physical fact, Sophocles neglects to explore the relationship of the body's mediating function with respect to Oedipus's kingly subjectivity. Either his "crippling" results in an insignificant physical difference, or the detailing of his difference can be understood to embody a vaguely remembered history of childhood violence enacted against him by his father. The disability remains a physical fact of his character that the text literally overlooks once this difference is established as a remnant of his repressed childhood. Perhaps those who share the stage with Oedipus either have learned to look away from his disability or have imbibed the injunction of polite society to refuse commentary upon the existence of the protagonist's physical difference.

However, without the pinning of Oedipus's ankles and his resulting lameness two important aspects of the plot would be compromised. First, Oedipus might have faltered at the riddle of the Sphinx like others before him and fallen prey to the voracious appetite of the she-beast; second, Sophocles' protagonist would lose the physical sign that literally connects him to an otherwise inscrutable past. In this sense, Oedipus's physical difference secures key components of the plot that allow the riddle of his identity to be unraveled. At the same time, his disability serves as the source of little substantive commentary in the course of the drama itself. Oedipus as a "lame interpreter" establishes the literal source of his ability to solve the baffling riddle and allows the dramatist to metaphorize humanity's incapacity to fathom the dictums of the gods. This movement exemplifies the literary oscillation between micro and macro levels of metaphorical meaning supplied by disability. Sophocles later moves to Oedipus's self-blinding as a further example of how the physical body provides a corporeal correlative to the ability of dramatic myth to bridge personal and public symbology.

What is of interest for us in this ancient text is the way in which one can read its representational strategy as a paradigm for literary approaches to disability. The ability of disabled characters to allow authors the metaphorical "play" between macro and micro registers of meaning-making establishes the role of the body in literature as a liminal point in the representational process. In his study of editorial cartoonings and caricatures of the body leading up to the French Revolution, Antoine de Baecque argues that the corporeal metaphor provided a means of giving the abstractions of political ideals an "embodied" power. To "know oneself" and provide a visual correlative to a political commentary, French cartoonists and essayists deployed the body as a metaphor because the body "succeeds in *connecting* narrative and knowledge, meaning and knowing" most viscerally (5). This form of textual embodiment concretizes an otherwise ephemeral concept within a corporeal essence. To give an abstraction a body allows the idea to simulate a foothold in the material world that it would otherwise fail to procure.

Whereas an ideal such as democracy imparts a weak and abstracted notion of governmental and economic reform, for example, the embodied caricature of a hunchbacked monarch overshadowed by a physically superior democratic citizen proved more powerful than any ideological argument. Instead of political harangue, the body offers an illusion of fixity to a textual effect:

> [Body] metaphors were able simultaneously to describe the event and to make the description attain the level of the imaginary. The deployment of these bodily *topoi*—the degeneracy of the nobility, the impotence of the king, the herculean strength of the citizenry, the goddesses of politics appearing naked like Truth, the congenital deformity of the aristocrats, the bleeding wound of the martyrs—allowed political society to represent itself at a pivotal moment of its history. . . . One must pass through the [bodily] forms of a narrative in order to reach knowledge. (4–5)

Such a process of giving body to belief exemplifies the corporeal seduction of the body to textual mediums. The desire to access the seeming solidity of the body's materiality offers representational literatures a way of grasping that which is most unavailable to them. For de Baecque, representing a body in its specificity as the bearer of an otherwise intangible concept grounds the reality of an ideological meaning. The passage through a bodily form helps secure a knowledge that would otherwise drift away of its own insubstantiality. The corporeal metaphor offers narrative the one thing it cannot possess—an anchor in materiality. Such a process embodies the materiality of metaphor; and literature is the writing that aims to concretize theory through its ability to provide an embodied account of physical, sensory life.

While de Baecque's theory of the material metaphor argues that the attempt to harness the body to a specific ideological program provides the text with an illusory opportunity to embody Truth, he overlooks the fact that the same process embeds the body within a limiting array of symbolic meanings: crippling conditions equate with monarchical immobility, corpulence evidences tyrannical greed, deformity represents malevolent motivation, and so on. Delineating his corporeal catalog, the historian bestows upon the body an elusive, general character while depending for his readings almost exclusively upon the potent symbolism of disabled bodies in particular. Visible degeneracy, impotency, congenital deformity, festering ulcerations, and bleeding wounds in the passage previously quoted provide the contrastive bodily coordinates to the muscular, aesthetic, and symmetrical bodies of the healthy citizenry. One cannot narrate the story of a healthy body or national reform movement without the contrastive device of disability to bear out the symbolic potency of the message. The materiality of metaphor via disabled bodies gives all bodies a tangible essence in that the "healthy" corporeal surface fails to achieve its symbolic effect without its disabled counterpart.

As George Canguilhem has pointed out, the body only calls attention to itself in the midst of its breakdown or disrepair (209). The representation of the process of breakdown or incapacity is fraught with political and ideological significance. To make the body speak essential truths, one must give a language to it. Elaine Scarry argues that "there is ordinarily no language for [the body in] pain" (13). However, we would argue that the body itself has no language, since language is something foreign to its nonlinguistic materiality. It must be spoken for if its meanings are to prove narratable. The narration of the disabled body allows a textual body to *mean* through its long-standing historical representation as an overdetermined symbolic surface; the disabled body also offers narrative the illusion of grounding abstract knowledge within a bodily materiality. *If the body is the Other of text, then textual representation seeks access to that which it is least able to grasp.* If the nondysfunctional body proves too uninteresting to narrate, the disabled body becomes a paramount device of characterization. Narrative prosthesis, or the dependency upon the disabled body, proves essential to (even the essence of) the stories analyzed in the chapters to come.

Chapter 3

Montaigne's "Infinities of Formes" and Nietzsche's "Higher Men"

As was suggested by the previous chapter, the history of disabled people inevitably involves a contemplation of a variety of mechanisms for enforcing their social segregation and even their extermination. The ancient Athenians assessed the physical and financial status of "infirm paupers" in order to determine those who qualified to receive "two obols a day from the state for their support" and a "treasurer . . . appointed by lot to attend to them" (Aristotle 92). The Romans established a council to determine which newborns, according to the heartiness of their cry and their apparent physical integrity, would survive and which were to suffer exposure to the elements.[1] The Old Testament preached the eradication of the lame and blind and the ouster of the blemished and unsightly from temples of worship,[2] while the New Testament defined the morality of a new religious ethos based largely upon the cure of cripples and their subsequent admission to the realm of the sacred.[3]

In the classical period, cripples served as the sign and symptom of a social disorder writ large—a symbolic function that continues across all historical epochs. During the late Middle Ages the "crooked and deformed" were sometimes consigned to the fate of a draught of hemlock because of their association with earthly malignancy and witchcraft.[4] The eighteenth century played host to the practice of physiognomy as an outgrowth of the Enlightenment's unfaltering faith in visible aberrancy and irregularity as indicative of moral nature.[5] And the Victorian era gave rise to the study of medical pathology and the use of statistical norms that began the process of sorting physical anomalies into taxonomic catalogs of deviancy.[6] Numerous societies have sought to ensure the vitality and genetic purity of the races by espousing genocidal solutions based upon an ethics of eugenics and euthanasia against those designated as crippled and infirm.[7] In our own era, a multivarious medical catalog is invoked to provide evidence of something gone awry in the master blueprint of biology.[8] The arbitrary social grouping of cripples collects and segregates disparate physicalities as a means of managing biological deviancies and their attendant metaphorical monstrosities. These groupings create a prosthetic effect by artificially yoking disabled people to narrative fantasies of difference. This narrative prosthesis produces the paradoxical situation of a population of social outcasts even as it maintains physical deviants as inimitably singular in their biological predicament.

The "disruptive presence" that cripples have historically provided for the management of aberrant bodies by social states has also pervaded their representation in literary narratives.[9] Unlike the marginalization of disabled people by the state, however, literary narratives tend to fixate upon this defining disruptive potential as critical to their challenge of cultural beliefs.

In this chapter we outline two antithetical approaches to the function of disability in cultural systems of representation. At opposing ends of a philosophical tradition, the early pre-Enlightenment writings of Montaigne and the post-Enlightenment thought of Nietzsche provide linchpins for ethical discussions in a philosophical tradition. Both move philosophy toward a disruption of the tradition's formulas of ethical discourse through direct challenge to the normative expectations that surround disabled figures. We contend that both of these philosophers of "the body" mobilize the power of narrative prosthesis—or the metaphysical dependencies upon disabled bodies—as a pivot for key philosophical interventions.

First, Montaigne stresses the disabled body as merely an incidental expression of the diversity of God's works, which he calls "infinities of formes." He thus critiques the early modern penchant for interpreting disability as a sign of divine disfavor and superstitious revelation. Montaigne's pragmatic approach to deformed bodies prefaces the emergence of Enlightenment science and a refusal to interpret bodies as conveyances for hypersocial meanings. In stark contrast, Nietzsche ironically champions the value of disability as extreme devalued difference. His segregated community of cripples, "inoculated" from the insipidities of mainstream German culture by virtue of their exiled status, interrogates the ambitions of Enlightenment philosophy. They refute philosophy's curative claims even as their own figures, in Nietzsche's critique, serve as the foundation for Christianity's "debased" premise of a faith in salvation. Nietzsche's cripples emerge as central haunting figures in his critique of Christianity's curative propositions. We establish these contrary impulses of disability figuration—in Montaigne's efforts at the erasure of difference, as opposed to Nietzsche's ironical celebration of the socially marginal—for their possibilities and limitations in narrating disabled lives.

Both Montaigne and Nietzsche have been discussed as antisystemic philosophers because their writing tends to value the "open-ended" products of narrative storytelling rather than resolute findings of a more scientific philosophical pursuit. This open-ended (or literary) quality directly parallels their representation of cripples as those deemed "corporeally deviant." We contrast Montaigne and Nietzsche's writing about "cripples" as exemplary of antithetical philosophical approaches: Montaigne rejects any extraordinary meaning (metaphysical or otherwise) invested in the disabled body, while Nietzsche harnesses the abject alterity ascribed to the physically "grotesque" within his philosophical speculations. Squaring off these differing approaches allows us to establish the poles of even the most contemporary debates about the politics of disability. Like Montaigne, many theorists expunge the association of difference with disability; other scholars parallel Nietzsche in their attempt to deploy the power of difference against cultures that would make outcasts of disabled people.

Both Montaigne and Nietzsche derive critiques of prevailing norms and social pieties by heralding the body as a counterintuitive ground to reason. Well known for their critiques of the immorality of social reasoning, Montaigne and Nietzsche assign cripples a role that has been neglected, their meaning-laden, insurrectional narrative function subordinated to a safer, more transparently consistent, thematic concern. For example, both Donald Frame, Montaigne's primary twentieth-century English translator and critic, and Marianne S. Meijer argue that chapter 11, "Of Cripples," blemishes the otherwise perfect organization of Montaigne's massive three-volume work. As Frame and Meijer consign Montaigne's cripples to a form of "not-being" themselves, one recalls the ironic critiques of the philosophers who "exercise their judgment even in inanity" and to a "non-being" ("Cripples" 791). Likewise, in the most discussed chapter in Nietzsche's *Thus Spoke Zarathustra*, "On Redemption," the presence of cripples at the bridge and their pivotal role in spurring the invention of eternal return by the philosopher is almost entirely overlooked by an extensive critical tradition on the topic.

Montaigne's and Nietzsche's cripples function as vehicles of popular superstition that are made to deflect a more healthy and necessary encounter with a wider cultural degeneracy. For Montaigne, the social fantasies invested in cripples and physical monstrosities underscore a dangerous cultural penchant for containing that which is foreign within the self. By deflecting the need to believe in the physical evidence of monstrosity back upon those who desire to solidify their own normalcy and superiority, Montaigne evolves an alternative ethics of the "infinities of formes" that sees diversity as a law of human nature.

In the case of Nietzsche, cripples pose a devastating illocutionary force that threatens even the philosopher's own beliefs in his ability to identify the coordinates of a livable life. Nietzsche's writing establishes an inverted hierarchy of physical forms wherein the physically grotesque are ironically "protected" from the rampaging disease of Western nihilism. Shielded from some of the more debasing influences of human community, the cripples and grotesques of Nietzsche's work become primary weapons in his radical critiques of Christianity and philosophy proper.

Yet at the same time, Nietzsche's protagonist in *Thus Spoke Zarathustra* ultimately displays incomprehension in the face of the challenge that cripples pose to the integrity of an ethical system of precepts and values grounded in the life of body. If the Nietzschean body organizes competing drives, wills its own overcoming, and shapes the quality and nature of its thoughts and desires, crippled bodies pose the conundrum of damaged goods and their potentially unruly intellectual offspring.

Montaigne's Ethics of the "Infinities of Formes"

As pointed out above, Frame and Meijer detect a disharmony or misshapenness to the conceptual order in the concluding *essais* of book 3 that mars its aesthetic integrity and formal logic. Frame suggests that a more traditional and logical philosophical ordering would be chapter 9 ("Of Vanity"), chapter 2 ("Of Repentance"), and chapter 13 ("Of Experience"). Such a recommendation excludes from the acceptable topics of the *Essais* the two chapters that deal most directly with cripples—11 ("Of Cripples") and 12 ("Of Physiognomy"). Citing Frame's reordering, Meijer remedies this potential "flaw" by playfully suggesting a change in the English translated title, "Of Cripples," to "Of Witches" or worse, "Of Crippled Thinking" (167–68). She finds cripples a euphemistic topic of consideration, and in its place she substitutes the subjects of religious superstition or intellectual dishonesty that, she argues, were simply too dangerous for Montaigne to address directly.

This consternation over the placement of the essay "Des Boiteux" in the larger volume makes Montaigne's critics susceptible to what we will term Montaigne's ethics of the "infinities of forms." Montaigne might point out that such arguments demonstrate that cripples do not fit into our systems of thought because they have been historically jettisoned from the socially permissible shapes that the human body is allowed to manifest. With characteristic irony, Montaigne might accuse Frame and Meijer of asking him to conform to a conventional mold that proves too restrictive and narrow for the associational logic that guides the *Essais* in general. The essence of Montaigne's critiques of a normative notion of form (linguistic or bodily) stems from his argument that "[w]e call contrary to nature what happens contrary to custom" (539) [Nous appellons contre nature, ce qui advient contre le coustume] (67).[10]

In this same essay, "Of a Monstrous Child" ("D'un enfant monstrueux"), Montaigne denounces the common practice in the late Middle Ages of attempting to merge the definitive diversity of bodily life beneath a single rubric. This essay provides a detailed anatomy of a "double bodied" child whose parents sought to gain money by displaying his physical "strangeness" to passersby. Montaigne observes, "In all other respects he was of ordinary shape; he could stand on his feet, walk, and prattle about like others of the same age" (538) [Il estoit, en tout le reste, d'une forme commune et se soubstenoit sur ses pieds, marchoit et gazouilloit, environ comme les autres de mesme aage] (66). This display of the boy with a "double body" and the narrator's correspondent refusal to identify his physicality with any extraordinary sign demonstrate that Montaigne's ethics are not targeted at any grotesquerie of the body itself. Instead, superstitions and common wisdom give evidence of the fantastical contortions of the imagination projected out upon the material world.

In large part, Montaigne's rebuke of the invention, festishization, and exoticization of physical monstrosity develops from the doctrine that one's responsibility is first to know oneself. Because cripples represent a social grouping about whom social derision and absurd speculations are produced, Montaigne's *Essais* devotes three different efforts to the contemplation of physical differences and their illusory association with what Marie-Helene Huet has called a "monstrous imagination." For Montaigne, the diversities of physical forms serve as a humbling reminder that no singular truth can encapsulate the dynamic laws of which humanity is evidence and to which it is subject. The infinite differences that best characterize "nature's work" are transformed by the essayist into evidence that in the "immensity of [God's] work" he sees "the infinity of forms that he has comprised in it" (539) [Ce que nous appellons monstres ne le sont pas à Dieu, qui veoid en l'immensité de son ouvrage l'infinité des formes qu'il y a comprinses] (67). A diversity of physical forms may provoke awe, but the desire to graft a singular rule of the universe merely exposes man's pretensions to mastery and control.

As with the majority of his essays, Montaigne's most vituperative criticism is reserved for those whom Tacitus described as "[m]en [who] put greater faith in those things that they do not understand. . . . By a twist of the human mind, obscure things are more readily believed" ("Cripples" 789) [Maiorem fidem homines adhibent iis, quae non intelligunt.—Cupidine humani ingenii, libentius obscura creduntur] (274). In other words, the human will to knowledge is more readily exercised upon that which seems most unfamiliar. This wayward tendency inherent in the act of perception itself—which, as Michel de Certeau has argued, forms the core of Montaigne's theories of the cannibalization of the Other—takes on the characteristics of a travelogue (or travel writing) where the active subject leaves "home" to encounter the exotic object of difference (69). In doing so, the perceiver positions himself or herself as the measuring stick of normalcy and constitutes the realm of the Other as that which is distinctly inferior and separate from his or her own essential being. Thus, the knowledge of the self's inherent instability is momentarily staved off by the projection of its own volatility onto another.

The refusal to take up the normalizing function by which others are measured, assessed, judged, and distanced is the crux of any "system" in Montaigne's philosophy. Rather than designate the "double body" of the "monstrous child" as an aberration of nature or as a sign of divine disfavor, Montaigne stands stoic in the knowledge that he has drawn no moral superiority for himself from the encounter. His circumspect and measured reaction to the "monstrous child" proposes an alternative response to the hyperbolic demands of freakish spectacle.

In chapter 11, "Des Boiteux," a similar phenomenon can be observed in relation to the social construction of cripples. Just as the narrator of the essay "Of Cannibals" makes various tangential asides that seem to diverge from the issue of cannibalistic behaviors observed in the New World, the speaking persona adopted in "Of Cripples" haphazardly and "lurchingly stumbles" upon his proposed subject at various points in his essayistic journey. The first appearance of cripples in the essay occurs after a brief, but denunciatory disquisition upon the ease with which men sentence other men to death. To believe oneself to possess the "illumination" to execute another is tantamount to the belief in one's life as "too real and essential" [vie trop reelle et essencielle] in its makeup—that one is possessed of such a clear interpretation of life's meaning and value that one also feels authorized to judge the truth and value of the life of another ("Cripples" 789). During his own era, Montaigne argues that monstrosity had become the sign for everything mysterious, and thus "against nature." Thus the body had been transformed into a symbolic surface that manifests the truth of a malignant morality in need of judgment and susceptible to extermination. As a counter, Montaigne argues that the invocation of monstrosity should alert us to the inclination for creating fantastical landscapes where we encounter only our own ignorance and grotesquerie:

> Let us not look for outside and unknown illusions, we who are perpetually agitated by our own home-grown illusions . . . I follow Saint Augustine's opinion, that it is better to lean toward doubt than toward assurance in things difficult to prove and dangerous to believe. ("Cripples" 789–90)

> [Ne chercons pas des illusions du dehors et incogneues, nous qui sommes perpetuellement agitez d'illusions domestiques . . . et suys l'advis de saint Augustin, "Qu'il vault mieulx pencher vers le doubte que vers l'asseurance, ez choses de difficile preuve et dangereuse creance."] (274)

This reproof of the travel narrative's formula of cataloguing the exotic and different as a means of looking "outside" for that which is foreign to ourselves shares a thematic continuity with the reading of de Certeau cited above. However, unlike "Of Cannibals," the narrator in "Of Cripples" does not rely upon second- and thirdhand accounts of his investigative object. Given that the identification of monstrosity provokes the rashest and most inhumane of acts, "Of Cripples" gathers its own evidence about those cataloged beneath the headings of "monstrosity" or "marvel" ("Cripples" 787).

The linguistic poles of "monstrosity" and "expresse wonders" in the *Essais* directly echo the terminology of Ambroise Paré's influential medical treatise, *Des Monstres et Prodiges*. Published in 1573, just twelve years prior to the composition of the majority of essays in Montaigne's book 3, *Des Monstres* continued the medieval tradition of documenting deformities and monstrosities as a voyeuristic preoccupation of early medicine.[11] While critics have discussed Jean Bodin's excoriation of witches in *De la Demonomanie des sorciers* as the likely source of Montaigne's critique in "Of Cripples," Paré's medical fetishization and taxonomy of deformity and physical differences makes an even more likely intellectual opposition (Meijer 169).

The Infinities of Monsters

In contrast to "Of Cripples," which begins with a digression into the superficial changes instituted by the introduction of the Gregorian calendar in 1582, *Des Monstres* begins with a bold definition of monsters as "things that appear *outside* the course of Nature (and are usually signs of some forthcoming misfortune)" (Paré 3; emphasis added). In an attempt to explain what constitutes a human form "outside the course of Nature," the author cites three aberrant physicalities as preface to a stunning catalog of bodily characteristics that classify one as maimed or monstrous:

> Il y a d'autres causes que le laisse pour le present, parce qu'outre toutes les raisons humaines, l'on n'en peut donner de suffisantes et probables: comme, porquoy sont faicts ceux qui n'ont qu'un seul oeil au milieu du front, ou le nombril, ou une corne a la test, ou le foye s'en dessus dessous: Autres naissent aians pieds de griffon, comme les oiseaux, et certains monstres qui s'engendrent dans le mer: bref, une infinite d'autres qui seroient trop longs á d'escripre. (*Des monstres* 3)

To secure this point of an inexhaustible catalog, the English translation adds on several more examples of the category from Paré's lengthy footnotes:

> Maimed persons include the blind, the one-eyed, the hump-backed, those who limp or [those] having six digits on the hand or on the feet, or else having less than five, or [having them] fused together; or [having] arms too short, or the nose too sunken, as do the very flat-nosed; or those who have thick, inverted lips or a closure of the genitals in girls, because of the hymen; or because of a more than natural amount of flesh, or because they are hermaphrodites; or those having spots or warts or wens, or any other thing that is against Nature. (*On Monsters* 3)

The attempt to fully catalog physical deviancy gives way to the final rhetorical indeterminacy embodied in the phrase: "or any other thing that is against Nature." Such scientific determinations are acknowledged as being beyond the ability of the physician to record absolutely, for differences begin to multiply indefinitely once one sets to the task of specifying them. A voyeuristic principle is at stake here, for *Des Monstres* rides a fine line between the human and inhuman, reality and myth, in order to couch a leering curiosity within the respectable professional interests of medicine. Like the parents who stake their fortunes upon the spectacle of their son's "double bodied" deformity, Paré's work exploits his audience's fascinations in an equally spectacular manner. His parade of physical grotesqueries depends upon the lure of the body as a liminal point that can undermine seemingly stable cultural distinctions between self and other. In these "believe-it-or-not" presentations, the physician must maintain his professional credibility by establishing his empirical accuracy while simultaneously acting as witness to the extraordinary tales that give flesh to fantasy.

While many scholars have noted the similarities between these two late-sixteenth-century writers, Montaigne dismantles the categories of miracles and monsters as the products of philosophical speculation and folk superstition. In direct contrast to Paré's exotic travel narrative of human aberrancy across the globe, Montaigne poses as a conscientious skeptic on the certainties of medicine and jurisprudence. In the essay's climactic scene, the narrator mimics Paré's own collecting tactics by visiting the country of a "soveraigne Prince" who promises to alleviate the skeptic's disbelief in monsters by parading "tenne or twelve" imprisoned examples of the genre before him. The narrator reports that he interviews one of the prisoners at length, an

> old woman, indeed a real witch in ugliness and deformity, long very famous in that profession. I saw both proofs and free confessions, and some barely perceptible mark or other on this wretched old woman, and I talked and asked questions all I wanted, bringing to the matter the soundest attention I could; and I am not the man to let my judgment be throttled much by preconceptions. In the end, and in all conscience, I would have prescribed them rather hellebore than hemlock. ("Cripples" 790)

> [une vieille entre aultres, vrayement bien sorciere en laideur et deformité, tresfameuse de longue main en cette profession. Je veis et preuves et libres confessions, et ie ne sçais quelle marque insensible sure cette miserable vieille; et m'enquis, et parlay tout mon saoul, y apportant la plus saiue attention que je peusse; et ne suis pas homme qui me laisse gueres garotter le jugement par preoccupation. Enfin, et en conscience, je leur eusse plustost ordonné de l'ellebore que de la cigue.] (275)

The passage functions in the guise of a pseudo-scientific proof complete with hypothesis, testing of the evidence, and conclusion. Montaigne sets up the inverse logic of a culture that interprets external signs as the symptoms of behavioral improprieties. The "old woman" begins as a "real witch" by virtue of her dual cultural qualifications of "ugliness and deformity," and her identity is further supported by the duration of her renown as a practitioner of witchcraft. The passage continues with the marshalling of scientific evidence as the narrator examines physical evidence—the "barely perceptible mark"—and bears witness to her "proofs" and "free confessions." Yet, the evidence fails to cement the initial hypothesis into fact, for the exchange can neither overcome his skepticism nor his personal credo, to lean toward doubt rather than certainty. The woman reveals nothing extraordinary in regards to her frame of mind during the interview, and the narrator reaffirms his earlier conclusion that such a belief "puts a very high price on one's conjectures" ("Cripples" 790).

Physicality does not prove trustworthy as an interpretable surface, and consequently the narrator circles back to his original disquisition upon the flippancy of men's abilities to prescribe death as the antidote to perceived deviancy. The ethical dilemma of death and deformity is explicitly coupled in the text in the aftermath of the interview with the "beldam witch," for the narrator contents himself with an argument against the extremity of execution rather than take on (for the moment at least) the larger issues of physicality's presumed relationship to internal malignancy. The joke about preferring hellebore (the ancient remedy for madness) to hemlock upsets the formulaic proceedings of the proof and returns the reader to a less-than-scientific first-person discourse. Montaigne reinstates the personal equilibrium he finds in his own ethics of the "infinities of forms" by refusing to read physical diversity as exemplary deviance. To complete this inversion and subvert more insidious cultural equations about the body, the narrator conjures up an image of the philosophers and physicians of his day as "sorcerers [who] would thus dream materially, if dreams can thus sometimes incorporate themselves in reality" (790) [sorciers songent ainsi materiellement; si les songes par fois se peuvent ainsin incorporer en effects] (275). Denying the malignant fantasies associated with physical differences undermines the many cultural investments in deviance. Montaigne would undercut the self-serving morality of those who view themselves as the embodiment of natural laws and physical norms.

The essay concludes not with a final return to Montaigne's critique of the arbitrariness of death sentences, but with a further discussion of cultural misinterpretations of cripples. Thus, unlike Meijer, who argues that the apparent subject of "Des Boiteux" is a deflection from the actual concerns of the essay, we want to examine Montaigne's use of physical differences as an alternative economy of value.

An Erotics of Cripples

Following the interview with the beldam witch the essay flirtatiously centers the question of cripples and value as a means for interrogating various cultural assumptions about physical differences. Beginning with a metaphor about the tenacity of opinion that can cause one to be "bent and prepared on one side," the narrator argues that only stubbornly clinging to certainty makes one crooked in the habits of thinking. This sudden deployment of "crooked" physicality as a metaphor is surprising since it works against the author's refusal in the essay to read bodily difference as symptomatic of imperfect reasoning. As if to balance this metaphorical opportunism, the narrator shifts tactics in his quoting of a common proverb: "he does not know Venus in her perfect sweetness who has not lain with a cripple" (791) [on dict en Italie, en commun proverbe, que celuy là ne cognoist pas Venus en sa parfaicte doulceur, qui n'a couché avecques la boiteuse] (275). Such a disconcerting introduction of the sexually potent *boiteuse* into discourse accomplishes two objectives: (1) a direct challenge to the devaluing of physical difference through an alternative belief exported from another cultural context; and (2) the recycling of the essay's primary critique that one cannot rely upon the physical exterior as a means for assessing less tangible behaviors. While the exoticization of physical difference is by no means undermined by the narrator's equation of physical incapacity with heightened sexual potency, the challenge to an absolute devaluation of aberrant physicality requires the strategy of a radical inversion of cultural precepts.

In part, the narrator's sexualization of the *boiteuse* rhetorically appeals to patriarchal desires for feminine objectification. The addition of physical difference to an economy of masculine erotics complicates the issue of desire (and desirability) by disrupting the visual field of the patriarchal gaze itself. Perhaps, suggests the narrator, the voyeuristic designs of patriarchy should reroute its conventions of erotics to incorporate the "deviant" characteristics of female cripples in its formula of desirability. From this enticing possibility, the narrator partially revises the proverb of the limping woman by making the observation less of a truism than a belief that may prove as fraudulent as the standard that devalues crippled bodies: "Fortune, or some particular incident, long ago put this saying into the mouth of the people; and it is said of males as well as of females" (791) [La fortune ou quelque particulier accident ont mis, il y a long temps, ce mot en la bouche du peuple: et se dict des masles comme des femelles] (275). If "fortune" or "accident" produced the proverb's veracity, the erotics of a *boiteuse* (limping woman) and subsequently the potency of the *boiteux* (limping man)—"Le boiteux le faict le mieulx"—nonetheless remains newly ambiguous, and thus, *physicality as value is transformed into an open question*. Montaigne's object is the destabilizing of cultural discourse itself—that which is most taken for granted becomes the most likely candidate for his ethical challenge. "The infinities of formes" opens out upon a dynamic whose instability becomes synonymous with his own alternative economy of value, and certainty becomes the bastard child of conformity.

The discomfort that Montaigne's narrator feels with resorting to the insertion of the limping woman into the sexualizing discourses of patriarchy causes him to further revise and balance his rhetorical tactics. The narrator immediately relays a story of an Amazonian feminine commonwealth that purposely seduces and maims men in their "arms, legs, and other parts" to "escape the domination of the males" (791). Anticipating the rebellion in his male readership at the "barbarity" of such a practice, the story ends with an ironic and self-reflexive cultural critique of patriarchy, for the gendered violence of the Amazons is parallel to the use "which we make . . . of our women over here" (791). The multiple inversions and challenges to cultural assumptions in regard to the bodies of cripples is accomplished in the skillful orchestration of diverging cultural beliefs. Italian proverbs unbalance French sayings, which in turn upend practices in the Amazon, and vice versa. Montaigne's bodies fail to cohere to any normalizing symmetrical aesthetic, and the challenge of his ethical perspective lies in the unnerving deployment of their unruliness and idiosyncratic "imbalance."

Reforming Physiognomy

The subject of Socrates' deformities also merited a critical assessment by Montaigne and helped him to return to the relationship between physique and psychology. In "De la physionomie" ("Of Physiognomy"), he creates a physical hierarchy between unsightly blemishes and true deformities, and puts Socrates in the less dire camp. As a challenge to a social propensity for devaluing the bearers of any superficial difference, Montaigne argues that

> we also call ugliness an unattractiveness at first glance, which resides chiefly in the face, and often arouses our distaste for very slight causes: the complexion, a spot, a rugged expression, or some inexplicable cause, when the limbs are symmetrical and perfect. (809–10)

> [nous appellons laideur aussi, une mesadvenance au premier regard, qui loge principalement au visage, et nouse desgouste par bien legieres causes, par le teint, une tache, une rude contenance, par quelque cause souvent inexplicable, en des membres pourtant bien ordonnez et entiers]. (291)

Montaigne critiques his physiognomically obsessed contemporaries, who, in contrast to the Athenians, would not be capable of discerning the beauty of Socrates. In Montaigne's schema, such a beauty would emanate from internal soulfulness and bear expression in a range of features—in such a manner he substitutes trustworthiness and reliability as personality traits that can be discerned across a range of features, even repulsive ones.

Yet, in distinction to the egalitarian and democratic spirit of physicality that the narrator self-consciously cultivated in "Of Cripples," Montaigne makes several equivocating distinctions in "Of Physiognomy." While deformity and facial blemishes supply his case in point for the inner beauty of Socrates, Montaigne concedes that bodily "deformity" and limitations do invariably work their effects upon the interior disposition:

> This superficial ugliness, which is very imperious for all that, is less prejudicial to the state of the spirit. . . . The other, which is more properly called deformity, is more substantial and more apt to strike home inwardly. (810)

[cette laideur superficielle, qui est toutesfois la plus imperieuse, est de moindre prejudice à l'estat de l'esprit. . . . L'aultre, qui d'un plus propre nom s'appelle difformité, plus substancielle, porte plus volontiers coup jusques au dedans.] (291)

This exception to, rather than contesting of, physiognomic principles applied to the body proceeds from Montaigne's absolute faith and certainty that Socrates' merit did not come by way of rigorous training (as the Greek philosopher claimed), but rather was present from the beginning. Unlike the common folk superstitions and governmental tyrannies that sentence deformity to death in "Of Cripples," "Of Physiognomy" gives some ground in order to rescue one of the principal founders of Western philosophy. For Montaigne, Socrates' perfect mind precedes and conditions any interpretation of an imperfect body—inciting the first "body theorist" to develop, not an exception(ality) of his figure, but a more complex physiognomic reading that would challenge other less accomplished "soul readers" such as he detects among his contemporaries.

Montaigne's method of bodily interpretation continually expands the discernible range of types and, in the process, so stretches taxonomical efforts that they nearly collapse from the necessity of all-encompassing individuation. In acting as the cautious guide to the tricky nature of belief in surfaces and their "revelations," Montaigne nonetheless acknowledges that the body is not a completely unreliable symbol of the soul: "Not every shoe of smooth leather but every well-formed shoe shows the form of the foot within" ("Physiognomy" 810) [non pas tout soulier de cuir bien lissé, mais tout soulier bien formé montre l'interieure forme du pied] (291). For Montaigne, the best exterior, of course, is that which does justice to the relatively elastic interior of the mind. In proclaiming this to be so he opens the door to a future of renewed interrogations of the body/soul relationship that have proven so historically devastating to the bearers of physical differences.

Nietzsche's Crippled Inversions

> Of Montaigne's playfulness I have something in my soul, and
> perhaps—who knows?—in my body.
> —Nietzsche

Right up front, we should point out that Nietzsche's unabashed metaphorics of physical monstrosity and bodily breakdown mean to metaphorize human degeneracy and incite confrontation over the questionable morality of widely held cultural beliefs. Nietzsche positioned himself as a diagnostician of a foundational cultural illness permeating the West; he spent his career accusing Christian and Platonic principles of fermenting the "poison of the doctrine equal rights for all" out of which the sick individual became "so important, so absolute, that he could no longer be sacrificed" (Nietzsche, cited in Ahern 131). How then do we read his jest, "Of Montaigne's playfulness I have something in my soul, and perhaps—who knows?—in my body" [Etwas von Montaigne's Muthwillen im Geiste, wer weiß? vielleicht auch im Leibe habe] (cited in Förster Nietzsche 367). How could the proponent of an overman, the philosopher who challenged an ethics of equality upon the premise that life operates according to a hierarchy in nature, propose to bear anything in common with the essayist who insists that human diversity evidences the "immensities of [God's] work"?

Montaigne sought to disprove any subhuman propensities in physical differences. In contrast, Nietzsche's cripples appear in the shape of grotesques and needy supplicants who have been exiled from human society either by force or by choice. These roles challenge the premises, and the possible ethical applications, of a valuing of human life grounded in a body that is the taskmaster of the will—such a philosophy as *Thus Spoke Zarathustra* attempts. Nietzsche's project of compiling a "genealogy of morals" and arriving at a "transvaluation of all values" sought to expose a resident immorality in systems of moral governance. Furthermore, Nietzsche's embrace of the body as a key component of human subjectivity serves as the precondition for the promise of a more robust and discriminating philosophical program. The fact that Nietzsche's Zarathustra heralds an indissoluble link between physical experience and identity prepares the way for him to pay intellectual visits to the nightmare sites occupied by physical outcasts. This does not mean that he can credit the "lower man" with having anything to teach him *or* that he openly seeks rapport with those on the social margins.

At moments, the character Zarathustra recognizes the virtues of the dark corners of the world he comes to occupy—those inhabited by rejected bodies—while at other times the poet-philosopher dismisses their longings as emblematic of the corruptions of the human predicament. Unlike his philosopher-character Zarathustra, Nietzsche ends up expounding extermination and euthanasia as logical, rational solutions for the "parasites" in human societies: "The invalid is a parasite on society. In a certain state it is indecent to go on living" (*Twilight* 99) [Der Kranke ist ein Parasit der Gesellschaft. In einem gewissen Zustande ist es unanständig, noch länger zu leben] (*Götzendämmerung* 154).

While Montaigne naturalizes physical difference so that it bears no key interrogative point, Nietzsche would extend the idea of sickness until it acts as a diagnosis that extends to the entirety of the human condition. Such a move simultaneously "liberates" cripples from their more traditional status as outcasts and reifies them as the metaphorical embodiment of the stigma that must be overcome. In general, however, Nietzsche tends to pose organismic weakness as a resoundingly intangible and interior predicament—a problem of personality more than physicality. In this manner, he resisted the nineteenth-century predilection for emphasizing the reliability of the physiognomic surface as a mirror of internal malignancy. Nietzsche proposes that sick individuals are preeminently those who "stand in a negative relation to life." Theoretically deprived of their exceptional physical differences, cripples nevertheless retain a symbolic and cultural potency for Nietzsche. Or to put it conversely, whenever the Nietzschean narrator would openly accommodate a range of physical incapacities and intellectual differences into his theories, he stumbles.

Up until the climactic chapter, "On Redemption," the philosophical protagonist of *Thus Spoke Zarathustra* espouses an exalted doctrine that promises a new pathway through the debasements of culture and tradition. His ringing critiques of the "poison of the marketplace" and of the "sheepish followers" who trail behind commonplaces and folk wisdom in the illusion of "chasing a higher thought" position Zarathustra as a prophet of the highest order. Halfway through the narrative, the "rainbow bridge" that Zarathustra approaches in "On Redemption" would serve as a metaphor for his successful metamorphosis into the suprahuman entity he has celebrated as the *Übermensch*. Paradoxically, "On Redemption" also presages an end to Zarathustra's teaching career and the beginning of a phase of contemplative retreat or convalescence. This chapter contains the key narrative reversal from an achieved quest narrative to an episodic series of encounters with disabled and disreputable outcasts. Many critics and commentators have noted that the protagonist's abrupt downward spiral occurs subsequent to the end of book 2, but most have not linked this sudden change of modes—from preaching to introspection—to the direct challenge that his crippled interlocutors pose. Zarathustra is confronted with explaining the merits of a teaching that resembles prophecy yet excludes the promise of a tangible "cure." Most significantly, Zarathustra's exclusion of cripples from his audience of address, when cannily observed by a hunchback near the conclusion of the chapter, shores up a limitation that pervades his philosophy of transcendence, overcoming, and sublimity. From this chapter on in his life and work, Zarathustra's narrative becomes more recognizable as dark comedy—one that inaugurates his encounters with a series of grotesques, cripples, and physical misfits—but makes little in the way of intellectual progress.[12]

Cripples at the Bridge

Acting as an agent of interception in Zarathustra's "progress narrative," and serving as a kind of toll collector for those who would make the crossing, is the figure of a hunchback *(Bucklichter)* acting as spokesperson for a population of cripples and beggars (137) ("Krüppel und Bettler" 150).[13] By the time their exchange is over, Zarathustra's philosophical project is in jeopardy. The poet-prophet has experienced an upheaval in his previous confidence that the world will follow him in his higher teachings. The crucial encounter with the cripples at the bridge marks a crisis point in Zarathustra's brief career as a philosopher not so much because of the nature of their query—their request for cure as proof of his prophetic agility—but rather because Zarathustra is forced, in a series of explanations, to generate a theory of the will that no longer maintains its clear difference from other vengeful acts in humanity. The hunchback provocatively tries to lure Zarathustra into the performance of a miraculous act that can release his followers and himself from the confines of their physical conditions, while also providing the philosopher with the opportunity for a salvaging act that would further his renown. Rather than accept the hunchback's offers to serve as mediator between the abstractions of philosophical reason and the material proof that secures belief from the people, Zarathustra engages in a series of rhetorical rebuffs that deflect his thinking away from the cripples' desire for a cure and into an associational logic spawned by their presence.

C. G. Jung and his students, in a series of published seminars on *Zarathustra,* one of the few accounts to interpret the significance of cripples in this most-discussed chapter in Nietzsche's oeuvre, note Zarathustra's syndrome of deflection and avoidance in his encounters with these "representatives of his unconscious." Jung's psychological allegory casts Zarathustra himself as crippled because he has become lopsided in his privileging of a grossly overcompensatory theory, that of the *Übermensch.* Ironically, then, Jung has Zarathustra fall prey to his own counternarrative equivalent to the *Übermensch:* the "inverse cripples" (138) [umgekehrte Krüppel] (151). For Jung and his students, the idea of the *Übermensch* compensates for Zarathustra's own internal crippling, which results from his inability to encounter the presence of the "inferior function" within himself. Jung's reading reincorporates the radical otherness of physical difference—its challenge to a normative model of human development—into a psychomythical framework that will explain Zarathustra's personal trepidation. In the process, Jung himself leaves behind the crippled interlocutors to serve as mere signs and symptoms of the philosopher's internal turmoil.[14]

In pointing out that Zarathustra cannot sufficiently encounter the figures who accost him, however, Jung takes an accurate pulse of this chapter. Zarathustra realizes for a moment that the cripples may have more valuable gifts to impart than he has prophecies to offer. But rather than act upon this recognition, he minimizes their significance for, according to Jung, "He is talking them away" (1234). However, unlike Jung, whose mythic incorporations result in a domestication of the challenge that cripples pose as a social group, Nietzsche allows their disruption to reverberate as a problem of integration, segregation, and intellectual discomfort. In rejecting the hunchback's clever gambit that Zarathustra prove his abilities on the altar of Christian parable—recalling Jesus' multiple healings of the crippled, maimed, defective, blind, and deformed—Zarathustra resorts to some clever deflections. In an atypical gesture aimed to refute the terms of the hunchback's request, Zarathustra offers up an insulting reminder of the essentialist proposition that one's identity derives from one's physical anomalies: "When one takes away the hump from the hunchback one takes away his spirit—thus teach the people" (137) [Wenn man dem Bucklichten seinen Buckel nimmt, so nimmt man ihm seinen Geist—also lehrt das Volk] (151).[15] In this manner, he cleverly inverts the grounds for seeking cure in the first place: the social ostracization of the blind, for example, shields them from the horrific sights of human atrocity. Zarathustra condemns healing practices, tongue-in-cheek, by arguing that they make those who seek them subject to the commonplace debasements of modern existence: "For when he can walk his vices run away with him—thus teach the people about cripples" (137) [denn kaum kann er laufen, so gehn seine Laster mit ihm durch—also lehrt das Volk über Krüppel] (151).

Not only do these folkloric suppositions parody the direct relationship between body and disposition that Zarathustra has argued for as one of the bases for his new philosophy, they also condemn the blind and lame to a sterile innocence wherein Zarathustra would patronize and protect them. Zarathustra speedily discharges these superstitious commonplaces in order to digress to a further point about the deformity of the human condition itself. Suspecting the hunchback will refuse the tenets of his philosophical doctrine of overcoming, Zarathustra bypasses the issue in favor of an ironic reversal, "inverse cripples." While cripples are traditionally designated as those who *lack* some necessary aspect of their physical being, inverse cripples are those who *cultivate* one trait or characteristic to the detriment of all others: "human beings who are nothing but a big eye or a big mouth or a big belly or anything at all that is big" (138) [Menschen, welche nichts weiter sind, als ein grosses Maul oder ein grosser Bauch oder irgend etwas Grosses] (151). Physical ability in this formulation becomes a liability, and disability could be understood as no more limiting an existence than any other bodily feature. Are the cripples therefore to assume that Zarathustra comprehends, in Montaigne-like fashion, *their* physical aberrancies as relatively inconsequential and thus preferable to moral and intellectual weakness? Should the cripples rejoice in Zarathustra's refusal to accord them any special concern when there are "many things so vile that I do not want to speak of everything" (137) [mancherlei so Abscheuliches, dass ich nicht von jeglichem reden und von einigem nicht einmal schweigen möchte] (151)?

Stanley Cavell has pointed out that Nietzsche's inverse-cripples formulation most likely derives from Ralph Waldo Emerson's essay "The American Scholar."[16] Cavell shows that like Nietzsche, Emerson employs a catalog of fragmented bodies and body parts for the sake of an all-purpose metaphor of hypertrophied humanity, or "walking monsters." Cavell links Nietzsche to Emerson through their shared questioning "on the existence of humans by sensing a problem with their gait" (Cavell 46). While Cavell does not explore the reasons or dangers behind this crippling metaphorical device in the writings of either philosopher, he does remark upon it as an unusual rhetorical move that allows him to assert that Nietzsche borrowed from Emerson directly. In contrast, Rosemarie Garland Thomson has argued that Emerson's robust, fully able ideal of American citizenship depends upon the invocation of disabled people as its contrastive mechanism: "The freak, the cripple, the invalid, the disabled—like the quadroon and the homosexual— are representational, taxonomical products that naturalize a norm comprised of accepted bodily traits and behaviors registering social power and status. . . . With the body's threat of betrayal thus compartmentalized, the mythical American self can unfold, unobstructed and unrestrained, according to its own manifest destiny" (*Extraordinary Bodies* 44). For Thomson the threat of cripples and other "extraordinary" physical types surfaces as a repression of bodily variation and is contained by their accompanying social pathologization. She exposes Emerson's metaphorical ploy as appealing to populist desires and fears by setting up cripples as the term from which the ideal American must distance himself. Cripples stand for that which is definitionally undesirable, for they are locked into a predicament of eternal, unchanging, and absolute deviancy.

If we accept Cavell's premise, it would seem that Zarathustra pulls out Emerson's tactic as another arrow in his quiver of intellectual evasions on the social meaning of cripples and their place in philosophical registers. Nietzsche has Zarathustra try out Emerson's metaphorical formulation as a way of extricating himself from answering their discomforting request, and in the process exposes its insufficiency as a rhetorical conceit. "Inverse cripples" abstracts the point into an argument about cultural insipidity and, at the same time, dangerously reifies cripples as the undesirable locus of his definitional inversion. By generating a contest between undesirable lives, Zarathustra momentarily places himself above the fray. Like Emerson, he pontificates upon degrees of monstrosity in humanity as a means of claiming the "hard line" in the necessary discriminations that philosophy must make. As if Zarathustra senses that the cripples are simultaneously dismayed and critical of his exploitation of their physical differences in metaphor, the poet-philosopher turns his back to them and addresses the remainder of his remarks to the disciples who are watching the exchange.

This pointed address away from the cripples allows Zarathustra to seek refuge for a third time from the request for a cure that initiates the exchange. In a parallel to the Christian myth of Christ's three falls with the crucifix and Peter's three denials of his acquaintance with Christ, Nietzsche positions his protagonist as vulnerable to the burden of the cripples' request. Can the hunchback and his fellow outcasts join the ranks of Zarathustra's philosophical disciples? Because the cripples pose the extremity of a life that one wills to escape in Zarathustra's mind, he employs them as a test case in the formulation of his most radical theory, that of eternal recurrence. The core element of Zarathustra's philosophy of eternal return is the idea that the respectable life can be fashioned only if one is willing to live it over again in every detail for eternity. How then can cripples seeking a cure for their conditions live up to such a postulate? By the very nature of their request, a cure seeks the alleviation of an undesirable condition that one would rather not live out into perpetuity. How does the hunchback's applying a distinctly biblical paradigm of cure to Zarathustra's teaching result in what Martin Heidegger points out as the location for Nietzsche's only substantial elucidation of the idea of the repetitive nature of time and experience?[17]

This elucidation depends upon Nietzsche's conjuring up these cripples as a test case for each of his protagonist's "proofs" underpinning eternal recurrence. The evidence of corporeal "imprisonment" bodied forth by the

assembled cripples and the failure of Zarathustra to dispose of their challenge inspire his alarming reflection that the will too suffers bondage: the
force that would liberate a "fragmented" humanity is itself imprisoned by
time. In thrall to the past envisioned as dreadful accident, and poised only
toward the future, the will is itself *disabled:* "Powerless against what has
been done, he is an angry spectator of all that is past" (139) [Ohnmächtig
gegen das, was getan ist—ist er allem Vergangenen ein böser Zuschauer]
(153). For Zarathustra, cripples represent the literal manifestation of a past
that cannot be revised or changed after the fact. Furthermore, Zarathustra
intends this parallel between the will's temporal imprisonment and the
body's physical imprisonment to resound with the malignant associations
cast upon vengeful cripples who vent their wrath indiscriminately at an
unjust nature.

Zarathustra argues that the need for revenge emerges particularly when
the past seems unjust, as in the case of cripples and physical suffering. Even
more deadly, revenge disguises its violence in the form of "just punish-
ments" that are predicated on calling attention to a misdeed. Zarathustra
points out that punishment cannot redeem the past because it originates a
guilt that repeats itself from one generation to the next. Among the many
dangers of this utter deconstruction of retributive justice is that Zarathustra,
by implication, derives his critiques of mad vengeance out of his contact
with cripples. He points to a universal condition but makes cripples, as the
ones who most forthrightly embody resentment against nature, the evidence
for his observation's validity and appropriateness. (This tradition of associ-
ating cripples with those who seek vengeance will continue to be borne out
in our next chapter, on Shakespeare's Richard III.) The representation of
disability in narrative provides this motivation as one that has been consistently reiterated from the earliest texts. Thus, Zarathustra's critique of
human revenge in front of the hunchback invokes a long-standing literary
ascription of vengeance to disabled people.

Of course, revenge presents a serious problem for a theory of an *Übermensch* predicated on the transcendence of *ressentiment*—one that has prevailed up until this point in Nietzsche's narrative. Still, at this moment, the
theory of the *Übermensch* that has predominated until this scene is eclipsed
by the proposition of eternal return—a method for redeeming the past.
Montaigne argues that revenge is usually exacted upon another in order to
shore up limitations within oneself. As a result, cripples emerge in his work
as scapegoats rather than avengers, with their wrongful sacrifice appearing
to salvage a social system. Zarathustra's point that the law of time makes
past deeds ineradicable would render the cripples' search for a cure mis-

guided. He provocatively points out that their desire for deliverance from physical maladies or bodily "monstrosity" ensnares them as participants in a more generally shared denigration of their forms; they, in effect, solidify their own stigmatized grouping by seeking its annulment. In contrast to the cripples' belief about their own tragic circumstances, Zarathustra's parable of the will's imprisonment has a definitive salvational conclusion: the present can be ennobled through the affirmation that one wills the past. This consent to the terms of eternal return—that one would welcome the prospect of living one's self-same life, in every minute detail, without the excision of any aspect, over again for eternity—would essentially place the cripples as the *willers* of their own impairments.

Yet, Zarathustra, his disciples, and the cripples are still left with the unnerving question of whether or not eternal return applies to cripples. Although it would seem unlikely that anyone with a significant disability would will the physical predicament again, Zarathustra asserts that if one cannot say, "Thus I willed it" (139) [So wollte ich es!] (153), one surrenders to an insignificant and devalued life. This absolute binary choice between the life of the willful creator and the life of the vengeful victim seems to exclude all the cripples within earshot (or lipreading view) from Zarathustra's redemptive model. While he rightly points out that the treatment of bodily affliction as punishment results in the debasing cycle of vengeance and guilt, his address to the disciples about the need to answer in the affirmative to eternal return is never posed to the cripples themselves. Would not an affirmative answer on the part of bearers of visible physical stigmas be the most compelling evidence for the value of eternal return as a guiding principle? Nietzsche and Zarathustra hold out such a challenge to the cripples but by refusing them an answer leave the question provocatively unresolved.

This instance points to the definitive ambiguity surrounding Nietzsche's attitudes toward cripples. While we would not desire Nietzsche to hold up any romantic illusions about their ability to become superior converts to the doctrine of eternal return, *Zarathustra* explicitly trades off their momentarily tantalizing voicelessness. The book both illustrates their desire for cure as the most retrograde for a philosophy of willfully affirming the past and holds them out as the most extreme test case for eternal return's radical promise. A time line of bodily breakdown in a lifespan holds intact an idea of biological normativity and makes outcasts of those who defy it as cripples. Nietzsche's contemplations of the will's imprisonment in time, therefore, are drawn to cripples as embodiments of both temporal defiance and temporal logic. Conceivably cripples dispute the idea of a normative chronological disintegration—though we do not see Nietzsche forthrightly take up this factor. Rather, for him cripples confirm an "imprisonment" in the nature of time—the past as past rather than as willed experience—that philosophy, to liberate mankind for the sake of a new respect for embodied, earthbound life, must contest.

Breaking the silence following Zarathustra's soliloquy is the hunchback's worried retort that the teacher speaks one way to the cripples and another way to his disciples. The hunchback wonders why the philosopher has not offered his version of a "curative" principle to cripples as well. By pointing out the explicit shift in tone and rhetoric that Zarathustra deploys, the hunchback calls the bluff on philosophy's inability or stubborn unwillingness to address a variety of interested audiences simultaneously. Nietzsche's authoritative benediction that punctuates each chapter, "Thus spoke Zarathustra," is upstaged by the hunchback's own words. His interlocution is given primacy over Zarathustra's lofty proclamations because his philosophy proves incapable of responding to the desires of those outside the circle of his immediate discipline (and, as is evidenced by the disciples' dismay, possibly those inside as well). When Zarathustra tries to dismiss the hunchback by turning him one last time into a vengeful metaphor—"With hunchbacks one may well speak in a hunchbacked way" (141) [Mit Bucklichten darf man schon bucklicht reden!] (156)—Nietzsche redresses his protagonist's derision with the hunchback's own snappy retort: "and one may well tell pupils tales out of school" (142) [und mit Schülern darf man schon aus der Schule schwätzen] (156). This enigmatic pun charges that Zarathustra is spinning "yarns" as if they were scientific theorems while also pointing out that one should value the capacity to speak to audiences in a variety of contexts. In other words, if one can teach students outside of a classroom setting, then why can he not teach hunchbacks?

The hunchback matches Zarathustra's patronizing response about gearing his comments to the appropriate context (to speak crossly to a hunchback because his form mandates a crude address) with his own diminutive point that Zarathustra is little more than a parablist incapable of speaking outside of the pseudoprofundity of parables—in other words, the hunchback counters with a reduction of Zarathustra to a rhetorical form rather than a physical one. Furthermore, the hunchback finishes his critique by pointing out that Zarathustra even speaks differently to himself than to his disciples. This identification of the layered and contradictory nature of the philosopher's rhetoric exposes Zarathustra as one who furtively withholds valuable information. He picks and chooses how much and when he will speak his beliefs, and thus his authority is undermined. The hunchback ends by pointing out that Zarathustra and his philosophy participate in the general cultural segregation of cripples and, thus, disputes the validity of the philosopher's self-proclaimed desire to "redeem the people."

The Aesthetics of Exile

The exchange between the hunchback and the poet-philosopher initiates the destabilization of Zarathustra's more exalted desires for philosophical transcendence and throws him into consort with those banished from the company of polite society—a freak show that necessarily debases both philosophy and humanity. The author banishes his protagonist to take up residence with the grotesques that he had emphatically tried to dismiss in "On Redemption." Such a decision on Nietzsche's part transforms Zarathustra into a wanderer rather than a poet-philosopher, and his domain on the mountain is no longer sacrosanct or exclusively his own. He is forced to surrender exclusive claims to the idea of the "highest man" while taking up a more interdependent relationship with the ironically titled "higher men" (286) [Vom höheren Menschen] (317).

Unlike Zarathustra, who has tenaciously maintained faith in his own superiority to the subordinated wills of other men, the "higher men" embrace their own debased conditions and feel compelled to explain the reasons behind their self-willed exile from society. Like the cripples in "On Redemption," the isolation of the highest men bears a direct relation to, and is symbolized by, their intellectual and physical misshapenness. Their rejected bodies become the source of their unlikely identification and force them to share segregated quarters. However, unlike the anonymity of their crippled predecessors, the "highest men" become distinctly individualized—they are the bearers of their own unique subjectivities. As Zarathustra encounters each grotesque, he is forced to contemplate the reasons for their social rejection that have brought them to this intersection of exiles. In the midst of these encounters Zarathustra does not relinquish his own self-importance, but the text openly suggests that the "highest men" proffer a vision of ennoblement. Each has acted upon a desire to affirm his own socially derided identity in a manner that recalls Zarathustra's championing of "Thus I willed it."

While none of the characters who populate books 3 and 4 is provided with the narrative space necessary to realize a fully developed character on the order of Zarathustra himself, "the ugliest man" does offer a developed theory about his decision to consciously seek exile. Rather than chide Zarathustra for his "profound sense of shame" upon encountering a form "shaped like a human being, yet scarcely like a human being," the ugliest man expresses his satisfaction with the fact that Zarathustra "blushed" but did not feel pity when he looked upon him:

> Everyone else would have thrown his alms to me, his pity, with his eyes and words. But for that I am not beggar enough, as you guessed; for that I am too rich, rich in what is great, in what is terrible, in what is ugliest, in what is most inexpressible. Your shame, Zarathustra, honored me! With difficulty I escaped the throng of the pitying, to find the only one today who teaches, "Pity is obtrusive"—you, O Zarathustra . . . And to be unwilling to help can be nobler than that virtue which jumps to help. (265)

> [Jedweder andere hätte mir sein Almosen zugeworfen, sein Mitleiden, mit Blick und Rede. Aber dazu—bin ich nicht Bettler genug, das errietest du— dazu bin ich zu reich, reich an Grossem, an Furchtbarem, am Hässlichsten, am Unaussprechlichsten! Deine Scham, o Zarathustra, ehrte mich! Mit Not kam ich heraus aus dem Gedräng der Mitleidigen,—dass ich den Einzigen fände, der heute lehrt 'Mitleiden ist zudringlich'—dich o Zarathustra! . . . Und Nicht-helfen-wollen kann vornehmer sein als jene Tugend, die zuspringt.] (293)

The ugliest man's espousal of his need to reject the sentiment of "pity" as the most debasing human sentiment directly parallels Nietzsche's own diagnosis of this universal syndrome. Nothing debases the human experience, in the ugliest man's terms, such as the disgust of pity, for pity denigrates human experience by encouraging *ressentiment* in both the pitied and the pitier alike. In order to refuse the guilt and personal resentment that accompanies the daily navigation of social derision, the ugliest man ennobles himself (in Nietzschean terms) by removing himself from the source of his own degradation. Nietzsche's ethical lessons lie in his efforts to push philosophical interrogation to a breaking point where the limitations of an espoused "system" are exposed. As a result, Zarathustra's encounter with the freakshow exhibit, "the Ugliest Man in the World" (263) [Der hässlichste Mensch] (290), yields access to a perspective that sees disabled life as necessarily, and nobly, contesting the insults and subordinations of pity.

To the extent that he is unwittingly pulled into communion with the agenda of these social outcasts, Zarathustra does become a man of the margins. As the outcasts of culture, the grotesques, like the cripples before them, have curiously immunized themselves from the degraded practices of society by their expulsion from it. Interestingly, Nietzsche's disdain for pity presages the contemporary disability rights movement's rejection of this most debased "universal" sentiment, and thus *Zarathustra*, which seeks no politicized context for identity, ironically offers a politicized critique that is espoused by a would-be representative of this later constituency in history. In the end, all we can do is wonder why Nietzsche could not reiterate the limits he found for the espousal of his new philosophy in the text that enacts a fictional testing grounds of its premises. We cannot interpret the metaphorical and philosophical utility of cripples in Nietzsche's texts without also recollecting that he authored the dogmatic justification for one of the most devastating attacks ever waged against those who embodied the later Nazi ideology of "lives unworthy of living."

When Nietzsche did venture into social theorizing, the result was brutal solutions such as those in *Twilight of the Idols* and acted out upon the bodies of more than seventy thousand disabled people at the beginning of the Holocaust and countless numbers thereafter (Proctor 179). Nietzsche's philosophy could not accommodate the social realities encountered by those who live with physical, cognitive, or emotional disorders. The German philosopher never did explicate the lines of social contact between his own predicament as an exceptional aphasic during the last ten years of his life and the lives of other rejected bodies in the neighborhood. We know, however, that suicide did not lure him into the kind of solution he advocated for others: "When one *does away with* oneself one does the most estimable thing possible: one thereby almost deserves to live . . . *life* itself derives more advantage from that than from any sort of 'life' spent in renunciation, green-sickness, and other virtues—one has freed others from having to endure one's sight, one has removed an *objection* from life" (*Twilight* 100) [Wenn man sich abschafft, tut man die achtungswürdigste Sache, die es gibt: man verdient beinahe damit, zu leben . . . Die Gesellschaft, was sage ich! das Leben selber hat mehr Vorteil davon als durch irgend welches "Leben" in Entsagung, Blechsucht und andrer Tugend,—man hat die andern von seinem Anblick befreit, man hat das Leben von einem Einwand befreit] (154).

Deforming Socrates

Another prime example of Nietzsche's ambivalence toward the cripples he conjured up in the tale of Zarathustra occurs in his readings of Socrates' deformities in *Twilight of the Idols*. Unlike Montaigne and Socrates' followers, who described a mind "bursting with figures of virtue" (Plato 75), Nietzsche claimed that Socrates' body disrupted the Athenian faith in the direct parallel between bodily beauty and goodness: "ugliness, an objection in itself, is among Greeks almost a refutation" (40) [Aber Hässlichkeit, an sich ein Einwand, ist unter Griechen beinahe eine Widerlegung] (89). Socrates' deformities exercised a fascinating pull upon Hellenes who had been schooled in classical ideals that reaffirmed a direct accord between physical appearance and interior disposition. As a result of his disruptive physical presence, Nietzsche accords Socrates a truly exceptional and idiosyncratic role in the Athenian state—his visage commands both repulsion and fascination for the standard-bearers of classical aesthetics. Nietzsche himself seems fascinated with his own psychological version of the ancients, imagining Socrates' power as that of a grotesque who touches "on the agonal instinct of the Hellenes" (42) [an den agonalen Trieb der Hellenen] (91), and therefore "introduces a (physical) variation into the wrestling-matches among the youths and young men" (42) [brachte eine (physische) Variante in den Ringkampf zwischen jungen Männern und Jünglingen] (91). Socrates' apparently repellent visage, combined with his exceptional status as an intellectual "fencing master," sponsors his ironic renown as "a great erotic."

However, Nietzsche points out that much of Socrates' appeal for the Athenians was based upon a freak-show-like spectacle of a philosopher who champions rationality as beauty in spite of physical evidence to the contrary. Nietzsche's Socrates dishonestly ignores the corporeal source of his power and, in doing so, diminishes the master's mythic stature to little more than a symptomatic conformist (as Nietzsche was wont to do in characterizing philosophers in general): "Rationality was at that time divined as a *savior;* neither Socrates nor his 'invalids' were free to be rational or not, as they wished—it was *de rigueur,* it was their *last* expedient" (43) [Die Vernünftigkeit Wurde damals erraten als Retterin; es stand weder Sokrates noch seinen "Kranken" frei, vernünftig zu sein,—es war de rigueur, es war ihr letztes Mittel] (92). Arguing that Socrates' visible presence introduced the destabilizing power of an aberrant corporeality into philosophical discourse, Nietzsche nonetheless berates Socrates and his followers for sacrificing a power akin to that espoused by "the ugliest man" to the banal superiority of abstract reason. For example, Nietzsche tells us that when a Greek physiognomist studied Socrates' face and proclaimed the philosopher to be a monster who harbored "every evil lust" (43) [aller schlimmen Begierden] (92), Socrates assented to the charge and ironically retorted, "But I have become master of them all" (43) [Dies ist wahr, sagte er, aber ich wurde über alle Herr] (92). Rather than interpret this exchange as indicative of Socrates' superior wit—his turning of the physiognomist's indictment to his own advantage—Nietzsche shows that Socrates was willing to forgo the challenges his deformities represented to classical idealism. Socrates' willing sacrifice of his "unsightly appearance" to a claim of superior reckoning with base instincts causes him to elide, in Nietzsche's mind, the irrational power of the body.

The Socratic embrace of "the daylight of reason" (43) [das Tageslicht der Venunft] (92) casts a shadow upon the influence of his own extraordinary body and diminishes the true source of his potency. Nietzsche, who would locate, and even perversely celebrate, the intellectual insurgency implied by a deformed Socratean figure's challenge to Athenian precepts, can therefore find Socrates' willing participation in his own self-destruction, his self-dosage of a draught of hemlock, to be an obscene, immoral act. Nietzsche's most vehement critique of Socrates comes in the Greek philosopher's staging of his own death as an act of heroic self-sacrifice. Socrates' deathbed claim that "life is suffering" unwittingly confirms the deviant associations cast upon his deformity. By seeking salvation in self-effacing virtue, Socrates becomes complicitous in the final objectification of himself by the state, and therefore sins against his own influence and against Nietzsche's belief in a necessary ethical commitment to life as will to power.

Nietzsche's own struggles with suicidal impulses emphasize the importance of his critique of Socrates' role in his own death. In 1883 he confessed to Franz Overbeck that his own physical condition had brought him to the brink of this same immoral possibility: "[I find] the barrel of a revolver . . . a source of relatively pleasant thoughts" (Nietzsche cited in Ahern 145). Were we to imagine Nietzsche living out the last ten years of his life in the midst of this ethical crisis, we might understand the imperative he felt to resist the extremity of the Socratic answer. A dedication he inscribed for an asylum orderly underscores his commitment to examine even the most debilitating condition as worthy of prolonged scrutiny: "There are losses which exalt the soul, so that it forebears to whine, and walks silently under tall, black cypresses" (cited in Förster Nietzsche 396). We read this poetical claim from Nietzsche's "insane" years—an era written off by critics and followers alike—as a purposeful description of the philosopher's investigative purpose in the final years of his life. An exaltation of bodily loss sends the aphasic Nietzsche off on his last stoic mission—to contemplate the perdurable cypress as if in a refusal of the cynicism of hemlock. In this manner we finally find Nietzsche to be most like Montaigne in his adherence to the body as the source and subject matter of philosophical inquiry.

Toward a Philosophy of Cripples

Tracing out these discursive treatments of cripples allows us to discern two available philosophical positions with respect to the representation of difference (physical or otherwise). The first recommends a program of recognized limits on what we know and are capable of knowing about others. Representative of this approach are Montaigne's interpretive disputes that suggest an ultimate lack of access to cripples as the bearers of a range of social, psychological, and metaphysical meanings. His championing of a predominantly essentialist position would maintain a respect for individual embodiment to the point where only the individual involved could adequately articulate a fair account of his or her own experience, history, and perception. He poses alternative, disputatious interpretations that counteract the presuppositions of other perceivers without establishing a credible alternative beyond the practices of skepticism and self-knowledge. The experience of the deformed, the lame, and the monstrous may bear a social meaning, but Montaigne's methodological tact can only dispute the terms of reception and refute their metaphysical and supernatural signification. Cripples become subalterns, incapable of reconfiguring the terms of contrary normalizing accounts, silenced beneath the incapacitating projections onto their figures. Capable of wielding contrary and fantastical social meanings, they become the bearers of none.

Montaigne therefore emphasizes respect for social difference and epistemological positions—a respect that cannot bridge essential differences in prosthetic narratives about bodily appearances. At best, our different bodies divide us in unbridgeable multiplicity. At worst, we all act on physiognomic principles and therefore need to extend our range of interpretive detection so that we better discern enticing nuances and become more cautious in flat ascriptions of meaning to physical surfaces. Cripples, however, become liminal cases—Montaigne leaves them as the extreme evidence of the soul impinging upon the shape of the "shoe" it wears. Physical differences, in being so pronounced, cannot help but signify some part of a soul's disproportion in the majority of cases, and yet it is better to lean toward a healthy skepticism of our own predilections for discerning them.

The second narrative strategy in the approach to cripples hinges upon a belief that knowledge comes only out of a willingness to interrogate principles to their logical breaking point—that conceptual rigor exposes the contingency of all truth. In direct contrast to Montaigne's cautious handling of cripples, Nietzsche boldly forwards their disruptive appearances as a crisis in his own philosophical project. In this model of narrative prosthesis, cripples embody the extreme case that Nietzsche openly wonders if his theories can encompass and "seduce." He binds their disputatious perspectives to their wrongfully incapacitated figures. In doing so, Nietzsche locates a philosophy of the "body" that acts as an organizing medium for the creations of the self. Nietzsche flirts with a dangerous essentialism while also demonstrating that their stigmatized bodies become the impetus for the cripples' proto-Nietzschean critiques of widespread societal debasements.

Whereas the cripples in "On Redemption" are assembled as an ostracized social grouping who participate in denigrating societal attitudes about their bodies, the individuated grotesques of books 3 and 4 proffer the only tangible examples of what Nietzsche's earthly philosophy might ennoble. Thus, cripples become the perpetuators of their own disenfranchisement and also those who are the most redeemed—since they have the farthest to rise—in Zarathustra's alternative rehabilitation program. The body of this more conflict-ridden approach becomes the supremely idiosyncratic legislator of what is "best" for the individual, and thus civilization is turned into the source and subject of the body's unruliness and discontent.

Montaigne's and Nietzsche's speculations upon the body's prosthetic relationship to subjectivity provide them with the opportunity to both calm and discomfort readers with the unsightly appearances that cripples make in their writing. People with disabilities can endorse neither their own absolute inaccessibility nor the essentialist foundation of their physical beings. Yet both provide possibilities for a more thoroughgoing revision of societal precepts about the fiction of the normative body and the necessity of physical and attitudinal accommodation. The surrender or rejection of either option limits the development of a more substantive arsenal of discursive weapons to combat an entrenched history of oppression. Yet the continuous representation of cripples as the liminal test cases for distinctions between life and death, human and inhuman, life as value and lives unworthy of being called life, throw into question the humanity that people with disabilities take for granted. In the next chapter we demonstrate the dangers of this ambivalence toward disability as the prosthetic nexus of Shakespeare's invention of the disabled avenger, Richard III.

Chapter 4

Performing Deformity: The Making and Unmaking of Richard III

I need motivation. Just a *little* hump.
—Richard Dreyfus playing Richard III in *The Goodbye Girl*

One must speak in a hunchbacked way with hunchbacks.
—Zarathustra in *Thus Spake Zarathustra*

I've heard this story before. Except the way I heard it, it wasn't a fisherman. It was an escaped mental patient who had a hook for a hand.
—Sheriff in *I Know What You Did Last Summer*

The previous chapter contrasted Montaigne's "infinities of forms" with Nietzsche's "higher men" to test limits in disability figuration. The present chapter is largely devoted to tracing out historical variations in the performance and interpretation of William Shakespeare's disabled protagonist Richard of Gloucester. Richard III remains a popular disabled icon largely through the character's revival in filmed dramatic versions of the play. Therefore we will begin this chapter with an overview of the role that narrative prosthesis plays in film traditions—a role largely inaugurated by the highly acclaimed and influential adaptation of Shakespeare's drama to the medium in a 1912 feature-length extravaganza.

Film Art's "New" Physiognomy

The film adaptation of Michael Ondaatje's *The English Patient* (1996) sets out an important quandary for disability studies scholars. Unlike Ondaatje's novel, the film version portrays the character Caravaggio's tracking down "the patient" as a matter of linking his motivation to revenge for the amputation of his thumbs by Nazi agents. The film's transformation of Caravaggio into a mutilated avenger, one determined to seek out and kill the man he believes responsible for suffering, allows the incalculable narrative complexities of postcolonial fiction to fall into line with popular film conventions. A focus on his amputated thumbs lends the film a singular narrative motive absent in the original.[1]

Film adaptations, by necessity, seek to realize a narrative's textual explanations with visual cues. Physical anomalies, such as that supplied by Caravaggio's amputated thumbs, provide photographic opportunities for filmmakers to display the titillating subject matter of disability. Amputations, mutilations, and twisted, "misshapen" bodies encourage audience fascination with overt displays of physical differences. In narrative filmmaking, internal and textual abstractions require visual display. Whereas written narratives name and label experience, film "tricks" are even organized around tactics to visually evoke, as opposed to voiceover or label, dramatic content. Thus film often resorts to a spectacle of corporeal aberrancy as a matter of narrative expediency. But this narrative convenience produces further effects: in the protected theater darkness audiences are given permission to stare at the socially "inappropriate fact" of disability—a habit discouraged in other public settings! In this case, shots of Caravaggio's thumbless hands frame "rack-focus" shots of the burned patient supine in bed. The audience is invited to look and look and look while Caravaggio's lack of thumbs is used as a quick means to imply a world of relationships and "deeper" meanings.

Film narratives rely upon an audience's making connections between external "flaws" and character motivations in a way that insists upon corporeal differences as laden with psychological and social implications. We refer to this production of disability as a visual indicator of fathomless motivations as film art's "new physiognomy"—the visually expedient "twist" to what we have theorized in previous chapters as narrative prosthesis. Our use of *physiognomy* here underscores that "art that has to be reinvented . . . to codify our pragmatic understanding of [physical] appearance as a clue to character" (Barton 95). Film narratives' use of artistic codes in the portrayal of disabilities supports Barton's contention that physiognomic habits continue across time periods in spite of nineteenth-century refutations of physiognomic science.[2]

Barbara Maria Stafford's genealogy of physiognomy can guide our quest for the origins of film's tactics of disability. According to Stafford, the "science" of a relationship between an inaccessible psychic makeup and bodily characteristics emerges out of "visualizing strategies" in aesthetic and medical practices developed during the eighteenth century (xvii). Early moving pictures pick up and exploit physiognomy in an effort to turn motion images into story lines—to achieve a condensed method of exposition.

Rather than ask why a surface might be perceived as a mirror to the intangible workings of psychology, then, we will seek out the invocation and recirculation of this equation in film. In this, we are suggesting that the point for disability studies is not simply the discovery or denunciation of the equation. Rather, we need to analyze the effects of the repetitious framing of this question over time in our most influential storytelling medium.

The Question of Vengeance

In film, the coupling of an interior motive with a "visible cripple" (to borrow Mark Jeffreys's phrase) begins with the physical language of a silent era of cinema largely dependent upon gesticulation, expression, dramatic action, and intertitles. Certainly physiognomics had been overturned as a science in the nineteenth century. Yet would-be film storytellers, young and innovative directors such as D. W. Griffith, were not so confident they could turn moving images to developed storytelling purposes. In 1902 Auguste Lumière had declared that film was a medium with no future, yet by 1910 a new breed of filmmakers was seeking every expeditious means available to get plotlines into a visual format. In this, they readily borrowed Victorian concepts of melodramatic villainy as physical monstrosity. As a result, early cinema often instructs audiences to uncover a character's hidden disposition from the presentation of visible disabilities. Frederick Warde's film of *Richard III* in 1912, the translation of a largely verbal drama to a silent intertitled film medium, remains a landmark in film history, even as it remains troublesome for disability studies.

Even today film narratives retain, and even deepen, the original ambitions of film's new physiognomy. Any quick glance through film archives will find an abundance of quirky disabled characterizations. Physiognomy orders the film universe of psychic discordance through a recognizable portraiture of external deformities and visible ticks of character: psychotic villains limp, political tyrants grow immobile and corpulent, vapid beauty queens become static amputees, a defeated culture's idols are decapitated or defaced, avengers act out of their own physical deprivation. Distortions of the physical surface provide a window onto the soul of motivation, desire, and psychic "health"—all aspects of character that would otherwise be difficult to narrate within film's representational repertoire.

In this catalog, the mutilated-avenger motif stands out for its deployment of disability as direct, embodied motivation: Caravaggio's hands are a convention borrowed from the horror genre itself, where amputations, limps, and other disfigurements provide steady explanation for "deformed" psyches. We are likely to think of horror films as central in the recirculation, unveiling, and display of anomalies that would return us to an explanatory origin of psychic wounding. Indeed, Caravaggio bears kinship with another recent thumbless avenger, played by Dennis Hopper, in *Speed* (1994) who time-wires city buses with explosives to avenge his bodily sacrifice while on his police beat. Much like the "high art" *English Patient,* the "logic" of physical loss supplies an immediate explanation for motive and method. Digital amputation as a harbinger of malevolence has historical notoriety: Alfred Hitchcock's hero Hannay from *The 39 Steps* (1933) can identify the demonic spy by way of a spectacular shot of his missing finger. Then there's always *Goldfinger* and *The Man with the Golden Arm.* One telling distinction separates the detective thrillers from the high-art *English Patient:* character recognition and reversal. The more complex artistic rendering will also aim to school Caravaggio in the error of any effort to avenge physical loss.

Caravaggio's change of heart, his satisfaction that personal motives excuse war crimes, and his forgiveness of the enemy operator Almasy also focus the audience's reversal: "It gets to the morning, and the poison just melts away," he helplessly muses. This mutilated avenger is cured of his need for personal retribution, rehumanized, and reintegrated from morphine country to postwar Italy. In coming to terms with the fact that even bodily torture bears no single causal agent, a mutilated avenger is robbed of a target and "restored" to a modicum of health. The more complex titular protagonist, the English patient, has already reconciled himself to the idea that his own burns and mutilations have occurred in service of a higher romantic purpose. Caravaggio's "reversal" secures the character's complexity as issuing from a reconciliation to fate and disability—he puts away his vengeance and takes up residence with the more balanced characters.

These amputations, then, offer value as filmed spectacle *and* as narrative prosthetic. At the moment of revelation, Caravaggio uses his teeth to pull knit gloves off his truncated hands. This exhibition invites the audience to gaze upon his loss while the narrative takes the spectacle as a prompt to return us to the primal scene of torture. The visual cue dissolves to a flashback of personal disclosure where we witness Caravaggio's mutilation—the origin of his wounds—in graphic detail. Film operates by sound and image tracks yet works toward effects that simulate the infliction of impossible physical suffering. Filmmakers discuss the achievement of visceral effects as a matter of technical achievement. Rather than show the actual cutting off of thumbs or ears, the film cuts away and substitutes a character screaming on the premise that an audience will fabricate a more terrible experience than can be graphically portrayed.

Since the early Richard IIIs made their appearance in film, the technologies and acting innovations required to give a "realistic" appearance to simulated disabilities have taken over as a primary preoccupation of film. The "challenge" that disabled characters present to film's technological wizardry helps us to understand the preponderance of disabled characters and disability story lines circulating within cinema—and even the highly experimental efforts of the early silent era. Early in the history of the medium all story lines were overtly conceived as special effects. New moving-picture technologies exploited the combination of camera, costume, and editing that could appear to record the fearful "truth" of human oddities. (One finds early still photographers pursuing this same trend, recording neighbors as exotic, costumed creatures rather than mundane).[3] Suddenly, alien landscapes and lives from history and imaginative literature could be visibly, and magically, depicted on screen by the camera lens. The embedded ideology of disabled lives as inherently foreign lent silent-era cinema a serious moral purpose, as well as a means to display technological achievements in its portrayals, even as film worked to establish credentials as a storytelling (more than a peep-show) medium.

In these efforts, disability as a ploy, stratagem, and special-effects performance becomes a staple fantasy of the early screen, with horror film soon to become an influential genre. At the same time, disabled Shakespearean characters bestow a high-art context for these efforts. Likewise, film adaptations of Victor Hugo's *Hunchback of Notre Dame* in silent and early sound versions proved a huge success. These early films took and accentuated one interpretation of Shakespeare's play that generations of critics had found to be either an embarrassing Tudor anachronism or a misjudgment of Shakespeare's intent: that Richard sought vengeance because of his disabilities. Warde's feature-length effort at portraying a strictly visual Richard III—a limitation that could *only* transform Shakespeare's highly verbal character into a malevolent hunchback—resulted in spin-offs and revisions into the next decade. Such a central role in the film medium has resulted in an intermittent "conversation" across decades as new adaptations attempt to remedy, deepen, or simply exploit the successes of earlier Richards. Many mutilated avengers gain a steady high-art complexity by invoking Shakespeare or Melville in the portrayal of a hunchback or an amputee.

Film figures of disabled avengers range from Captain Hook and his latest manifestation, Ben Willis in *I Know What You Did Last Summer* (1997), to the avenger who is tracked by a trail of prosthetic arms in Roman Polanski's *Frantic* (1987). Orson Welles limped menacingly across the screen as Hank Quinlan in *Touch of Evil* (1958). Tod Browning's *Freaks* (1932) is notorious for its casting of freak-show actors in a story of vengeance upon "the norms"; even Darth Vader embodies the answer to his dark side allegiance in the revelation of his prosthetic arm. We might also recall that Frankenstein's monster seeks revenge upon his creator and that cyborgs in *Bladerunner* (1982) track down the engineer responsible for implanting them with early death time-clocks. Even a double-amputee Vietnam veteran gains prosthetics and a vengeful purpose upon uncomprehending "normals" in *Blackenstein* (1972).

In many of these cases a question of authorship is at stake. Who has brought disability into the world, and what is its purpose? Avengers supply ready and usually irrational answers to this question. Ultimately, the mystery that true origination remains allows the endlessly permeable depths of character implied by corporeal anomaly, even as the anomaly itself supplies an immediate answer to the question of motive.[4] In this way film markets narrative prosthesis as no medium before it.

Disabled avengers in film history promise to mobilize an apparent "depth" of character while providing for the easy interpretation of caricature. As a result, the figure of the disabled avenger resuscitates visual physiognomic cues, becoming prime producer of an ideology that equates physical differences with psychological disorder. The ready answer and ineffable mystery of "evil" motivation finds perfect expression in an anomaly for which there is ultimately no fixed source. Significantly, Shakespeare presents us with a deformed hero who receives his physical differences not from an "accident" but from nature.[5] "Half made up," an Elizabethan idea that birth anomalies stem from an unfinished gestation period, Richard describes himself as "so lamely and unfashionable / That dogs bark at me as I halt by them." Uncertain of the exact cause of his physical liabilities, Richard takes vengeance upon a world that casts him as "unfit" and a family that conceives of him as a "curse." Like *Bladerunner*'s cyborgs, Richard III *appears* to seek compensation for built-in "defects"—the trouble is that his "vengeance" invents multiple and shifting targets of revenge. Critical history has postulated that Richard's true contest is with a nature or a universe that spites him. Finding little in the way of salvation for his "lowly form," he throws in his lot with the misshapen and disfigured realm of demonic nature. The only critical certainty has been that in Richard's own "distorted" features his character recognizes an avocation.

Silent cinema's first "film d'art" movement embraced Shakespeare's *Richard III* as a play that would lend serious purpose to film's efforts to install itself as an educational medium of public taste. Vitagraph, Biograph, and the Co-operative Cinematograph Company had begun efforts in 1908 to make films that countered the medium's reputation for popular peep-show aesthetics (Norden). It was in this context that turn-of-the-century performers, such as Frederick Warde, toured with their film products in order to school audiences in Shakespearean drama. The play's centrality to early film shorts and the film's status as one of the earliest feature-length films (it is the oldest surviving feature in cinema history; a lone print was recently discovered in a garage in Portland, Oregon) provided material for a series of hunchback and avenger films during the next decade. *Richard III*'s high-art display of physical anomalies provided early filmmakers with a dual intrigue of high-art characterization and low, popular conventions that film has continued to seek.

Today film has largely taken on the task of editing and rearranging Shakespearean drama into an appealing entertainment package. Al Pacino *(Looking for Richard)* explicitly names as his goal making Shakespearean drama accessible to a wide-ranging public. In this effort, *Richard III* remains one of the most popularly performed of the plays, with adaptations continuing to streamline all plot contrivances around a central preoccupation with the king's disabilities. Yet an earlier dramatic tradition had already begun this retooling of the play around a disability fulcrum. In the next section of this chapter we will offer a cultural history of the performance of Richard III's disability onstage in order to better assess more recent, highly successful adaptations of the play.

The (Un)Making of Richard

Tracing out the history of performances in theater and film situates Shakespearean performance history as a primary resource for mining the shifting artistic and cultural expectations that infuse physical disability itself. Prior to the advent of film, theaters in the United States and Europe often staged *Richard III* for its perceived popularity with a mass audience.

Shakespeare's "crookback'd king" embodies the chaos of a moment in England's history, while his physical differences underline his own metaphysical unfitness to govern. The fascination with this metaphorical tactic on Shakespeare's part has been evidenced for four hundred years in the play's undying popularity; critics have speculated that it has been performed more often than *Hamlet;* it was probably the first of Shakespeare's plays to be performed in the colonies (in New York in 1750).

As a Renaissance version of late medieval attitudes toward deformity, the play sits at a crucial threshold between a flat, static understanding of disability as a definite aesthetic impropriety (as in classical renderings) and the more mysterious complexity of full-blown maladies sketched out by medical science in the eighteenth century. It draws the same bold equations between external deformity and psychic immorality that are embodied in the medieval grotesque; Renaissance audiences would readily understand Richard's misshapen figure to invoke the demonic figure of Vice from morality plays of the previous era. The play's appeal to the masses, however, has militated against acclaim by critics. For centuries, critics and commentators have derided the egregious Renaissance superstition embedded in Shakespeare's character. In this line of critique, Shakespeare unknowingly reiterates a Tudor myth concerning Richard of Gloucester's deformities.

It can indeed be shown that Shakespeare culled his disabled Richard from an account by Sir Thomas More—a version of which is traceable to Bishop Ely, who, historians suggest, *invented* the deformity of the king as a stratagem for proving the wholesale malignity of the previous regime. In this, Richard's disability serves to guarantee the House of York's illegitimate governance. In the same vein, the Richard III Society points to Richard's hump, withered arm, and limp as indicative of Shakespeare's belief in a Tudor distortion of historical reality: "In reality, Richard was quite normal looking . . . [he] was known as an accomplished solider. He would not have been able to fight on horseback with heavy armor and weapons if he were Shakespeare's hunchback with a withered arm." (<www.richardiii.net /deformity.htm>) Efforts at rescuing the historical Richard from the slander of physical deformity were begun as early as the middle of the eighteenth century by Horace Walpole. Unfortunately, the restoration of Richard's physical form in an effort at historical accuracy reiterates a much more resonant equation at the root of cultural mythologies of disability—that between external shape and internal disposition. Likewise, the Richard III Society's insistence that Richard disproves the slander of physical liabilities by the very fact of his accomplishments reinstates the belief that wherever accomplishment exists, disabled people do not. Even if the "real" Richard were not the disabled provocateur of Shakespearean drama, cultural history must accept that the historical protagonist has secured notoriety by the very virtue of the exploits he undertakes as a disabled avenger.

Scott Colley's influential performance history *Richard's Himself Again:*

A Stage History of "Richard III" divides four hundred years of productions into two opposed camps: those who exaggerate his deformities in order to supply the play with an otherwise absent motivation; and those who downplay Richard's disabilities as an archaic characterization device and focus instead on the rhetoric of intrigue. He also poses the actor's dilemma as a question: To limp or not to limp?

In order to understand the historical attitudes toward deformity that are marshaled by Shakespeare's original text and production, we need to examine the play's mediating position between the publication in 1588 of Montaigne's *Essais* and the publication in 1622 of Francis Bacon's Enlightenment treatises. In his study of Montaigne, Jean Starobinski characterizes the politics of the sixteenth century in terms of political intrigue and courtly deception. Montaigne's essays point to a critical moment when philosophy attended to the disjunction between signifier and signified that allowed kings and magistrates to perform "lies" and "deceits" with impunity. According to Montaigne, courtly life had become rife with the tactics of dissimulation and deceit: "People massacre one another under cover of noble pretexts which, in reality, merely mask base interests" (cited in Starobinski 1). Montaigne's published exposé of the political intrigue rampant in linguistic machinations provides a historical context for Shakespeare's drama of duplicitous stratagems and murderous plots. As we discuss at length in chapter 3, at the same time that Montaigne assesses the performative behaviors of courtiers and counsel, he argues for a politics of disability that relinquishes belief in the idea that deformities convey a divine message. In this, he contests the medieval belief that disabilities signify a wonder or marvel of nature.

These contestings of medieval belief lay the groundwork for a dramatic character to be seen exploiting ambiguity and irresolution in significations of deformity for his own personal ends. In Shakespeare's play, with the significance of Richard's deformities unmoored from a fixed meaning—after all, the play enfolds a late Renaissance perspective upon medieval habits of court and "superstitions" about disability—Richard is liberated to "refashion" a performance. Richard's character fashions disability, then, as a full-blown narrative device that accrues force for his own machinations. He sets to work performing deformity. That history records audiences' marveling upon the character's singular capacities for deceiving his courtly audience has much to do with the fact that Richard is singularly endowed, by Shakespeare, with a late Renaissance perspective on the narrative mutability of disability. He wields this perspective amid a cast of his contemporaries who cling to medieval interpretations of disability as a sign for misfortune.[6]

A brief overview of this aspect of what is, after all, one of Shakespeare's lengthiest plays will demonstrate the point. As Richard's opening monologue descends from a comment upon the peacetime world that will arise out of the ashes of the War of the Roses, his promise to "descant on mine own deformity" intones the play's method of compiling the myriad inflections and impersonations that are traceable to the shape of Richard's "extraordinary" body. If an ordinary crippled body presents a simple melody—the pathos of a discarded life—Shakespeare's protagonist immediately and directly assures the audience that he will improvise a personally advantageous song from these basic social tunes. This is not just a matter of *overcoming* liability, but of *employing* apparent liabilities as weaponry in the rhetorical dispute over his intentions and ambitions. He proposes to reclaim the myriad associations placed upon his form to his own advantage even while divulging his tactics to an audience that thereby becomes an accomplice to his treachery. The audience, in its own turn, can be titillated by a knowledge of the extremity of a deceit denied to that of Richard's many victims. One among many examples occurs when Richard schools us in his methods of feigning religious piety: "And thus I clothe my naked villainy / With odd old ends stol'n forth of holy writ, / And seem a saint when I most play the devil" (I.iii.324–38). The pointed exhibition and concealment of multiple corporeal deformities furthers these same ends. Richard brazenly displays a "withered" arm in order to accuse Hastings of colluding with witchcraft; he puns upon a "hump" in his "humble" acquiescence to assume the "burden" of national leadership; he endures his nephew's mockery of him in the pointed request that his uncle bear him on his back.

In all these figurations, a politicized disability critique of representation and stereotype has much to guide it. After all, Shakespeare solidifies an array of perverse motivations for a character otherwise bent on political survival, and he ventriloquizes these associations through the mouth of a disabled character, thus lending Richard's evil motive the cast of factuality. Among the contradictory significations of disabled corporeality that Richard's figure is made to mobilize, we would include these: social burden; metaphysical sign of divine disfavor; evidence of the workings of a divine plan in England's monarchy; the retribution a disabled child bears for parental wrongdoing; a disabled subject's binding to a determinate life; Richard's bearing an entrenched identity (pathetic or vengeful); his serving as literal evidence of the Fall; his personifying the fiendish specter of war; his being singular and exceptional rather than common or ordinary, most interior to a social order and most "human" in his suffering, most exiled from society and lacking in natural human affections. Finally, a scapegoat patterning to the play reiterates exile as a culturally sanctioned historical solution to the social disruption that disabled people are perceived to present to an otherwise harmonious social order.[7]

The pre-Enlightenment challenge to the long-established equation between deformity and metaphysical meaning also initiates a host of many other mutable and *social* meanings for disability. In this, Richard's dispute with the terms of his own embodiment of physical monstrosity enables him to employ to his singular advantage the many social and metaphysical insults that swirl around him. In repossessing himself of slanders against disability—cripples as infantile, for example ("I am too childish-foolish for this world")—he initiates absurd and entertaining ironies. Finally, we have argued that the character's overt identification of disability as a matter of restrictive narrative constructs and beliefs makes him a medieval jester in possession of Renaissance savvy. In the end, corporeal "defects" that would otherwise appear as those most "fixed" and resolute aspects of personal "makeup" become the very stuff of multiple impersonations. For example, in *3 Henry VI* the young duke of Gloucester had bragged: "I can add colours to the chameleon, / change shapes with Proteus for advantages, / And set the murderous Machiavel to school." Chief among these dramatic ploys is that he who would appear most incapable of physical alteration becomes most adept in the acquisition of new "forms" of presentation.

Our reading of Richard's deformity is meant to complement the Renaissance historian Stephen Greenblatt's influential argument that a more fluid idea of self-fashioning came to characterize Renaissance self-conceptions. Yet Greenblatt's paradigm loses applicability when we seek to collect the multiconflictual ideologies of disability that inform the play. Even as the protagonist negotiates strategic deployment of the many social meanings ascribed to his figure, he expresses the suspicion that his own efforts remain doomed—possibly by his own deformed makeup. To complicate the show of political bravado, Shakespeare has Richard brood over a predetermined physical fate that slowly overwhelms his best displays of linguistic prowess. Intruding into his musings is the possibility that he exemplifies true *abomination*, rather than an exceptional perversion of nature:

> Cheated of feature by dissembling Nature,
> Deformed, unfinished, sent before my time
> Into this breathing world, scarce half made up,
> And that so lamely and unfashionable
> That dogs bark at me as I halt by them.

(I.i.19–23)

The derision of dogs (and later the numerous equations of his figure with curs, toads, boars, and cacodemons) underscore Nature's perhaps inherent, instinctual disdain for him, leaving Richard with only the monster's lament toward the creator (reminiscent of the cyclops in Virgil's *Aeneid*) that cheated him of a worthy shape—dissembling Nature—and the belief that the natural world automatically distinguishes between rightful forms and malignant ones. This original slight against his person extends to his family, with his own physical shape providing an outward expression of the House of York's internal malignity—their moral corruption issuing forth in his physical shape. In this he would believe himself to be selected to pay for the sins of his forebears. The extent to which the character partakes of the social scripts he performs receives variant emphasis from production to production.

This portrayal of self-doubt as to the nature of one's own role in a universal drama undergirds the premises of emergent Enlightenment philosophies that reinstate singular and psychological portraits of a mirroring relationship between physical "defects" and personal disposition. Perhaps Montaigne's dispute with disability as a sign taken for wonders helps to usher Shakespearean figuration of disability into cultural traditions as much as Bacon's essay "Of Deformity" provides a companion to discussion of the topic thereafter. Bacon begins with a suspicion about the potential for violence that Shakespeare's drama secures for the sake of narrative momentum. Bacon theorizes that deformity breeds resentment of the deformed individual toward the world, for "as nature hath done ill by them, so do they by nature" (Bacon 158). Espoused as an error of nature that results in a "void of natural affection," physical deformity penetrates beneath the surface and leaves its impression upon the mind as well—"where nature erreth in one, she ventureth in the other" (Bacon 158). Shakespeare may ventriloquize common cultural prejudices toward disability and deformity through his titular character, but "Of Deformity" revels in its ability to expose the concealed key to the production of a character of Richard's barbaric proportions.

Rather than criticizing the public scorn that could trigger resentment, Bacon draws a series of equivalences against which the nondeformed world must be on guard:

> Whosoever hath anything fixed in his person, that doth induce contempt, hath also a perpetual spur in himself, to rescue and deliver himself from scorn. Therefore all deformed persons, are extreme bold. First, as in their own defence, as being exposed to scorn; but in the process of time, by a gen-

eral habit. Also it stirreth in them industry, and especially of this kind, to watch and observe the weakness of others, that they may have somewhat to repay. (158)

The oscillations between moral contamination, boldness, and industry evidence the slippery slope of deformity's meanings for Bacon. The Baconian deformed subject may be oriented in multiple directions by "the spur" that corporeal difference provides. Despite the wholesale conjecture involved in these observations, empiricism would prove loathe to follow up these possibilities in any romanticized project of rescue. Bacon prefaces the above discussion with a caution against interpreting deformity as a "sign" of internal malignancy—for that could prove misleading—and encourages his audience to consider it a "cause that seldom faileth of the effect" (158). The emphasis upon "cause" provides the philosopher with the desired complexity by seeming to modulate the absolute condemnation of his opening remarks. Yet the essay winds up by revealing that "deformity is an advantage to rising" up the ladder of political power. Just so, Bacon warns that the assumption that physical deformity might signify a correspondent inability on the part of the afflicted could lull the nondeformed into a dangerous complacency. His is a cautionary tale: do not distrust the apparently natural correspondence between deformity and disposition.

During the Restoration, John Dryden and Nathaniel Lee would claim that Shakespeare's characterization of Richard III served as muse for their own rewriting of *Oedipus*. In Dryden's portion of the work, a similar ideology of physical correspondence lures the audience into the mystery of whether discernible defects divulge a defective moral and civic character. Claiming imitation of Richard, Dryden satirically depicts a deformed Creon in order to lampoon his real-life disabled archrival, the earl of Shaftesbury. (Emphasizing the antipathy that informs this portrait of Creon, even one of Dryden's recent biographers cites these debates over deformity only to point out that, while unfortunate, the Shaftesbury being satirized in "Creon" *was indeed* someone who "never attained normal height . . . and walked hunched over, and with the aid of a cane" [Winn 312].)

In order to place this narrative "twist" to Sophocles' drama center stage, Dryden's *Oedipus* begins with an argument over the meaning of Creon's multiple deformities, one that is waged by the deformed man himself and Eurydice. In Dryden's version, the very mystery of Creon's "unnatural" form returns as the play's central preoccupation and largely displaces the investigation into the murder of Laius by Oedipus. Like the litany of epithets hurled at Richard by Lady Anne and Queen Margaret on his physical unsightliness, Eurydice marshals her own series of taunts toward Creon as her illegitimate and distasteful suitor:

> Nature her self start back when thou wert born;
> And cry'd the work's not mine:—
> The Midwife stood aghast; and when she saw
> Thy Mountain back and thy distored legs,
> Thy face itself,
> Half minted with the Royal stamp of man;
> And half o'recome with beast, stood doubting long,
> Whose right in thee were more:
> And knew not, if to burn thee in the flames,
> Were not the holier work.

> (Dryden 359)

What informs the allure that must have accompanied these feminine curses upon masculine deformity? In both plays the "unnatural" thirst for political power is presaged by lengthy scenes where scornful epithets mock ambition by hurling insults at appearance. Moreover, each play anticipates that the repulsion felt by the would-be maidens is justifiable and sympathetic in the audience's eyes. In Lady Anne's case, her hatred derives from her knowledge that Richard is the murderer of both her husband and his father. She can come up with nothing worse than pointing out to Richard that he is only a "diffused infection of a man" (I.ii.78). Queen Margaret comments that the inborn nature of Richard's political treachery was the result of a genetic anomaly: "But thou art . . . like a foul misshapen stigmatic [congenital cripple]" (3 Henry VI, II.ii.136–37). By the end of the seventeenth century, the allure of Richard's obscene ability to woo the wife and daughter of the men he has murdered is refused in Oedipus. Dryden ennobles Eurydice's repulsion at the sight of Creon's deformities and, in the process, reveals the depths of the satirist's own classical repugnance for physical difference.

Barbara Maria Stafford argues that the Renaissance would ultimately compensate for its lack of information about the internal body by overdetermining the symbolic significance of surfaces. The excessive nature of the curses heaped upon Richard (and later Creon) sought to reveal the truth of character by hyperbolical comment upon the contorted nature of physical form—its antithesis to a reigning classical aesthetic of human nature based upon symmetrical forms. The relation between exterior and interior provides a matter of serious dispute, however, because in each case, the insulted suitor counters the dehumanizing terms with the proposition that his own external deformities provoked nature to make up for the error by "stamp[ing] the mind more fair" (Dryden 359).

Indeed, Bacon himself had allowed that Socrates and Aesop, among a few exceptional others, had overcome the "stars of natural inclination . . . by the sun of discipline and virtue," implying that one could counteract external deformity with a conscious cultivation of virtue. Bacon launches this narrative of a requisite overcoming of nature, one that can be accomplished by only a few stellar deformed men. The range of Bacon's influence is indicated by the contemporary disability movement, which disputes "overcoming narratives" that leave all remaining, unexceptional cripples as victims of their own psychological inevitabilities. Forty years before Dryden, Bacon had not contended that nature might "stamp the mind more fair"; but he had believed that extraordinary individuals in history could overcome a natural propensity for malignant acts or abusive behavior. Dryden's furthering of a story of intellectual compensation would proffer another significant strain in the historical narration of disability.

Socrates, then, could continue to be championed by numerous philosophers as one whose physical ugliness was overtaken by an extreme virtuosity of his soul. Likewise, the writer of the 1687 *Life of Aesop* could end a catalog of the fabulist's numerous disabilities, a crooked back, splayed feet, an enlarged head, and knotty knees, with the compensatory emphasis upon "th'Endowments of his mind, and skill in Arts" (Aesop 276). By heralding the value of an exemplary imagination and visionary capacity, these more romantic versions of disability emphasize stark contrasts between interior and exterior in order to demonstrate a few exemplary cases of reversals in natural expectations.

The more romantic "reversal" of a "mind more fair" would prove to be less intriguing than direct correspondences between mind and matter, consecrated through an interpretive tradition quickly consolidating around *Richard III*. Well into the eighteenth century, scholars located direct evidence for the relationship between physical laws and moral instruction in Shakespeare's drama. William Dodd, editor of *The Beauties of Shakespeare,* published in 1757, selects a series of moral lessons on deformity, deceit, and high birth directly from *Richard III*. In quoting several diatribes from the play, Dodd coolly distills a universal truth from Shakespearean text: "It has long been observed, that *Distortun vultum sequitur distortio morum*. A face distorted generally proclaims distorted manners." In this same vein, Mrs. Griffith in *The Morality of Shakespeare's Drama* (1775) looks to *Richard*

III for lessons in a moral education. She notes a skillful contrivance in Shakespeare that results in the proper conjoining of pity and disdain for Richard:

> [O]ur poet, zealous for the honour of the human character, most artfully contrives to make Richard's wickedness appear to arise from a resentment against the partiality of Nature, in having stigmatized him with so deformed a person, joined to an envious jealousy towards the rest of mankind, for being endowed with fairer forms, and more attractive graces. By this admirable address, he moves us to a sort of compassion for the misfortune, even while he is railing an abhorrence for the vice, of the criminal. (311)

Griffith admires Shakespeare's schooling of an audience into comprehension of Richard's natural rage against unfair Nature. Her ideas of Richard's understandable, yet criminal, conduct entrenches a deterministic view of deformity—this one stemming from Richard's jealousy of those with "more attractive graces."

Not only would *Richard III* influence future artistic grappling with disability, disabled artists would be forced to navigate the social and moral quagmire of public perceptions now given a high-art sanction. For instance, Alexander Pope would endure efforts by Restoration critics and artists to undermine the authority and influence of his work by fielding an array of epithets that were excerpted, by his detractors, from both *Richard III* and classical Greek literature such as depictions of a raging Thersites. Pope's translation of the *Iliad* was crudely lampooned by references to his physical stature in a pamphlet engineered by Joseph Addison.[8] These lambastings have been critiqued as a product of crudeness in the eighteenth century by twentieth-century biographers, who, while downplaying Pope's disabilities, are forced into commentary on disabled people's psychology and social status. Rather than analyze the integral role that Pope's disability played in his poetics, Maynard Mack interprets Pope's disability as a sympathetic, yet general, psychological predicament: "He longs desperately—as he did in all his relationships with women,—and as we know today that cripples and other afflicted persons regularly do—to know the degree and nature of his acceptance" (306). Here the biographer becomes a psychologist counseling the reader about the psychic truth of embitterment, while making an artificial distinction between poetical achievement and the social text of a disabled life.

With disability studies methodology, biographers can conceive of Pope's embrace of the spider as a personal emblem, in all its Shakespearean resonance, as a poetical resignification—a perverse embrace of self-denigrating terms. These poetical rituals of deflection both refuse social imposition and reappropriate a linguistic slander to artistic ends. Hence the cultural context of disability makes more evident the logic of efforts to claim *Richard III* as an insightful drama. From his own disability-centered perspective, Lord Byron hails Kean's enactment of Richard: "By Jove, he is a soul! Life—Nature—truth without exaggeration or diminution. Kemble's Hamlet is perfect; but Hamlet is not Nature. Richard is a man; and Kean is Richard" (cited in Hankey 10). For Byron, Richard's deformity stands as a wound of nature that makes him a tragic victim and, in a perverse fashion, most imperfectly and paradigmatically human. His own play, *The Deformed Transformed,* provides bold contrast with a "high art" camp that finds fault with the Renaissance's immature perception of the implications of disability.

Today, general critical acclaim for the play rests upon the belief that *Richard III* is Shakespeare's first depiction of a modern subject. The character conceives of the world as a stage—a key figure for Shakespeare—and thus, self-consciously fashions himself through a multitude of deceptions and performances. Through his "self-fashioning," this critical viewpoint would contend, the Richard III stands as the first dramatic personage to embody a modern sense of a singular self. In this respect, Richard's idiosyncratic makeup yields the very stuff that individuality is made of—the multiple psychic "depths" alluded to by disability.

The opposed view believes that the play reveals the immature work of a not yet accomplished dramatist. Therefore, while the protagonist wields the rhetoric of his noble successors in the tragedies—Hamlet, Macbeth, Othello, Lear—he does not arrive at the necessary insights. Thus, he comes off as more caricature than character. This contrary response would contend that Richard's disability ruins the drama by supplying a too-obvious motive. It also undergirds a widespread conviction that the play's stunning popularity stems from the rabble's preference for the simplifications of an anti-Shakespearean Shakespeare. Detractors who complain about the play's mass appeal include George Bernard Shaw, who denounces the drama as sheer carnival: "[Richard's] incongruous conventional appendages, such as the Punch hump . . . leave nothing lacking to the fun of entertainment, except the solemnity of those spectators who feel bound to take the affair as a profound and subtle historical study" (Wilson 164).

Shaw and Henry James see Richard's character, exposed by the naturalistic acting techniques of their own era, as a ludicrous fantasy—at best an antiquated theatrical convention. Their dismissals of the play express distaste for the Renaissance's unscientific linkage between disability and disposition. Their views were authenticated by the sciences of physiognomy into the nineteenth century. With his blatant deformities, Richard seems too obvious for a more nuanced literary physiognomy's developed methods of discernment. The "Punch" caricature that critics find in Richard's figure resonates with the critical opinions of the juvenile strategies of cartoon entertainment, in which a physical form is drawn to identify a character's status as villain, victim, or hero. The simplistic associations between exterior form and psychic disposition in cartoons help to explain our perennial association of cartoons with children's entertainment, even though more sophisticated interpreters may "transgress" this presumption and find value in them.[9]

In the twentieth century, the Victorian distaste for Richard III's buffoonery was remedied by the infusion of medical ideology into cultural interpretation. Critics and performers alike came to view medical diagnoses and taxonomies as providing for nuances of character that were understood as absent from Shakespeare's original. We would contend that recourse to medical taxonomies helps to explain the steady modern recourse to a figure that has been dismissed as a gross historical anachronism. Perceived as lacking the insights of contemporary medicine, the play has been transformed into a vehicle for improvisational reworking beyond that of other Shakespearean dramas. In this process, Richard is more vessel for innovative performance than fixed theatrical stereotype. And Colley Cibber's recentering of the history plays around Richard's figure serves as a benchmark, with Laurence Olivier even crediting his indebtedness to Cibber onscreen.[10]

Ironically, historical shifts in ideas concerning "authentic" impersonations of Richard's "misshapen" form and medical disorder lie at the heart of the play's popularity into the twentieth century. Many theorists have sought to restore "authenticity" to performances of Shakespeare's character by properly diagnosing his "true" impairments. In this effort, an authentic impersonation of medical verities becomes the grounds for critical evaluation, as in this interpretation of Peter Glenville's performance in 1934:

> The severe thoracic kyphoscoliosis of the left side is both hidden and suggested by the cape and the arm akimbo. The flexion deformity of the left wrist is well represented. The legs of unequal length are depicted by the bent left knee joint and the rigid right leg. Richard's "grim visage" was doubtless more repelling. (Miller 360)

Miller and Davis even suggest that modern prosthetics might have corrected Richard's scoliosis and, thus, rehabilitated history itself!

> Let us examine the congenitally archdefective in all literature who, unfortunately, was not fictional. If his malformations had not so warped and made evil his character, if modern corrective measures had then been available to

the infant who was to become Richard III, history might have told another story in England. ("Orthopedics" 361)

If only modern treatments could be applied to Renaissance ills! Here medical practitioners demonstrate their own belief in warped psychology issuing from corporeal "anomalies." Yet who believes any longer that disability signifies a crime against a natural order? With the original play's avalanche of social scripts covering over any explicit motivation, scholars express a compulsion to verify or disprove a psychology of disability. Many critical appraisals of Richard performances make recourse to pop psychology. For example, an influential critique of Olivier's performance by Constance A. Brown argues that Richard's "quest for power is a substitute for normal sexual activity" (27). Given the nearly universal critical acclaim for Oliver's performance, the few critiques waged of it concern his neglect of the psychodrama of disabled characterization. James E. Phillips argues that

> the film falls short of Shakespeare in failing to make convincing, on the one hand, the physiological basis of Richard's psychological warp; and on the other hand, the psychological disintegration that was both cause and effect of his downfall from power. As for the first, Shakespeare was at pains to indicate that Richard's deformities were indeed monstrous—a hunched back, a withered hand, and a dragging leg that was more than a slight limp. Sir Laurence's Richard displays . . . little more than the familiar scholarly stoop. . . . the preliminary explanation that he was motivated by compensatory drives loses much of its power to convince. (407)

Finally, performers seeking more original and earth-shattering portrayals of Richard have found solutions by conducting their own investigations into a "psyche" of disability.[11] In these ventures, Shakespeare's play is presumed to lay out the broad strokes for a psychology of disability that contemporary scientific diagnoses will yield.

For Anthony Sher, Richard represents a pathological specimen in need of an accurate psychological and medical diagnosis. In *The Year of the King*, Sher narrates a personal odyssey, his actor's research undertaken in nursing homes, doctor's offices, and psychoanalytic sessions—and while watching late-night television. Sher studied for the role by visiting mental institutions, incognito, where he was horrified by the blank stares of those incarcerated therein. These ventures lead to the demonstration that Shakespeare's portrait contains psychological truths about disabled persons—ones that reveal the same "natural," yet necessarily understandable, rage discerned by the author of *The Beauties of Shakespeare* in 1775. Sher's acclaimed portrayal of Richard lent him crutches along with the developed tics and psychological abnormalities medical culture ascribes to physical impairment: repression, self-pity, aggression, sexual dysfunction, and an essential inability for self-reflection. *Year of the King* makes apparent one explanation for the many revivals of the play into the film era. Increasing medical study of congenital anomalies has provided for a steady interest in taxonomies of physical aberrations. With Sher, multiple diagnoses can be tackled with glee for their further performative possibilities.[12]

Presumed Anachronistic: Richard's Film Legacies

Disability studies, in launching critiques of stereotyping tendencies in film, initially found Richard an example of the presumption that disabled people have personality disorders. Noting that Bacon had formulated a pseudoscientific precept that has been reiterated as profound insight until recently, scholars necessarily contested the "fixing" of disability character in a portrait of rage and criminal affect.[13] With the benefit of these earlier disability studies critiques, recent scholarship tries to assess the pleasure that audiences, disabled and nondisabled alike, continue to find in the performance. This effort of critical retrieval sorts through the shifting cultural investments in Richard's deformities in order to unearth reigning cultural attitudes.[14]

Though Richard appears on film as early as a 1908 short, he will remain forever notorious as the protagonist of the first extant feature-length film. Frederick Warde's performance as a villainous hunchback now predates the racially deformed avenger of D. W. Griffith's *Birth of a Nation* (1914). Like *Birth of a Nation,* Warde's *Richard III* was lauded in reviews for its historical verisimilitude. In this case, an estate on City Island, New York, served as the setting for the play's Tewkesbury, London Tower, and Bosworth Field. The claim for an unparalleled historical authenticity dovetailed with the new film art's need to expand audiences, among them the crowds that attended freak-show entertainments.

Unlike Griffith's later extravaganzas that make copious use of cross-cutting and close-ups, Warde's *Richard III* is "primitive" in its arrangement of a series of tableaus for murder. In the early scenes, Richard commits the deeds in person: a hulking Warde bludgeons Edward VI with his sword, walks onto a balcony to wave to a roaring crowd, then sneaks back inside to deliver a few more vengeful stabs. Later, continuity editing lets the film audience witness Richard's sponsorship of each murderous act: he lurks in the corridor with payoff money for the princes' deaths or Queen Anne's poisoning. With this staging, film audiences are given a superior knowledge of

Richard's character, one lost to the characters onscreen; the observational vantage supplied by a hidden camera caters to a knowing voyeurism in the audience. This visual tactic supplants silent film's loss of Richard's soliloquies, beginning with "Now is the winter of our discontent. . . ," that have given the play renown. After all, a play famous for eloquent speechifying would seem to make a poor candidate for adaptation to a silent medium. Because the actors perform as if the camera were an unobserved witness, film audiences spy Richard's villainy without being enlisted, as the soliloquies direct, as knowing parties in the villain's motives and plans. As a result, Richard's figure, his hulking shape on screen, substitutes as the only origin for treacherous acts.

Because film follows the lead of theater in developing metaphors out of props and location, Richard's unfitness for the throne can be illustrated by having him nearly topple over from the weight of the crown during his coronation. Metaphorical equivalencies can be marshaled to fill in the interpretive vacuum evoked by the performance of Richard's many disability tricks: a limp, a twisted spine, a withered hand, a hunched-up shoulder, and difficulties in breathing.[15]

The play itself seems to encourage the creative alignment of physical aberrancy with Richard's canny awareness of the multiple and conflicting metaphysical and social meanings ascribed to congenital anomalies in Renaissance England. Shakespeare's "original" Richard, in a perverse adoption of courtly dissimulation, sets upon his physical aberrancy with performative glee. The very absence of clear explanation for his condition make it possible for actors to perform Richard's social roles as a disabled subject in ways that accrue to his own advantage: as a burden upon the resources of the state; as a metaphysical sign of divine disfavor; as the product of a perverse maternal imagination; as the most human in his suffering; or as lacking in natural human affection. Without mobilizing and commenting upon these commonplaces of early modern society, later Richards may lose track of his uncanny ability to manipulate the contempt brought about by his physical person to his own advantage.

For much of the twentieth century, Richard's mad-dash vengeance upon the world of God and king, his slaughter of innocents and perversion of natural order, served up an amusingly anachronistic spectacle. Ian McKellen, who published an interpretive narrative of the play, situates his recent filmed remake within proto-fascist Britain in the 1930s. Unlike Sher, who medicalizes and diagnoses Richard's character, McKellen attributes Richard's behavior to his response to the social reception of his disabilities:

> Before 1990, I had had no interest in playing Richard III. Indeed, I had long dismissed the play as not fit for modern consumption. Its sell-by date had surely expired, once modern psychology had questioned the cruel assumption of Shakespeare's contemporaries that physical deformity was an outward expression of some inner moral turpitude. Studying the play reveals an opposite proposition—that Richard's wickedness is an outcome of other people's disaffection with his physique. . . . Academics can be too adamant when exploring the origins of Elizabethan drama. They note the symbolism of characters in those medieval morality plays with which Shakespeare was undoubtedly familiar. They miss what actors discover, that Shakespeare fleshed-out those types and made them human. (McKellan and Loncraine 22)

McKellen contends that the play dramatizes the social outcome of cruel presumptions about disability held by the protagonist's family and associates. In an effort to make the politics of his own interpretation clear, McKellen refuses to allow Richard's disabilities to appeal to a purely objectifying interest in the audience. McKellen's Richard disrupts the power dynamic of staring with numerous direct addresses to the camera. This Brechtian tactic uses the theatrical convention of the monologue to destabilize a film audience's reception of Richard as merely another physical spectacle. McKellen's Richard vies with his fellow actors and contemporary onlookers for interpretive authority over his own definition. By putting Olivier's idea of Richard as the "Big Bad Wolf and Hitler" into action, McKellen's Richard threatens to exceed the restrictions of caricature with a portrait of a disabled man as a dynamic product of personal and social interactions. Yet by emphasizing Richard's and Hitler's stereotypical qualities as larger-than-life historical tyrants, the film also comments upon each era's need to condense evil into a manageable singular figure outfitted in the readily identifiable physical "costume" of disability.

After all, historical repetition has so naturalized this connection between physiology and psychology, between deformity and derangement, that even if it does not bear the markings of factuality and truth, it yields the pleasure of universal recognition. Al Pacino's recent film restaging, *Looking for Richard* (1996), sets into motion (once again) the search for the meaning of the mystery that Richard's character embodies. When he hits upon the term "deformity" in the opening monologue, Pacino is transformed from New York City street clothes into the Renaissance garb of Richard III. "Deformity" is fed into an echo chamber as both a stumbling point and a figure of universal recognition. The generational imperative to "look for" the essence of such an elusive figuration brings Pacino full circle, to what every generation of critics has discovered: disability *is* motivation embodied. This tautological equation between the visual surface and the invisible interior becomes the artistic holy grail of the new physiognomy of film; what begins as the most alien and inexplicable of life-forms yields the most commonplace and familiar of explanations.

Looking for Richard sets out on a high-art pilgrimage that every generation has made since the original production hit the stage in 1593. This ritualized artistic travel narrative searches for the assurance that the mystery of the relationship between the body and psychology can be resolved and fixed once and for all. Whether or not the relationship between physical disability and psychic malfeasance is reconfirmed, as in many performances of *Richard III*, or refuted, as in the restorative "cure" that concludes *The English Patient,* comes to be beside the point—filmed disabilities beg the question of their suspected linkage, and thus moral decrepitude shadows physical anomaly in the most intimate sense. In perpetually invoking this equation filmmakers confirm that disability's physical and psychological disorder can be recontained and domesticated from the safe distance of an artistic stare.

Chapter 5

The Language of Prosthesis in
Moby-Dick

Physiognomy, like every other human science, is but
a passing fable.

—Ishmael

The Inflexibility of Prosthesis

Critical attention brought to bear on Melville's *Moby-Dick* during the past twenty years has largely circulated around the novel's critiques of American ideologies of race, manifest destiny, and capitalism. Michael Paul Rogin links the social subtext of the novel to national "fears of disunion," controversies surrounding the incorporation of California, and the growing antagonism with Mexico in the first half of the nineteenth century (107). Marsha C. Vick argues that Melville's novelistic technique of "defamiliarization" allowed him to "call into question the use of racial characteristics as criteria for determining identity and worth" (331). Wai-Chee Dimock discusses the centrality of growing class divisions in the industrializing North as prompting the novel's contemplations of bountiful space as a solution to economic tensions, urban crowding, and the disgruntled poor (16). Each of these commentators recognizes that mid-nineteenth-century political upheavals in the social, economic, racial, and geographic identity of the country precipitated Melville's allegorical representation of "bourgeois individualism's historical conflict with liberal democracy" (Markels 1).

Unlike the important attention bequeathed to questions of race, class, and nationalist identifications, little attention has been focused upon the novel's vehement insistence upon the relationship between Ahab's "monomaniacal" personality and his dismemberment by Moby-Dick.[1] Our emphasis here is not upon the parallel between monomania and dismemberment (there is a substantial critical tradition on this relationship alone), but rather the peculiar and unnatural insistence in the narrative that these two facets of Ahab's identity are inexorably linked. The fact that Ahab's "monomaniac mind" is said to be forged out of "the direct issue of a former woe"—namely the instant of his crippling—runs counter to the novel's overarching strategy of demonstrating the ultimate indeterminacy of meaning embedded in the relations of signifier and signified (385, 463–64).[2] This chapter analyses the reasons why Ahab's crippling accident and subsequent prosthetic alteration bequeath to him a static identity that resists even Ishmael's fluid interpretational practices. Ahab's disability proves recalcitrant to the linguistic ambiguity that destabilizes the truth-telling systems of human knowledge addressed in the novel.

There are important questions to be unearthed in the novel's inability to place the meaning of Ahab's disability into its universe of mutable and forever mutating discourses upon the production of meaning and ways of knowing. Why does a disabling condition unquestionably precipitate Ahab's obsessive and vengeful quest to kill the white whale?[3] Why, in the critical tradition, is Ahab's disabling condition not subject to the same definitional and multiperspectival scrutiny as are other "physical" identities such as race, masculinity, and national origin? What challenges do the material circumstances of physical incapacity pose to the novelist's philosophy of indeterminate meaning? How do the conventions of literary romanticism constrain less deterministic interpretations of Ahab's dismemberment?

Our contention is that there is a short-circuiting of narrative purpose that crystallizes around the physical *fact* of Ahab's prostheticized difference. The repaired leg signifies a physical and metaphysical *lack* that cements the captain's identity as obsessive, overbearing, and overwrought. Yet, curiously, this static identity bequeathed to Ahab also provides the contrast against which the linguistically permeable universe of *Moby-Dick* unfolds. From the moment that Captain Peleg explains to Ishmael that the source of Ahab's "desperate moody, and savage" behavior commenced with the "sharp shooting pains in his bleeding stump," the riddle of Ahab's identity is largely solved (79, 77). Ishmael's access to the story of Ahab's dismemberment provides a physical myth of origins that the novel never sincerely interrogates. Thus, just as "the most poisonous reptile of the marsh perpetuates his kind," the "miserable event" of Ahab's dismasting "naturally beget[s its] like" (385, 464). Although the argument for the source of Ahab's compulsive behavior and violent vendetta is revisited on numerous occasions, the monomaniacal result of his prostheticized body eventually becomes novelistic doctrine.

As Rosemarie Garland Thomson observes, "Ahab's outrage compensates for his vulnerability, rendering him both a sublime and a threatening version of the disabled figure" (*Extraordinary Bodies* 45). The literal "threat" posed by disability in Melville's novel centers upon one (human) monster's indefatigable pursuit of another (mammalian) monster that places the lives of the rest of the able-bodied crew at risk. While the monstrosity of the latter issues from its definitional inaccessibility, however, the former's monstrous nature is secured by a largely unchallenged story that yokes disability to insanity, obsessive revenge, and the alterity of bodily variation.

Ahab's Accessibility

The novel's singularizing explanation of Ahab's physical loss can be traced directly to nineteenth-century attitudes about bodily differences and physical incapacities. Unlike previous historical moments that ascribed physical "hardships" to a sinful fate bequeathed from God or as the surface manifestation of satanic possession, the Victorian period witnessed the rise of an increasingly professionalizing medical ethos and ideology. The nineteenth-century study of pathology, as medical historian Georges Canguilhem has documented, developed out of a belief that bodily permutations could be empirically quantified as degrees of deviance from an idealized norm (154–55). Nineteenth-century diagnostic taxonomies in the medical writings of Bichat and Bernard, for instance, sought to not only describe and devise interventions for a variety of physical incapacities but also to arrange them in a hierarchy. Catalogs of pathology that slotted biological differences into hierarchies of human deviancy situated medical doctors, pathographers in particular, as authoritative legislators of biological nature who upheld a fiction of bodily normativity. In doing so, Canguilhem argues, medicine surrendered its professed ideal of diagnostic objectivity by applying a generalized and theoretically abstract model of the body to evaluate organisms that are inherently adaptive, fluctuating, and idiosyncratic.

Ahab's "demasted" body sets this key contradiction between biological deviation and organismic adaptation into motion. While Melville's captain alters himself and the maritime world around him to better accommodate his disability, he nonetheless fails to escape the fate of a medicalized determinism that pervades the novel. The captain's endeavors to provide himself with a "foothold"—both literally and metaphorically—in a traditionally able-bodied profession ironically solidifies the evidence of his single-minded arrogance and overreaching nature. A catalog of Ahab's physical alterations of topside life fends off potential doubt that a one-legged captain could function in such a precarious environment: the "auger hole, bored about half an inch or so, into the plank" that steadied his "barbaric" bone leg

(110, 124), the "iron banister" that he grips to "help his crippled way" (112, 127); the winch hook and specially designed saddle that carries him aloft into the ship's rigging; his unsuccessful request for a special allotment of "five extra men" from the ship's owners (Ahab fulfills this need secretively in the smuggling of Fedallah's crew on board); the "making [of] tholepins with his own hands for what was thought to be one of the spare boats"; the addition of an "extra coat of sheathing in the bottom of the boat, as if to make it better withstand the pointed pressure of his ivory limb"; and the "shaping of thigh board, or clumsy cleat, . . . for bracing the knee" (198, 230). The final commentary on these transformations to accommodate Ahab's disability comes in an exhausted exclamation by Ishmael on the superfluous nature of his efforts: "Hence the spare boats, spare spars, and spare lines and harpoons, and spare everythings, almost but a spare Captain and duplicated ship" (89, 96).[4]

Each of these innovations and inventions is paraded not as evidence of Ahab's resourcefulness, but as proof of the extent to which he will go to fulfill his "singular" quest: "But almost everybody supposed that this particular preparative heedfulness in Ahab must only be with a view to the ultimate chase of Moby Dick" (198, 230). The paradox for Ahab is that his need for physical alterations aboard the ship supplies the tangible evidence of his "unhealthy" perseverance. Suspicions of his "monomania" in the first half of the novel are largely buttressed by these insistent endeavors to reconfigure ship to altered man, and yet suspicion of these outward signs of Ahab's personal willfulness is not enough to cement the truth of these readings. Ahab, like our previous readings of other high-ranking characters such as Shakespeare's Richard III and Dryden's deformed Creon, must ultimately condemn himself by confessing his own malignancy.[5]

In fact, when the novel drops Ishmael and installs Ahab as the narrative's focal point, it does so largely to allow the ill-fated captain to confirm the suspicion that he is "demoniac" and the personification of "madness maddened" (147, 168).[6] Once Ishmael via Captain Peleg lays the explanatory foundation for interpreting Ahab's character through his physical incompleteness, his first-person narrative largely concludes, and the "path to [the novel's] fixed purpose is laid with iron rails" (147, 168):

> Unwittingly here a secret has been divulged, which perhaps might more properly, in set way, have been disclosed before. With many other particulars concerning Ahab, always had it remained a mystery to some, why it was . . . for that one interval, [he] sought speechless refuge, as it were, among the marble senate of the dead. Captain Peleg's bruited reason for this thing appeared by no means adequate; though, indeed, as touching of all Ahab's deeper part,

every revelation partook more of significant darkness than of explanatory light. But, in the end, it all came out; this one matter did, at least. That direful mishap was at the bottom of his temporary reclusiveness. (386, 464)

The passage's oscillations between a definitive explanation for Ahab's behavior in his disablement and the "mystery" of his "deeper parts" cannot avoid the revelation of an "explanatory light." Although this interpretation is offered in the above passage only in terms of Ahab's "temporary reclusiveness" following the accident when his ivory leg "pierced his groin" on a Nantucket beach, his incapacities—physical, sexual, and psychological— are all eventually chalked up to complications associated with his original dismemberment and subsequent acquisition of a prosthetic (385, 463). While the narrator alludes to a psychological reality that is more obscure, complex, and less interpretable than the loss of a leg, disability continually surfaces as an answer to Ahab's fathomless personality.[7]

This "secret" now explicitly divulged has been more than a novelistic rumor even at this point in the book, and it surprises neither narrator nor reader that the "direful mishap was at the bottom" of Ahab's character. Unlike the slippery multiple meanings of the "monstrousest parmacetty that ever chipped a boat," the linkage of Ahab's subjectivity with his disability functions as a mystery without the force of revelation (69, 72). The significance of disability as a prescription for Ahab's mysterious behavior suggests that people with disabilities can be reduced to the physical evidence of their bodily differences. Disabilities represent all-consuming affairs that become the sum of one's personality, canceling out all other attributes of one's multifaceted humanity (Murphy 143). Ahab's dismemberment and "incomplete" physicality—now simulated with a whalebone substitute— supplies Melville's characterization with both a personal motive and an identifying physical mark. These two aspects function in the novel as a deterministic shorthand device for signifying the meaning of Ahab's *being*.

In the next section we want to argue that although Ahab's single-minded identity is fixed by the presence of his artificial leg, there is a paradoxical purpose accorded to the captain's ivory supplement; prosthesis doubles as a metonym for the myriad "substitutions" that riddle the novel's plot (such as the shiplike pulpit from which Father Mapple sermonizes his congregation on land, or Queequeg's coffin that later serves as a life preserver for the sole survivor, Ishmael) and as a metaphor for the artificial operations of language that give "flesh" to that which is perceived as natural in the world.[8] Prosthesis functions in *Moby-Dick* as the mutable relation between natural and unnatural and as a deterministic principle buried within Ahab's identity. Such a paradox demonstrates that Melville simultaneously anticipated a primary postmodern conceit about the slippery function of language and condemned his disabled character to a limiting ideological myth of physical normativity.

The Language of Prosthesis

As we discussed in the introduction to this volume, David Wills's *Prosthesis* argues that the prosthetic relation between natural and artificial—the attempt to simulate a living appendage with a wooden or inorganic substitute—serves as the proper metaphor for the workings of language itself. Rather than assailing a living reality directly or absolutely, language disguises its inability to represent anything once and for all, and, thus, the sign acts as an elaborate system of deception. The sign's concealment of the artificiality of the relation of signifier and signified performs a prosthesis upon the "Real." For Wills, the word is an artificial extension of the body seeking to capture an elusive essence:

> Language inaugurates a structure of the prosthetic when the first word projects itself from the body into materiality, or vice versa; by being always already translation, constituting itself as otherness, articulation of the othernesses that constitute it, *language is a prosthesis*. Every utterance is as if spoken from a skateboard, written on crutches, relying on the prosthetic supplement. (300; emphasis added)

In taking an "incomplete" or "maimed" physicality and turning it into an organizing metaphor for the operations of language itself, Wills displaces our notions that either language or the body exists in a natural relation to the worlds it inhabits and of which it endeavors to make sense.

Within Wills's model the world of relations is turned into an "ever-shifting" and "obfuscatory" series of substitutions à la Derrida, all simulating their monopoly upon claims to the natural or truthful. Language, in Wills's analysis, cannot walk straight—its figures "limp or zig zag" (24). *Moby-Dick* also searches for an understanding of the question of linguistic relations and, in the end, anticipates Wills's deconstruction of language as prosthesis. Melville's sea captain becomes stubbornly welded to a whalebone supplement that, by its very presence, demonstrates that the natural world exists only in a constructed—or *prostheticized*—relation to the artificial workings of language. When Ahab woefully exclaims, "Oh! how immaterial are all materials," and "What things real are there, but imponderable thoughts?" he espouses a theory that Melville sought to exemplify in the elusive meaning of the great white whale itself (432–33, 528). Ahab's immaterial materiality arrives as a recognition that language functions as a frail and tenuous veil before the inscrutable workings of life, and that there is little substance beyond the realm of thoughts and the realities they constitute. Thus, in the much-discussed pasteboard masks segment (144, 164), Ahab lashes out at the ephemeral and contextual nature of knowledge and yearns for "something in this slippery world that can hold" (390, 470). This desire for solidity—to locate a concreteness in the object world that mimics or parodies a one-legged captain's perilous footing on a ship—parallels language's function as a simulacrum of the Real or as a prosthetic supplement. Ahab desires nothing short of a denial of this prosthetic relation and, in doing so, situates his bodily "loss" as an insult to an originary whole that he longs to reinstate.

Ewa Ziarek argues that Ahab's "inability to detect any transcendental design in nature articulate[s] the main epistemological difficulties in the text of *Moby-Dick*" (272). Why would Melville ironically employ the bearer of a prosthesis as the character who insists upon maintaining a belief in the promise of literality? For Ahab, language functions as a compensatory mechanism that guarantees an absoluteness to meaning and definition that it cannot deliver. Like the phantom pain that Ahab still feels, "though it be now so long dissolved," there is a remnant of fixed meaning—or a hint of a once intact Truth—in language that Ahab's prosthesis continually calls to his mind (391, 471). He is doubly haunted by the memory of his once "intact" body and by an unattainable ideal of physical completeness.

Here we arrive at one of the defining conundrums embodied in physical disability: it provides the "visible" and fixed evidence of a violated bodily wholeness while calling to mind the failure of our bodies to attain the ideal of completeness. In theorizing this foundational conundrum about bodily inadequacy, Lennard Davis makes a key parallel between race and disability to demonstrate the ideological investments in social constructs of marred physicalities: "As coded terms to signify skin color—black, African American, Negro, colored—are largely produced by a society that fails to characterize 'white' as a hue rather than an ideal, so too the categories 'disabled,' 'handicapped,' 'impaired' are products of a society invested in denying the variability in the body" (*Enforcing Normalcy* xv). The "Fall" from a biological ideal denoted by people with disabilities surfaces as an act of denial that situates the physically normative as possessing a nonvariegated, and thus normative, biology. Within such a formulation Davis might point out that Ahab's dismembered body surfaces as an example of Freud's *unheimlich* in that his body deviates from the expectations of the idealized cultural body. While Queequeg's muscular—albeit racialized and tattooed—physique can be assimilated into the topsy-turvy norms of Melville's shifting universe, Ahab's disability marks him as embodying a physical "hue" that exists outside of the bodily continuum enshrined aboard the *Pequod.*

Not only does Ahab's body distinguish him from the rest of the crew (just as the rank of captain places him above them in the hierarchy of shipboard life), it also serves as an alienating difference within his own psyche. In the chapter "Ahab and the Carpenter," he speaks desperately to the human "maker" of his artificial limb about the absurdity of experiencing pain in a limb "so long dissolved": "when I come to mount this leg thou makest, I shall nevertheless feel another leg in the same identical place with it; that is, carpenter, my old lost leg; the flesh and blood one I mean. Canst thou not drive that Old Adam away?" (391, 471). The "Old Adam" of a once intact body now lost recalls the biblical allegory of a fall from Edenic literality where signs enjoyed a more direct relation to their signified objects. To seek "knowledge" in the postlapsarian world of sliding signifiers means to enter into the insufficiency and discomfort of a prosthetic relation. Disabilities bear the stigma of a reminder that the body proves no less mutable or unpredictable than the chaos of nature itself.

Ahab's character becomes the tragic embodiment of this linguistic equivalent to original sin, and his prostheticized limb serves as the visual evidence of his metaphorical plight. Unlike the more fluid narrations on whaling and the whale offered up by Ishmael and the unspecifiable third-person narrator of the latter half of *Moby-Dick,* Ahab is sentenced to the inflexibility of a prosthesis. This treatment of his character is distinct from the narrative's musings upon the meanings of the white whale, whose multiple physical differences, including albinism and "snow-white wrinkled forehead," "pyramidical humpedback," and "deformed lower jaw," fail to secure any absolute definition of its mammalian essence (159, 183). The mythic whale defies any human-made system's ability to discern a reliable natural patterning to it existence, and thus its "monstrous" physicality eludes capture as *knowledge.*

Yet this mystery does not embed the anomalous organism in a deterministic identity—rather its inscrutability reflects back upon the limitations of humanity's ability to control the world through language. Melville's language of prosthesis demonstrates that meaning is inherently unstable and artificial, a product of the perceiver's will or desire projected upon a dynamic universe. Nature comes into conformity with that imposed meaning only in the sleight of hand that language performs. Any attempt to graft static meaning upon a dynamic nature only demonstrates the tenuous illusion of human desire.

Physiognomic Allegories

While the allegory of the whale may be explained as an exposé of the artificiality of language—a prostheticized bridge between the human verbalization of desire and "mute nature"—Ahab's own allegory is sedimented into a story of biological fact and personal, as well as physical, incapacity. Wai-Chee Dimock argues that the allegorical structure of *Moby-Dick* forwards characters who become agents of the textual exegesis rather than agents in their own right. This narrative strategy employed by Melville serves as a "personification" of character types that necessarily limits the "play" usually associated with developed characterizations:

> In short, what makes the allegorical character powerless is precisely his fixedness, his materialization within a form that never changes. To be personified at all, from this perspective, is already to submit to the dictates of the timeless, the dictates of destiny. This point becomes especially clear when we consider the nature of "agency" in allegory. . . . [If] allegory leaves no doubt about the character of its agency, that emblematic clarity is possible only because its "agency" is always represented as "image," a bounded figure in space. Personification is really a kind of reification then: it reifies the category of "agency," investing it and confining it within a material form—in this case, a human form. (25)

Interestingly, Dimock endeavors to prove her theory about the determinism of allegory through its numerous applications to the figure of Ahab: his character reveals a "blaming the victim" mentality in Melville's narrative because his agency is already delimited by the conventions of the novel's allegorized expression (109). Yet Dimock's theory overlooks Ahab's prosthesis as the organizational principle of the novel, while also ignoring the more political question of why Ahab's figure proves so available for allegorization in the first place. While Dimock significantly points out that Ahab's agency is thoroughly compromised by Melville's larger thematic objectives, his singular status as a "bounded figure in space" demonstrates that what is at work here is a cultural penchant for allegorizing disability itself. Culturally, we imagine agency to be precluded by the fact of a disability—one is transformed into the principle of passivity where agency is only a longed-for ideal available to the normative inhabitant of an intact body.

To demonstrate that what is at stake in the novel's representation of Ahab's physical difference is more than the workings of agency in allegory, we want to turn to Melville's brief reflections on the nineteenth-century sciences of physiognomy and phrenology in the chapters entitled "The Prairie" and "The Nut." While Ishmael ends up dismissing these two "semi-sciences" as little more than a passing fad—and thus, gesturing toward Melville's critique of nineteenth-century empiricism in general—we want to go on to demonstrate that the novel continues to rely upon the very tenets of these disciplinary perspectives wherever Ahab's visage and physique are concerned. The means by which Ahab's "personification" occurs is more strictly connected to the material facts of his physiology than Dimock's argument recognizes; and thus, we want to argue that disability's "material form" plays host to the "confining" logic of identity that Dimock chalks up to the process of allegorization in general.

In "The Prairie," Melville begins with a farcical commentary about the difficulty of applying the "tactile" methodology of physiognomy and phrenology to the head of a whale. Lacking the physical geography necessary to allow a reading of facial lines or cranial bumps, Ishmael nonetheless strives to "read" the whale's interior truth via signs made manifest on its external surface. His attempt to apply the teachings of the renowned physiognomist Lavater to the facade of the whale stems from a taxonomic desire to exhaust all of the available disciplinary tools for deciphering meanings in nature. In spite of gesturing toward the unfeasibility of such an approach to an understanding of Leviathan, Ishmael stoically argues in Montaignian fashion: "I try all things; I achieve what I can" (291, 345).[9] Yet by the end of the chapter, the "physiognomical voyage" around the full circumference of the whale's head leads Ishmael to dismissively conclude, "Physiognomy, like every other human science, is but a passing fable" (292, 347).

The flawed theory behind these pseudosciences proves twofold: first, Ishmael borrows an argument from a classist perspective that one would need to be extraordinarily perceptive to decipher the meaning of facial lines in even the "simplest peasant's face" (292–93, 347); and second, the absence of human features on the whale's head defies physiognomical and phrenological emphasis upon facial lines, cranial bumps, and individual countenances.[10] Frustrated in his attempt to identify the physiological criteria necessary for a physiognomic interpretation—"For you see no one point precisely; not one distinct feature is revealed; no nose, eyes, ears, or mouth; no face; he has none, proper"—Ishmael derides the applicability of the physiognomical catalog that sought to distinguish between virtuous and deviant physical characteristics in the first place (292, 346). The whale proves no suitable candidate for such a theory, and, consequently, physiognomy evidences itself as a flawed system based upon the deciphering of variable physiological elements. This exposé of scientific practices of bodily standardization that began in the eighteenth century situates Melville squarely in the tradition of other literary Romantics who embraced a symbolic representation of the human condition based largely upon bodily and cognitive differences (the importance of this influence upon Melville is discussed later in this chapter).

Consequently, physiognomy's—and later phrenology's—conceit of empirically mapping facial and cranial contours into a moral system is undermined by the novel's superior ethics of multiplicity. *Moby-Dick* confidently parades the fallibility and incompleteness of a multitude of discursive systems before its reader—biology, psychology, economics, astronomy, statistics, art, sociology, and so forth—in order to demonstrate the impossibility of unraveling the riddle of the whale's essential being. Each disciplinary strategy of attack stands as the symptom of a desire to control and subjugate nature to knowledge—all are elaborate systems of deception disguising the prosthetic artificiality of language itself. In slotting various explanatory methods into a novelistic exposé of interpretive limitations, Melville demonstrates that interpretation itself is historically contingent and contextual.

Such a strategy ultimately dooms the novel to a similar fate. If discourses are the products of their historical moment and cultural perspectives, then *Moby-Dick* can no more elude this fate than those disciplinary systems it critiques. While the whale's "lack" of facial features ennobles its visage with a "sublime" comportment, Ahab's missing leg debases his physical and psychological person by making him "too much of a cripple" (364, 437). The enigma of his figure translates into the static device that causes *Moby-Dick*'s philosophical pursuit of language's radical contingency to falter. In "The Sphynx," just nine chapters prior to the denunciation of physiognomy as a pseudoscience, Ahab offers up his own physiognomical correlative to the relationship between body and subjectivity: "O Nature, and O soul of man! how far beyond all utterance are your linked analogies! not the smallest atom stirs or lives in matter, but has its cunning duplicate in mind" (264, 312). Tellingly, this general principle, that the mind follows the course of the body (or matter), pigeonholes Ahab most vehemently. Yet this physiognomic philosophy fails when applied to the indeterminable meanings of the whale's external anomalies and to the other sailors' physical beings: "Only some thirty arid summers had [Starbuck] seen; those summers had dried up all his physical superfluousness. But this, his thinness, so to speak, seemed no more the token of wasting anxieties and cares, than it seemed the indication of any bodily blight" (102–3, 115). The narrative's refusal to assign any "bodily blight" to Starbuck's visible thinness demonstrates that neither human nor whale physiology provides a reliable surface for interpretation.

Ahab's self-condemning philosophy about the interrelated aspects of body and mind openly defies this pivotal aspect of the novel's moral lesson on the instability of language. In order to construct the narrative's insistence upon the mirroring relations of bodily surface and internal psychology, Ahab's confessions about his truncated humanity supply their own correspondent physical signs. The narrative's external vantage point on the character of Ahab could easily be refuted as mere projection upon his disabled figure, just as Dr. Bunger aboard the *Samuel Enderby* explains that "what you take for the White Whale's malice is only his awkwardness" (368). But there is a good deal of plot at stake in enforcing Ahab's unique and singular position with respect to bodily signs taken for internal symptoms.

Since Ahab's perspective cannot be rendered in the first person once the novel takes up Ishmael's point of view, the narrative shifts anxiously back and forth between recording the truth of Ahab's identity in his spoken monologues and sculpting a bodily surface that mirrors an internal state of mind. At numerous points a full-blown physiognomical principle is at stake in the narrative portrait drawn of Ahab from the outside.

> Ahab's soul, shut up in the *caved trunk of his body,* there fed upon the sullen paws of its gloom! (134, 153)

> Did you fixedly gaze, too, upon that *ribbed and dented brow;* there also, you would see still stranger foot-prints—the foot-prints of his one unsleeping, ever-pacing thought. (140, 160)

> [A]ll the added moodiness which always afterwards, to the very day of sailing in the *Pequod* on the present voyage, *sat brooding on his brow.* (162, 186)

> Till it almost seemed that while he himself was marking out lines and courses on the wrinkled charts, some invisible pencil was also tracing lines and courses upon the *deeply marked chart of his forehead.* (171, 198)

> His firm lips met like the lips of a vice; *the Delta of his forehead's veins* swelled like overladen brooks; in his very sleep, his ringing cry ran through the vaulted hull, "Stern all! the White Whale spouts thick blood!" (400, 483)

> Sweeping one hand across his *ribbed brow;* "if thou could'st, blacksmith, glad enough would I lay my head upon thy anvil, and feel thy heaviest hammer between my eyes. Answer! *Can'st thou smoothe this seam?*"

"Oh! That is the one, sir! Said I not all seams and dents but one?"

"Aye, blacksmith, it is the one; aye, man, it is unsmoothable; for though thou only see'st it here in my flesh, *it has worked down into the bone of my skull—That* is all wrinkles!" (403, 488)

The scalding steam shot up into Ahab's *bent face.* (404, 489)[11]

Ahab's "dented," "marked," "swelled," and "bent" forehead bears the signature of a violent internal upheaval that spills out upon the surface of his private physiognomy at nearly every point in his physical and psychological portrait. This pervasive emphasis upon correlations between external countenance and internal corruption effectively condemns Ahab as a product of his own physiological makeup. Since the primary use of physiognomic interpretations in the nineteenth century was to theorize a distinct visage of criminality and depravity, the relationship emphasized by Melville is exclusively debilitating to the reader's interpretations of Ahab's behavior. The captain's body serves as the medium that reveals his personality, and his physical inadequacy symptomatically belies his raging psychic life.

Despite Melville's insistence that the significance of Ahab's disability remains a riddle until the end, the narrative continuously bottoms out in its ascription of monomania to that particular cause. There is a narrative equivalent to scientific physiognomy at work here, and *Moby-Dick* falls prey to a methodology that it openly challenges and refutes. While the taxonomy of Nature proves fraught with misconceptions and thwarted ambitions of human mastery over diverse species and forms, the narrative itself pursues its own artistic classification system that would inculcate the plot in a similar reliance upon physiological hierarchies culled purely from the abstract workings of linguistic constructs of the body.

The Bodily Vulture of Narrative

Either the novel exhibits its own monomaniacal resort to this formative instance in Ahab's life, or Ahab's disabled exceptionality stubbornly thwarts authorial desire and the overarching thematic discourse upon the malleable nature of truth. Applying Melville's own commentaries upon the creative process to his physiological method of characterizing Ahab's disabled body, one may reveal the irony of the narrative's parasitical principles: "God help thee, old man, thy thoughts have created a creature in thee; and he whose intense thinking thus makes him a Prometheus; a vulture feeds upon that heart for ever; that vulture the very creature he creates" (202). This self-cannibalizing principle that Melville identifies in this passage involves a question of authorship. Whose creature is Ahab exactly—his own, as is speculated in the passage quoted, the "murderous" Moby-Dick's, or Melville's? From where does the vulture that feeds upon his heart hail, and who has set it upon him? Does the plea, "God help thee, old man," reflect upon authorial delusions of omnipotence that the Romantics were wont to challenge and punish in their overreaching authorial stand-ins?[12]

As many critics have pointed out, the literary predecessor of this allusion to a modern Prometheus is most likely Mary Wollstonecraft Shelley's *Frankenstein.* When the monster accosts his creator with a visceral complaint about the creative irresponsibility that resulted in his physical imperfection and social outcasting, he offers Victor's own journal entries as proof of his authorial culpability:

> Everything is related in them which bears reference to my accursed origin; the whole detail of that series of disgusting circumstances which produced it is set in view; the minutest description of my odious and loathsome person is given, in language which painted your own horrors and rendered mine indelible. I sickened as I read. "Hateful day when I received life!" I exclaimed in agony. "Accursed creator! Why did you form a monster so hideous that even *you* turned from me in disgust? God, in pity, made man beautiful and alluring, after his own image; but my form is a filthy type of yours, more horrid even from the very resemblance. Satan had his companions, fellow-devils, to admire and encourage him; but I am solitary and abhorred." (144–45)

We like to imagine this encounter as an allegorical moment in literary history where those constructed as physically deviant assail those who would create them in that image. The monster's lament, one that carries across a tradition reaching all the way back to the cyclops in the *Aeneid,* reviles not only one's own physical monstrosity but also the investment of the maker in the invention of monstrosity itself. Victor's abhorrence for his own creation could be read as a literary return of the repressed, where the bearers of physical differences in literary history demand accountability from their literary primogenitors. The irony of the monster's argument that he is "solitary and abhorred" proves inaccurate, for he is one among many in the ranks of the artistically defective.

Like Shelley's novel, *Moby-Dick* indicts the creator of monstrosity in the monstrous product itself. Yet Ahab is depicted as his own individual invention, and his invectives against the whale are widely discredited as self-destructive and egomaniacal. Melville's protagonist's attempts to blame the whale for his physical and metaphysical predicament prove unwarranted, for the sea monster is revealed to be merely a blank slate upon which humankind projects its own illusory meanings and malignant motivations. Thus, unlike Shelley's monster, who rails against his creator's monstrous insufficiency and is allowed sympathy in the wake of Victor Frankenstein's irresponsible neglect, "Ahab" is turned into a monster of his own devising. The "vulture feed[ing] upon that heart for ever" is set upon him by his own selfish devices, and in this way the novel "implodes" upon his character by turning him into source and subject of his own authorial insubstantialities.

As a product of the Romantic tradition, Melville recognized Ahab's disabling condition as the tragic mark of a "universal" suffering humanity, and, in this sense, Ahab is more of a prototype for humanity than Ishmael with his flexible and fluid speculations. At various points, the narrative comes close to openly implicating its own methodological sacrifice of Ahab to an artificial device of characterization: "The ineffaceable, sad birth-mark in the brow of man, is but the stamp of sorrow in the signers" (464). In *Moby-Dick,* Melville occupies the position of "signer," and the "stamp of sorrow" belongs to his own participation in the self-consciously crafted high-brow aesthetic of the American Renaissance. Melville, like many of his contemporaries, sought out the "tragedy" of disability as one antidote to what was commonly described as the facile sentimentality of a prudish (read feminized) Victorian literature. Ahab's external misshapenness represents an unflinching attempt to grapple with the deforming principles of man's insatiable quest for mastery over himself and nature. Yet Melville's use of disability in this manner proved neither unique nor a radical departure from nineteenth-century artistic appetites for contorting the bodies of its literary creations. As recent work by scholars such as Diane Price-Herndl, Maria Frawley, Cindy LaCom, and Rosemarie Garland Thomson has demonstrated,[13] writers of the Victorian period (especially women) relied heavily upon disabled characters in their artistic representations of femininity, sexuality, nationality, and race.

That this literary fetishization of disabilities and deformities did not go unremarked is evidenced in the writings of social moralists such as Anna Laetitia Barbauld. For Barbauld, a popular British commentator on the decaying virtues of Victorian society, the artistic desire to overload character portraits with "unsightly" physical and cognitive blemishes endangered the sensibilities of impressionable female readers. After running through a catalog of the reasons why violent tragedy offends rather than ennobles the reader's experience of a fictional world, Barbauld unleashes her most vehement criticism for the author who "deforms" or disables any character with whom the reader is intended to identify:

A judicious author will never attempt to raise pity by any thing mean or disgusting. . . . Nothing, therefore, must be admitted which destroys the grace and dignity of suffering; the imagination must have an amiable figure to dwell upon: there are circumstances so ludicrous and disgusting, that no character can preserve a proper decorum under them, or appear in an agreeable light. . . . Deformity is always disgusting, and the imagination cannot reconcile it with the idea of a favourite character; therefore the poet and romance-writer are fully justified in giving a larger share of beauty to their principal figures than is usually met with in common life. A late genius, indeed, in a whimsical mood, gave us a lady with her nose crushed for the heroine of his story; but the circumstance spoils the picture; and though in the course of the story it is kept a good deal out of sight, whenever it does recur to the imagination we are hurt and disgusted. (220–21)

In singling out the author as a potential violator of middle- and upper-class Victorian sensibilities, Barbauld further reified a wider societal belief in England and the United States that disability was an unsightly topic unfit for publication. Fiction, according to Barbauld, should be the province of an open collusion on the parts of the artist and moralist to hide or erase physical and cognitive differences from the map of human subjectivity and experience. Characters were to be endowed with "a larger share of beauty than is usually met with in common life." Any violation of this artistic contract threatened the frail moral fabric of Victorian values: "The mind is rather stunned than softened by great calamities" (Barbauld 218).

Such entreaties for writers to police their own voracious fascination with physical differences only underscores the pervasive recourse to this method of characterization. This reliance upon disability and deformity throughout the Victorian period evidences a growing obsession with the inflated symbolic significance projected upon physical differences. David Farrell Krell has argued that both Novalis and Nietzsche, two writers who were heavily influenced by literary romanticism, derive parallel investigatory and representational methods from a shared interest in conditions of biological extremity. Both were drawn toward contemplations of the body through their mutual poetical theme, "the attractive force of the dire" (Krell 201). Melville echoes this phrasing directly when Ishmael remarks, "Wonderfulest things are ever the unmentionable" just prior to discoursing upon the tragic fate of Bulkington at sea (97, 106). This penchant for foregrounding the wonderment of extreme conditions—particularly bodily afflictions such as illness, disability, and physical suffering—opened up a new literary area and mode of artistic exploration.

Melville's Ahab belongs within the tradition of this newly evolving literary aesthetic of *dire bodies*. The disabled body became an important means of artistic characterization, for it allowed authors to visually privilege something amiss or "tragically flawed" in the very biology of an embodied character. While disability had historically provided an outward sign of divine disfavor or monstrous inhumanity, the nineteenth century shifted the emphasis to a more earthbound principle of moral decrepitude and individual malfunction. The literary disablement of fictional bodies represented a tactile device for quickly individuating a character within a complex social network of relations. "Tics" of character abounded, and nineteenth-century writers—especially novelists—populated their fictional landscapes with "tragic" characters who embodied a range of physical and cognitive anomalies. The burgeoning of medical vocabularies and taxonomies of the body provided an impetus for the evolution of this *pathological aesthetic,* and nineteenth-century medicine and art mutually reinforced disabled bodies as sources of cultural fascination and leering contemplation.

Such disciplinary predilections on the part of medicine and art essentially preyed upon historical phantasms associated with disability by parading physical anomalies as spectacles of exotic interest. Although each approached disability with distinctively differing objectives—medicine solidified its professional authority by designating the need to institutionally manage bodies labeled as discordant, while art foregrounded bodies in various degrees of peril as a means of purposefully upsetting the staid morality of its upper- and middle-class readerships—physical differences were splayed, dissected, picked apart, and marveled at with a vulturish ferocity. The irony of this pervasive circulation was that people with disabilities were never identified as a bona fide social grouping or minority. Their conditions were viewed as rarities, and their lives remained thoroughly isolated examples of human deviance.

Medicine and art bolstered this perception of singularity by exploring physical differences without acknowledging the social context that authored them as Other. Ahab's isolated experience as the sole physically disabled denizen of the *Pequod*—with the exception of the "shuffling and limping" cook, Old Fleece, who is parodically described as having "something the matter with his knee-pans, which he did not keep well scoured like his other pans" (250, 294)—marks him as an unusual specimen among the multicultural human brood that occupies the ship. Disabilities are transformed into individually compelling idiosyncrasies bereft of their social stigma while paradoxically providing the means by which one becomes *interpretable* to an outside perspective. People with disabilities arrive with their limitations openly on display, and, thus, their bodies are constructed as the most transparent of surfaces. Consequently, their incapacities render them most incapable of eluding their textually bequeathed fates.

Sentencing Physical Difference

Yet in the nineteenth century the alterity of these textual dire bodies must eventually be punished or prove one's ultimate undoing. In a vein parallel to *Frankenstein,* where the monster eventually perishes as a punishment for its transgressive physiognomy and murderous responses to social ostracism, the narrative's tone in *Moby-Dick* becomes increasingly critical and denunciatory of Ahab's actions as it leads him to a similar apocalyptic fate. A sense of exasperation creeps into the final chapters as Ahab senses—or rather, sniffs—that the "whale must be near" (445, 546). Departing from the more speculative explanations about Ahab's personal motivations for captaining the *Pequod* after his accident, the narrative openly chides him for his physical and intellectual shortcomings: "Here's food for thought, had Ahab time to think; but Ahab never thinks; he only feels, feels, feels; *that's* tingling enough for mortal man! to think's audacity" (460, 563). This direct chastisement that issues from Ahab's own mouth situates him within an increasingly animalistic series of images—Ahab sniffs his prey, follows an unexamined instinct, and swamps human reason in the churning wake of his obsessive quest for violent retaliation. The narrative begins to abandon its own psychological theories of the captain's inscrutable behavior and places Ahab's physical incapacities on display as a means of forecasting the inevitability of the protagonist's final demise.

The singular marking of the "dazzling hump" now visible that designates Moby-Dick as identifiable, unique, and unrivaled in the teeming life of the sea, is paralleled by the highlighting of Ahab's physical singularity among his culturally diverse crew. During the sequence of events that make up the chapter entitled "The Chase—First Day," Ahab's bodily destiny surfaces as an ominous symptom that establishes the whale's superiority in what Ahab perceives to be their "mutual antagonism." When Ahab falls from his upturned whaling boat and Moby-Dick tauntingly circles him so as to cut off the crew's access to him, Melville objectifies his character's disability by describing him as "half smothered in the foam of the whale's insolent tail, and too much of a cripple to swim" (450, 551). The scene focuses upon Ahab's physical displacement in the unctuous and unstable medium of the ocean where his prosthetic leg's immobility is exacerbated. The quest to kill the white whale turns to farce, and *Moby-Dick* becomes a black comedy "whose centre had now become the old man's head" (450, 551).

Later, when Ahab is finally rescued and laid out in the bottom of Stubb's less accessible whaling boat, the captain is forced to come to grips with his own biological failings: "Dragged into Stubb's boat with blood-shot, blinded eyes, the white brine caking his wrinkles; the long tension of Ahab's bodily strength did crack, and helplessly he yielded to his body's doom: for a time, lying all crushed in the bottom of Stubb's boat, like one trodden under foot of herds of elephants" (450–51, 551). In this manner the narrative reaches its final objective: to force Ahab to admit that his human frailty defeats any designs he may have on the conquest of nature or personal renown. To punctuate such a revelation, Ahab finally declares: "Accursed fate! That the unconquerable captain in the soul should have such a craven mate [as his body]" (458, 560).

Ahab is increasingly singled out by the narrator, the crew, and in his own mind as the rarest creation of humanity—one who refuses to recognize that his soul is thoroughly subjugated to the dictates and (in)capacities of his body. The body surfaces in these final chapters like Queequeg's coffin doubling as an unsinkable buoy, for as Melville calls attention to the symbolic shortcomings of a prosthetic leg, he overdetermines its meaning as inescapable destiny. To call attention to the "affliction" and embedded limitations of Ahab's body demonstrates not a universal principle of human vulnerability, but rather that "Ahab stands alone among the millions of the peopled earth" (452, 553). This insistence upon Ahab's physical exceptionality characterizes Melville's use of the body as a corporeal vessel weighing down the metaphysical aspirations and longings of man *(sic)*; yet without the symbolically laden cultural meaning of disability as bodily imprisonment and damnable fate, this thematic strand of the argument would be significantly underemphasized. In this manner, the visible physical evidence of disability becomes transformed within the text as a form of embodiment with a vengeance.

Melville's concentration upon the disabled body as a controlling and constitutive feature of identity situates him within the Enlightenment tradition of representing the body as an earthbound and degraded aspect of human experience. Rather than allowing Ahab to expose this line of thinking as a throwback to the fallacy of Descartes's mind over body—where the latter term is jettisoned as insufficient and a nondefining coordinate of identity—the novel creates Ahab as a sacrificial victim to his body's dictates. While such a strategy significantly inverts the Cartesian tradition, Melville "overcorrects" for the philosophical discounting of human embodiment.

When Ahab points out in the culminating chapter, "The Chase—Third Day," that nature is comprised of ephemeral elements such as the wind that resist man's ability to confront, possess, and control them, he signifies the body as that which entraps one within its very materiality:

> Ha! a coward wind that strikes stark naked men, but will not stand to receive a single blow. Even Ahab is a braver thing—a nobler thing than *that*. Would now the wind but had a body; but all the things that most exasperate and outrage mortal man, all these things are bodiless, but only bodiless as objects, not as agents. There's a most special, a most cunning, oh, a most malicious difference! (460–61, 564)

A "body" would render nature assailable, and thus the comment comes as a self-reflexive revelation about the tragedy of Ahab's own inordinately *tangible* being. His prostheticized body serves as an object that makes his agency and mortality accessible to nature, to others, and to divine decree. Unlike the wind that strikes its target and whisks off out of reach, the disabled physical body cements one's being in time and space. Disability in *Moby-Dick* further concretizes this outrageous availability of human subjects to intangible processes, for it represents a distressed and fallible body calling attention to itself. Its deviations announce the material conditions by which it is apprehended by other outside perspectives and forces; its visible accessibility is imagined to disallow the subject any bodily subterfuge or physiognomic anonymity.

The "malicious difference" for Ahab between an embodied object and a bodiless agency suggests that the material vehicle of a body condemns one to a passive existence within its hull and, thus, precludes one from a more robust and direct interaction with the world (both physical and moral). Ahab would like to wrestle nature to the ground in submission to his will, but he cannot access it in any tangible "bodily" fashion. The body acts as a buffer zone effectively cutting one off from the environment while also making one physically subject to its own dictates as well as those imposed from without. Within such a paradigm, Ahab is held culpable for his actions in the narrative while paradoxically experiencing his life as already circumscribed by historical and mythological patterns: "Ahab is for ever Ahab, man. This whole act's immutably decreed. 'Twas rehearsed by thee and me a billion years before this ocean rolled. Fool! I am the Fates' lieutenant; I act under orders" (459, 561). Physical disability becomes synonymous in the text with the tragedy of a deterministic fate, for the body seems prematurely exposed to a future state of vulnerability and malfunction. The encounter with bodily deviations from an ideal of physicality challenges the expectation of a normative biological continuum.

Of course, time lines in literature are in themselves altered and "disordered" affairs. Characters necessarily capitulate to their generic conventions and the untimeliness of their melodramatic structures. Some five hundred pages into the narrative, *Moby-Dick* suddenly barrels toward its inevitable and fixed conclusion in the matter of three chapters. Ahab is doomed not so much to a "natural" fate bequeathed by the gods, but to an artificially contrived destiny that props up the captain's figure for a time and then "gives out" under the pressures of historically constructed assumptions about disability. The day before Ahab succumbs to the whale's indomitable power, he remarks, "I feel strained, half stranded, as ropes that tow dismasted frigates in a gale" (459, 561). This sense of being simultaneously immobilized and towed by another vessel proffers a vision of the disabled body firmly yoked to the tragically specular logic of nineteenth-century discourses on physical difference. Disability conjures up a ubiquitous series of associations between corrupted exterior and contaminated interior. The pairing is no more *natural* or aesthetically arresting than a truncated leg buttressed by an ivory shaft, but the language of prosthesis would make it seem so.

Chapter 6

Modernist Freaks and Postmodern Geeks: Literary Contortions of the Disabled Body

This boundless ocean of grotesque bodily imagery within time and space extends to all languages, all literatures, and the entire system of gesticulation; in the midst of it the bodily canon of art, belles lettres, and polite conversation of modern times is a tiny island. This limited canon never prevailed in antique literature. In the official literature of European peoples it has existed only for the last four hundred years.
—Mikhail Bakhtin, *Rabelais and His World*

A true freak cannot be made. A true freak must be born.
—Olympia Binewski

This chapter provides a contrast between literary representations of disability in American modernism and postmodernism. While the former has come to be synonymous with a particular aesthetic and coterie of writers, the latter has eluded classification. While modernism has taken up residence in the camp of "make it new," where literary experimentation proved paramount and sedimented symbolic systems underwent dramatic revision, postmodernism has been defined not in terms of its formal properties but rather with a variety of subject matters and "voices." The latter category has been explained as a celebration of literature's "hybrid potentiality" and the foregrounding of previously marginalized cultural perspectives. Brian McHale's *Constructing Postmodernism,* for example, explains that his prior work on contemporary literature had been criticized for applying a "fixed essence" to a literary category that by definition "refuses any solid identity of its own" (1).[1] In order for postmodernism to maintain its usefulness, McHale and other scholars suggest, the term must retain its own chameleon qualities.

Yet to develop a sense of what is distinct about these two literary movements, and to anticipate a series of arguments about the "future" of disability representation, one may look at the way each movement approaches disability. Since the literary components of postmodernism possess an identifiable "hereditary" pattern, the coordinates of its narrative structures and mythic contours provide a vantage point from which to understand some of its constitutive features. In other words, a comparison of the shared trope of disability can allow us to understand some of the distinctive styles and attitudes toward the landscape of literary endeavor itself, without restricting the category's fluid productivity. In each case we want to discuss the transformation of disability into a contemporary narrative prosthetic.

The epigraph from Bakhtin that begins this chapter proffers the "grotesque" as emblematic of literary characterization discussed to this point in the book.[2] If there is a "boundless ocean of grotesque bodily imagery" to be mined in the history of the "modern," then modernism and postmodernism have serviced this literary device as well. Along these lines, this chapter positions the well-worn literary trope of the grotesque in the interstices of these two literary moments in U.S. literary production. By contrasting two examples of narrative prosthesis from each period, Sherwood Anderson's *Winesburg, Ohio* and Katherine Dunn's *Geek Love,* we can assess the ways in which the grotesque continues to serve as grist for the writer's mill. On the one hand, our argument here is that while modernism unmoored the static languages of Victorianism from their "sterile" and more "puritanical" sources in the nineteenth century, writers nonetheless tended to reify categories such as the grotesque in their association with pathological cultural models of disability. On the other hand, postmodernist writers have tended to take up inherited tropes such as the grotesque from their predecessors and interrogate the very nature of their historical and artistic allure. In other words, while Anderson's novel exposes the prosthetic supplement of literary meaning-making with respect to metaphors of disability, Dunn interrogates the prosthetic reliance of literature, while developing a theory of disability subjectivity. Implicit in this distinction is an evolutionary model wherein the later generation assesses the mistakes and political proclivities of the previous, but the contrast of approaches also yields distinctions that address the historical moments of their invention and artistic utility.

The Modernist Freak

Sherwood Anderson's *Winesburg, Ohio* begins with an enigmatic dream sequence wherein the protagonist, a writer who is physically infirm, old, and has a white mustache, conjures up a "curious procession of figures" (22). This opening chapter, appropriately entitled "The Book of the Grotesque," acts as a myth of origins for our own formula of narrative prosthesis wherein the writer's creativity springs from the vision of "grotesque" imaginings. Instead of being terrified by this nightmarish vision, the writer is moved to leave his bed and compose stories about these "grotesques" that "represented all the men and women he had ever known":

> In the bed the writer had a dream that was not a dream. As he grew somewhat sleepy but was still conscious, figures began to appear before his eyes. He imagined the young indescribable thing within himself was driving a long procession of figures before his eyes. (3)

> You see the interest in all this lies in the figures that went before the eyes of the writer. They were all grotesques. All of the men and women the writer had ever known had become grotesques. (22)

Anderson posits this curious equation of creativity—"the young indescribable thing within himself"—and makes a link between this curious freak show of imagination and literature's exploitation of the world of physical differences. For the reader, the scenario proffers access to a "mysterious process": the moment of invention that compels the writer to leave the comfort of his bed and record a vision. What mobilizes this activity is a symbolic moment that transforms the everyday world of daily acquaintances into the acknowledgment of their "exceptionality." Just as with the story of *The Steadfast Tin Soldier* (see chap. 2), Anderson's writer writes only when he recognizes the formula of a worthy subject matter. Because these materials inevitably surface out of one's own socially produced experience, the unfamiliar "distortion" of the dream of the grotesque announces the arrival of a "full fledged" story.

Significantly, it is in this dreamlike state that the protagonist first encounters this "figural" world and connects it to the physical formula of the grotesque in an act of narrative prosthesis. Like Anderson's facade of small-town life that harbors an array of human abnormalities, the grotesque acts as a symptomatic visage that connects the deformities of a secreted internal life with distortions in the physical landscape. The writer's "dream" provides him with a necessary and fantastical transmutation of what he would otherwise find banal. The shadowy substance of a "character" barely discernible on the surface is suddenly unveiled to the writer in the physical landscape of the body. He metamorphoses the everyday into the literary "matter" of the grotesque.

In essence, Anderson's introduction illustrates, not that physicality mediates the personal coordinates of subjectivity, but that art, in this case literature, links the visible exterior world with the invisible interior life of the sub-ject.[3] As the narrative of the writer's dream continues and the "rationale" for the appearance of these grotesque figures emerges, Anderson yokes their unnatural visage with an analysis of individual pathology. As we discover in the second to last paragraph, what "made the people grotesques" were not physical properties but a more ephemeral "truth."

> It was the truths that made the people grotesques. The old man had quite an elaborate theory concerning the matter. It was his notion that the moment one of the people took one of the truths to himself, called it his truth, and tried to live his life by it, he became a grotesque and the truth he embraced became a falsehood. (24)

By objectifying truth in this manner, in making an abstract concept into material that can be snatched up like a valise or pocketed as a possession, the grotesque is constructed through a process of sublimation. To move from the nebulous world of possibility to the "falsehood" of solidity entails a kind of moral error in Anderson's fictional world.[4] The grotesque results from a delusion of mastery, a misprision of the fleeting nature of a concept. The writer's characters moor their identity to an absolute definition of self, and the consequence is a perversion of the dynamics of being itself. No longer are these formerly human subjects capable of change; they contort an inner reality into a restrictive mold that imprisons them within the corrupt world of an inelastic identity. The "evidence" of this *fatal fixity* for Ander-son's narrator is "embodied" in his own physical caricatures.

Thus, while Anderson's formula of the grotesque gestures toward an inaccessible interior landscape "deformed" by an unnatural desire for stasis, the writer supplies the physical realm as evidence for this distorting process. The figures of the dream world "parade" before his mind's eye as people who have been "drawn out of shape," and there are even those whose defor-mities "hurt the old man with their grotesqueness." An aberrant physicality commands interest in that it supplies both the fascination of a horrific dis-tortion *and* evidence of the artist's own perverse methodology. As evidence of creativity's obsession with the formula of the grotesque, the introduction ends with a crucial distinction. While the writer's fascination with the grotesque threatens to overcome him—even make him a victim of his own grotesque imaginings—he is saved from such a fate. "The young thing inside him" that previously served as the wellspring of creative vision preserves his own sense of integrity. In other words, he resists his own distortionary sys-tem by virtue of his mastery over the artistic mechanism itself.

The exoneration of the artist from implication in his own artistic landscape establishes an important moment in our understanding of literary modernism. Because canonical modernism openly embraced definitions of twentieth-century culture as inherently alienated and fragmented, its narrative method forthrightly sought out working symbols of this degraded malaise. Yeats's "rough beast" in "Slouching towards Bethlehem" announced the arrival of a moment that would find its most powerful expression in the perversion and contortion of physical and literary form themselves. Such an attempt to couple physical and literary form developed as a result of modernism's self-styled proclamation that language could act upon a Real in order to metamorphose its static properties. In *The Modern Tradition,* Ellmann and Feidelson describe this impulse to reorganize the reigning paradigms of social and individual perception as an inherently symbolist endeavor.

This strain of the modern tradition, which developed out of an imperative to use language to orchestrate a revolution of consciousness, imagined itself as a transcendence of a degraded nature. Instead of the artist striving to provide a mirror of perfect nature, as in romanticism, modernism began to characterize the artist as an actor who surpassed a defoliated, alien, and imperfect world:

> [M]any symbolists look at nature askance in all these senses, as a kind of brutal, massive, and crude encroachment of the non-human and sub-human. Their rebellion against it leads to Wilde's paradox that art holds no mirror up to nature, but is rather man's protest against nature's ineptitudes, his substitution of perfect imaginative forms for rudimentary natural ones. (Ellmann and Feidelson 7–8)

Through this artistic ideology the physical world would come to stand for the perverse and inept productions of a degraded material landscape. The symbolists would defiantly posit imagination as an aesthetic combat of symbols seeking to revise the monstrosities of nature.[5] To nail down this point, modernist poets, painters, and novelists consistently deployed the visible world as twisted and unidentifiable—a symbolic wreckage of romantic repression. The implementation of the symbolic order into a wrecked environment strategically upended audience expectations. Social codes, morality, aesthetic form, plot, and so on, all served as mediums for communicating a distinct upheaval in the times. Ironically, the extent of modernist experimentation left the symbolic order in disarray while entrenching artistic tendencies to pathologize cultural institutions through metaphorical perversions of the body itself.

Exploiting the "Private" Self

This key contradiction embedded in modernist artistic practice serves as the essence of postmodernist revisionist impulses. Instead of seeking to transcend the quagmire of an abject matter explicitly associated with the body, postmodernist texts investigate the site of metaphorical operations themselves. Katherine Dunn's "cult" novel *Geek Love* provides a useful case study of the contradictions embedded in modernist deployments of the grotesque, while steeping itself in the very "art" and language of the grotesque itself. Not simply claiming *Geek Love* as a "redemptive" site of postmodernist revision, we argue that the novel caricatures the artistic desire to yoke physical aberrancy to metaphors of denigration and perversity. Thus, while *Winesburg, Ohio* endeavors to "rescue" its characters from the horror and distance of the grotesque itself, *Geek Love* wallows in the very materiality that Anderson's novel establishes and then eschews.

In fact, it is the very subtlety of the grotesque imagery in the preface to *Winesburg, Ohio* that Dunn's novel would seem to challenge and celebrate. While Anderson's physical imagery of the grotesque never reappears outside of the dream life of the reporter, who stands in for the artist, it acts as a structuring device of the entire narrative that follows. Once set into motion, the story largely disassociates its characters from the physical correlative that initially calls them into being in the writer's imagination.

If we contrast the brevity of our voyeurism onto the visage of the grotesque in *Winesburg, Ohio* to the "traumatic" intimacy with physical disability in *Geek Love*, we recognize that the terms of artistic utility have shifted dramatically. The titillating glimpse that readers get of the grotesque in Anderson's novel and the full-scale "gimmick" of capitalist carnival in Dunn's work provide an important case study of the logic of the freak show itself in American literary history.

In the concluding chapter of *Freaks: Myths and Images of the Secret Self*, Leslie Fiedler argues that the literature of the freak has been transformed from the seductive peep of the prohibited to the lurid intimacy of "kinky sex and compulsory candor" (335). Within such a model, contemporary desires give way to a new kind of exploitation that thrives upon a once-taboo intimacy:

> Unreal, surreal to the point of making the whole tale seem more parable than history, that improbable juncture also opens up possibilities for the grossest scatological and sexual humor. . . . it is precisely such revelations about Freaks that we demand of those who reimagine them. What do they do on the stool? in bed? in all those private moments once considered out of bounds

to public curiosity? There have always been some who suspected that the appeal of the Freak show was not unlike that of pornography, and in the age of the explicit, the secret is out. (335)

The alarm that Fiedler sounds in this passage suggests exactly the kind of historical shift that we alluded to above. Such a "pornographic" intimacy can certainly be found in a novel such as *Geek Love,* where the narrative method hinges upon the promise of exposing what Fiedler terms the "private self." While Fiedler first critiques the exploitative voyeurism of nineteenth-century forms such as the freak show, he finds even less solace in the invasive conventions of contemporary literature.[6] Not only does he find the freak show alive and well in current literary metaphors, he argues that the artistic thirst for the freakish and grotesque now openly revels in that which the former century concealed and dissimulated. Not only is bodily aberration on display in the novel, the most intimate details of a life lived under the auspices of disability come into full view. *Geek Love*'s action goes behind the scene of public spectacle, and the reader walks into a world of "disturbing" familiarity.

The Postmodern Geek

Whereas the narrative of *Winesburg, Ohio* self-consciously distances its fictional subjects from the symbolic metaphor of physical aberrancy and bodily distortion, *Geek Love* mires its characters and readers in the *literality* of bodily metaphorics. As does its modernist predecessor, Dunn's novel begins with the fabricated "grotesque" as its own inspirational metaphor for the creative act. After introducing the key actors in "Binewski's Carnival Fabulon," *Geek Love* offers up its own parable for the originary moment of its freakish "conception":

> My father's name was Aloysius Binewski. He was raised in a traveling carnival owned by his father and called "Binewski's Fabulon." Papa was twenty-four years old when Grandpa died and the carnival fell into his hands. Al carefully bolted the silver urn containing his father's ashes to the hood of the generator truck that powered the midway. The old man had wandered with the show for so long that his dust would have been miserable left behind in some stationary vault.
>   Times were hard and, through no fault of young Al's, business began to decline. Five years after Grandpa died, the once flourishing carnival was fading. . . . Al was a standard-issue Yankee, set on self-determination and independence, but in that crisis his core of genius revealed itself. He decided to breed his own freak show. (7)

Such a paternal patterning of the carnival as family heirloom introduces the notion that freak shows, like genetic material, are passed on from generation to generation. Aloysius Binewski finds himself the unexpected inheritor of an economic enterprise subject to the whims of historical, cultural, and individual fate. Because the younger Binewski was "raised in a traveling carnival," he never questions the morality or redemptive value of the freak show. Instead he accepts the "carnival" as a natural outgrowth of patrilineal privilege, a legacy neither to be questioned nor refused by the rightful beneficiary. Thus, in one stroke the novel makes a key parallel between the social systems of patriarchy and the freak show as naturalized foundations of interpellation and systemic logic.[7]

By bolting the urn containing his father's ashes to the hood of the generator truck, Aloysius provides the novel with an ironic symbol of its own artistic legacy. Rather than distance itself from the legacy of "the grotesque" by leaving its progenitor's ashes to suffer the misery of "a stationary vault," Geek Love embraces the ashes of past literary traditions as the engine of its own narrative structure. In this way, the family dependency upon the freak show as an exploitative source of capital and personal survival establishes a parallel with the writer's own metaphorical opportunism. By beginning with an open commentary on the artificiality of the grotesque, the novel simultaneously embraces its own sordid literary origins and announces the object of its critique. When the father declares his decision to "breed his own freak show" as a means of revitalizing the failing business, the story unveils the artificiality of its own artistic method in order to candidly pursue the institutional forces that drive its desires.

Aloysius's "brain child" parodies a quintessentially modernist mechanism of "high" literature—the epiphany—by linking it up to a debased economic motivation. As he and his now pregnant wife, Lil, experiment with an array of fetus-altering chemicals, from the mundane effects of cocaine and amphetamines to the extravagant agents of insecticides and radioisotopes, an explicit connection is drawn between the daydreaming narrator of Winesburg, Ohio and the alchemy of a capitalistic underworld in Geek Love. The stated need to reproduce with an eye toward the "freakish" and "bizarre" locates an allegory for literature's dependency upon idiosyncratic, scandalous subject matter. Like the visible medium of the grotesque in Anderson's fantasy sequence, the characters of Dunn's parable formulate an artificial plot for reestablishing the visual evidence of the Fabulon's unique character. No longer content with the banality of performed behavioral oddities such as Lil's chicken-biting geek act, the carnival couple now searches for ways in which to provide sideshow-goers with the tangible fascination of bodily distortion itself.

This open nod to the material foundations of a past tradition in the grotesque provides a paradigm for the methodology of *Geek Love*. In her essay on postmodern narrative strategies in Dunn's novel, N. Katherine Hayles argues that shifts in historical paradigms occur within the metaphorical roots of narratives themselves. As one interpretive system's "metaphoric coherence" begins to dwindle and lose explanatory authority, another arrives to take its place. The interim of such a shift inevitably leaves behind its own historical residue: "In transition areas, where the power of one set of metaphors is not yet exhausted and the ascendancy of others not fully established, the systems interact with each other. The fading metaphors partly determine how the emerging metaphors will be understood, just as the newer metaphors cause the older to be reinterpreted" (396). This transitional moment can be discerned in *Geek Love*, for metaphors of the grotesque in its narrative structure signal the reverberations of a prior representational strategy *and* self-consciously privilege the very process of the category's revision. The "grotesques" of Dunn's story line pay lip service to their function as symbols of psychological horror and cultural collapse, while simultaneously "returning" these mythic selves to the realm of a thoroughly "embodied" experience.

While Anderson's narrator establishes a necessary distance between his grotesque vision and his own artistic project, Dunn self-consciously exploits the allure of the grotesque and indicts the dreamwork of art itself. Once the economic context of Aloysius and Lil's reinvention of the freak show is established, the novel immediately introduces the narrative perspective of one of the parents' "freakish" projects: the hunchbacked albino Olympia. Unlike Anderson's narrator, who views the world from the safety and artificially constructed vantage point of a raised bed (he begins his introductory parable by employing a carpenter to build a platform that will make his bed even with the window to better secure his voyeuristic tendencies), *Geek Love* begins with the perspective of the "grotesque" subject itself. In doing so, the novel effectively collapses the distance between its audience and modernist metaphorics of physical aberrancy.

In dispersed segments entitled "Notes for Now" that draw attention to the incompleteness of their "presentist" perspective, Olympia comments upon the meanings of her family's tumultuous past and her own contradictory contemporary moment. As the sole survivor of the conflagration that kills her family and destroys the Fabulon as a viable economic entity,

Dunn's narrator tells the story in retrospect from the "knowing" perspective of a second-generation freak. When Olympia acknowledges that her parents were secretly disappointed in the banality of her physical anomalies, she simultaneously introduces a division between the apocalyptic (and thus, more "valuable") freakish qualities of her brothers and sisters—Arty "the Aqua Boy"; Elly and Iphy, sisters joined at the hip; and Chick, the clairvoyant—and her own "less interesting deformities." Such defining distinctions allow Dunn to parallel the mythic fascination of physical difference that accrues around the "freak" to the more mundane experiences of individuals with disabilities. Each category interrogates the other, and in this way the novel thematizes and disturbs the associational lineage of physicality with metaphors of psychological alienation and moral corruption.

In reestablishing traditions of the literary grotesque as the artistic precursor of *Geek Love,* the narrative ironizes the "genetic material" from which the "grotesque" hails: Olympia and her freakish siblings "embody" the results of a past experiment gone awry. In a direct revision of the thesis of Simone de Beauvoir's *The Second Sex,* Olympia at one points states that "a true freak cannot be made. A true freak must be born" (20). The sentiment establishes one of the crucial paradoxes of physical disability in the novel: while the body hosts an array of parasitic social mythologies regarding abnormality and difference, it is also bound to a notion of biology as *inborn essence.* The Binewski children prove capable of adeptly manipulating fantasies of bodily difference in order to carve out a niche in a fetishistic commodity capitalism, yet such a manipulation leaves them ambivalently tethered to a physical fate. Faced with the dictates of a culture that confuses biology with destiny, Olympia embraces a dubious ideal that she and her siblings possess the "originality" of a "true difference," one that cannot be reproduced by pretenders to the throne of uniqueness and absolute individuality.

Such paradoxes can be seen throughout the novel as characters exploit their physical aberrations for their spectacular perversity while simultaneously contemplating the effects of their willing participation in the "meat market." In one early scene Olympia models for her daughter, who sketches portraits of physical suffering and unique bodily types, and the narrator is torn between rewarding her daughter's refusal to denote her as exceptionally disabled and feeling like an object in the service of artistic mimesis:

> Watching her work is comfortable. I feel invisible again, as though she had never spoken to me beyond "Good Morning." She is not interested in my identity. She doesn't notice it. Her eyes flick impatiently at me for a fast fix— a regenerative fusing of the image on her retina, the model she inflicts on the

paper. I am merely a utensil, a temporary topic for the eternal discussion between her long eye and her deliberate hand. (30)

The impulses that Olympia believes guide her daughter's art are both medicalized and artistic—as the poser she is simultaneously "a utensil" or the "temporary topic" of a conversation from which she is excluded, and an anonymous object in need of "a regenerative fusing." As she goes on to inquire about the origins of her daughter's artistic aspirations, she is quickly corrected with the reply, "No, no. A medical illustrator. For textbooks and manuals" (30). This critical connection between the creative impulses of art and the cataloguing objectives of medicine situates physical aberrancy as a foundational objective of both worlds. In either scenario Olympia feels her physical being extorted from herself, metamorphosed into a mere "model" inflicted on the paper and her own identity.

Yet paradoxically, the sketching scene also begins with a mood of tranquility—the narrator finds herself comforted by being sketched by one who is not "interested in my identity." Such longing for personal anonymity—to be provided a space where one's identity is not synonymous with the material properties of physical being itself—establishes the key coordinates of Olympia's subjectivity. Torn between the ethics of physical exceptionality championed by her family and her personal desire for assimilation, Olympia serves Dunn's theorizing of a psyche of disability that longs for a seamless integration into humanity in the midst of an experience of irreducible difference. As the artist's illustration passes from individual portraiture to the anonymous diagnostic catalog of the medical textbook, Olympia recognizes the risks of identifying with either the utterly individualized abnormality or the anonymous representative specimen.

Such competing desires send the disabled subject in a variety of contradictory and antithetical directions. Unlike the freakish performers of the Fabulon who extract a living by virtue of their own mythic existence as living anomalies, Olympia feels consigned only to the horror of her commonplace freakishness. In the street she is taunted by passersby who register shock over the "affront" that her physical difference poses. In her professional life she is relegated to a disembodied "voice" on the airways of a local radio station. And as an unexceptional "freak," she is relegated to the diminished role of barker outside the exhibit of her more famous brother. As one who is denied access to the larger-than-life authority of her circus-show siblings, Olympia is left to contemplate the insult of her own diminished standing within the family.

The ways in which Olympia is subjected to the cultural coordinates of her physical condition proves integral to Dunn's construction of disability as a less "spectacular" version of "the mythic prototype of the freak" (Fiedler 34). More than the uncanny shock of physical difference and the everyday terror of physical debilitation, the freak evokes associations with the monstrous and mythic fabulations of the most primordial kind:

> The true Freak . . . stirs both supernatural terror and natural sympathy, since, unlike the fabulous monsters, he is one of us, the human child of human parents, however altered by forces we do not quite understand into something mythic and mysterious, as no mere cripple ever is. (Fiedler 34)

This instrumental division between Fiedler's "fabulous monsters" and the "mere cripple" stakes out a terrain that *Geek Love* explicitly invokes. By foregrounding a world of characters who exist in this "no body's land" of physical deviancy, Dunn endeavors to trace out the process by which "cripples" are transformed into "monsters." Rather than reify the traditional distinction that Fiedler invokes—a division that "does not stray from the traditional view of 'freak' as a physiological condition" (Bogdan 7)—Dunn defines the designation as a matter of physical "packaging." As books 1 and 2 delve into the voyeuristic fascination of private lives and theatrical maneuvers that go on "behind the scenes" of a vaudeville of the flesh, Fielder's mythic monstrosities are unveiled in a myriad of exploitative conventions. Not only does *Geek Love* successfully manipulate the "lowest common denominator" of specular desire, the novel shamelessly refuses to "demystify" the grotesque moorings of its own literary lineage.

Technological Prosthetics

The coordinates of this "suspect" lineage of metaphorical properties are tied in the first half of the novel to the pontifications and promiscuous dimensions of Arturo, the armless and legless amphibian-boy. As the self-described mastermind of the Fabulon's flamboyant philosophy, which parades "deformity" as a seductive lifestyle and the symbol of the penultimate individualism, Arturo fashions himself into a cyborg of fleshy degeneracy and technological prosthetics. As Norval Sanderson, the journalistic follower of the Binewski "cult," compiles his data on Arturo's legend, he describes his enigmatic magnetism as a compilation of theatrical effects and boisterous self-assurance:

> Arty is sporadically self-educated with wide lacunae in his information. National and international politics are outside his experience and reading. Municipal power relationships, however, are familiar tools to him. He has no

real grasp of history—seems to have picked up drifts from his reading—but he is a gifted manipulator. His knowledge of science is primitive. He relies on specialists in his staff to provide him with effective lighting, sound technology, etc. . . . He has a sharp awareness of personal problems in others . . . professes no ethic or morality except avoidance of pain. (190)

While Sanderson, in good journalistic fashion, attempts to expose Arturo as a fraud by detailing the artificial apparatus of his "engineering," *Geek Love* contemplates the constructed nature of its own artifice. While Fiedler will draw a critical dichotomy between the "true Freak" and the "mere cripple," Dunn argues that the freak must be erected and molded from the outside. Constituted through an assortment of theatrical props and technological circuitry, Arturo stages his own public myth for mass consumption. Longing for a vision that can lead them away from the burdens that accompany the excesses of a bodily existence, the Binewski followers absorb Arturo's mythic ambiance with the zeal of the devout. For Sanderson, Arty's character is best defined in terms of the "lacunae" in his knowledge. Bereft of a working knowledge of history, politics, science, and technology, Arturo represents little more than an opportunistic manipulator of public beliefs about disability.

Such a catalog of negations casts "The Transcendental Maggot" as a vapid creation appealing to the basest instincts of human nature. Yet the journalistic exposé of Arturo's fabricated legend fails to explain the "power" his vision wields. Even after exposing Arturo as an intellectual fraud, the factual foundations of Sanderson's reportage fail to debunk his subject's mythic "meaning." Empty of content, Arturo's spectacle burgeons by virtue of the "authority" audiences invest in his self-conscious flaunting of physical aberrancy. Cut off from the historical traditions that have gone into the making of Arturo's freakish ambiance, his larger-than-life performance commands the attention of those who unwittingly act upon the culturally encoded "lure" of bodily deviancy. While Sanderson flippantly derides the performance—"Obvious horseshit" (190)—he fails to recognize that it is the "flesh" rather than the "flash" that ultimately constitutes the "material" of Arty's reign.

While the numbers of Arturans grow and the family's economic capacities increase, the special effects that "sell" the image of Arturo as the cornerstone in the architecture of the freak continue to expand. But as the apparatus of myth commands the attention of the Fabulon's audiences, the source of Arturo's cultish capital remains moored to the apocalyptic proportions of his physical presentation. The Zizekian "quilting point" of Arty's "appeal" has less to do with his technological augmentation than it does his philosophy of physicality as the bane of human existence. Rather than mourn the loss and limitation of his own biological capacities, Arty inverts the terms of public expectation by openly embracing the "terror" of his own physical banishment. In refusing to capitulate to an imposed definition of stunted humanity or private pathos, Arty declares that his biological condition offers access to the grotesque power of "difference" itself.

In other words, since Arturo understands that the realm of the biological represents the last outpost of material determinism, he flaunts his freakish disposition as the sign of his own idiosyncratic capital. When Al McGurk, the proficient electrician who later constructs the laser-like light show of Arty's performance, seeks to join forces with the Arturan ranks by virtue of his own disability, Arty distinguishes between the power of the freak and the insufficient model of physical impairment:

> "But I guess you want my credentials," McGurk said. . . . He slid his hand up the other trouser leg and both legs lay on the floor with steel shining out of the hollow tops of the knees. He pulled his pants leg up his thighs and showed the steel caps on the stumps. There were a groove [sic], a few grip protrusions, and a number of electrical contact points protruding from each unit. He looked up, calmly waiting. . . . "You figured it wrong. The whole thing," said Arty. He rocked slightly, chuckling. "You've got yourself a little old disability there, so you took pleasure in feeling sorry for me. Well. You figured wrong . . . You're just going along with what *they* want you to do. *They* want those things hidden away, disguised, forgotten, because they know how much power those stumps could have." (169–70)

Ironically, the scene pivots upon Arty's tactical inversion of McGurk's attempt to flaunt the secrecy of his physical "credentials." While McGurk's prosthesis involves an elaborate contraption made up of grooves, grip protrusions, and electrical contacts, the "unveiling" serves to secure his "membership" in the community of the norms through the proof of a nearly seamless bodily apparatus. Like Arty, McGurk also demonstrates the nature of his own prostheticized being in the narrative of his difference; yet while McGurk believes his "achievement" rides upon the success of his assimilation into an ambulatory ideal, Arty diminishes the power of the electrician's gambit by responding, "You've got yourself a little old disability there." Such masculine sparring exemplifies the key to Arty's deft manipulation of the conventions of disability—rather than cater to fantasies of physical wholeness and the sleight of hand that is the promise of prosthesis, he rewires McGurk's desires into the circuitry of the norms. For Arty, a prosthetic supplement geared toward a seamless integration reveals only a personal capitulation to the ideology of those who determine the standards of bodily aesthetic and physical capacity.

In Arty's worldview, "disability" (the "less" spectacular linguistic cousin of "freak") equates with an attempt to deny the "threat" that physical difference poses to cultural recitations of a holistic bodily mantra. In lieu of the disguise that even the most "lifelike" prosthesis affords to the contemporary cyborg, Arturo charges McGurk with an act of "re-membering" himself in order to cover up and downplay his own physical difference. Within this model the reconstruction of a body back into anonymity denies the "power" of an overt encounter with cultural perceptions of perversity and deformity that are part of the historical baggage of the tradition of the "freak." Since the body plays host to cultural fantasies about personal capacities and individual prowess, the flaunting of physical aberrancy promises a necessary rebuke to the ideology of biological homogeneity. In adamant refusal of a normative bodily "logic," Arty declares that the "norms" are the true freaks, for they are subject to the restrictive imperative of "sameness":

> Then there are those who feel their own strangeness and are terrified by it. They struggle toward normalcy. They suffer to exactly that degree that they are unable to appear normal to others, or to convince themselves that their aberration does not exist. These are true freaks, who appear, almost always, conventional and dull. (282)

The deployment of the category "norms" in *Geek Love* allows Dunn to invert the terms of a powerful hegemony of bodily types. In this way the novel deploys a definitional strategy that parallels Nietzsche's invention of the "inverse cripple." Arty's ironic psychologization of the "disabling" repression that characterizes the group identity of a physical constituency unexpectedly situates disability as the condition by which others are measured. Rather than casting disability as an inherently undesirable state, he defines the normative imperative to sameness as a "deforming" objective. To serve as a card-carrying member of the "norms," one inherently jettisons the idiosyncratic traits that would secure individuality and relative autonomy. While "freakishness" may jeopardize one's ability to exist in the indifferent and often hostile world of the "norms," Arty defines the "disabled" as a subjectivity mistakenly founded upon the repression of its own physical being.

Such a dissociation of disability from cultural "interest" leaves Arty to court his own mythic Other in the population of the norms. In another example of his "logic" of inversion, Arty not only embraces the "terror" that his physical aberrancy inspires in audiences, but he fosters a philosophy that makes his own physical condition the site of desirability. As his "Aqua Boy" performance becomes renowned and his audiences increase, the show metamorphoses into a platform for his own soap-box pontifications. As Olympia listens from the threshold of the big top, she begins to grapple with the meaning behind the reception of Arty's monologues:

> What Arty wanted the crowds to hear was that they were all hormone-driven insects and probably deserved to be miserable but that he, the Aqua Boy, could really feel for them because he was in much better shape. That's what it sounded like to me, but the customers must have been hearing something different because they gobbled it up and seemed to enjoy feeling sorry for themselves. (115)

What Olympia identifies as a shared longing in the community of the norms (or norm wanna-bes) is this desire to feel sorry for themselves. Such a longing, in Olympia's eyes, originates from a sense of the unbearable "weight" of normativity, which demands individual degradation and suffering from the *acceptable* body. Rather than imagining themselves as the possessors of a superior biology, Arty parades his "missing parts" and "deformed limbs" as the security of knowing he never has to worry about other people's perceptions of his appearance. Understanding that "severe disability" cloisters the bearer in the mythology of the leprous and monstrous, Arty espouses the doctrine that marginalization "frees" him from concern about the power of public scrutiny. As the audience acknowledges its own sense of subjugation to the surveillance and rejections of others, disciples of Arty's philosophy abdicate their membership in the normative and join forces with the Arturans. The price of membership: a contribution of all personal wealth, the swearing off of their allegiance to illusory bodily norms of health and wholeness, and a willingness to undergo radical amputation surgery.

It is in the collision of these hypermythological systems that *Geek Love* develops its political punch. In order to demonstrate that all belief systems entail their own martyrdom to a principle of self-flagellation and hegemonic devotion, Dunn deploys the "freak" as another example of allegiance to a powerful figurehead. Rather than identify the Fabulon as a location of "shock" where the audience is returned to the security of their own normative features, the lure and promise of the freak acts as a ritual catharsis for those seeking an alternative system of meaningful sensation and identification. To simulate the "jolt" that Arty imagines has been lost in the anesthetized halls of normativity, he has McGurk rig up electrodes to the aluminum bleacher seats in order to telegraph electrical surges into the audience's collective spinal column. Rather than the contrast that distances viewers from the spectacle of its "horrific" surface, the "freak" becomes a site of belonging and communal identity. If the ideal of anonymity in the life of the norms has proven deadening and mundane, the totem of the freak promises rejuvenation. This ironic exposé of the freak's appeal consequently provides Dunn the opportunity to define the sideshow as a regenerative model whose mythic packaging and "technotronic wiring" necessarily responds to an equally devastating cultural dictum.

The Evolving Grotesque

Yet it is the false opposition of "freaks" and "norms" that lets Dunn define the experience of disability within a more complexly human constellation of tropes and perspectives. While Arty's deployment of the spectacle of the freak rivals the equally magnificent banality of norms who stumble to his big top searching for a philosophy of individuation and difference, both categories sit ripe for novelistic caricature. Since, as Bakhtin has pointed out, the grotesque associations of the freak have been historically aligned with the bawdy excesses of the folk, the genre of satire has been most often typified as the literary location of this phenomenon. And while this is certainly the case in *Geek Love*, Bakhtin's critique of the narrowness of this linkage between the grotesque and satire points the reader toward alternative interpretations of Dunn's fantastical interests:

> Because Schneegans relied on the idealistic aesthetics of the second part of the nineteenth century and on the narrow artistic and ideological norms of his time, he could not find the right path to the grotesque. He could not understand *the possibility of combining in one image both the positive and the negative poles.* Even less was he able to understand that an object can transgress not only its quantitative but also its qualitative limits, that it can outgrow itself and *be fused with other objects.* (308; emphasis added)

Within this theoretical matrix, Bakhtin, who was disabled himself, begins to develop a series of associations that significantly characterize the work of the grotesque in folklore and literature. Unlike his characterization of his opposition, Schneegans, who limits the trope within a tradition of satirical purpose and "outlandish bodily caricature," Bakhtin argues through the work of Rabelais that the fluidity and instability of the grotesque determines its particular utility. Rather than provide an easy physical target for public laughter accompanied by the security of biological distance, the grotesque services a need to contain irresolvable polarities that exist in the mind of its audience. In other words, the grotesque in art proffers an ability to externalize colliding ideological systems into a metacritical allegory. Arty's packaging as the mythic freak taps into a need for an extravagant bodily image that can highlight its own illusory nature as well as that of its normative opposition.

In addition to commenting upon this ideological formation of the norms, Dunn also uses the freak to allegorize an array of bodily conditions that act as the host for numerous cultural pathologies. Bakhtin's theory of the grotesque crystallizes around his notion of "fusion," in which the "monstrosity" of his subject allows it to accumulate an expansive series of references and meanings. Because the grotesque body is an architecture that "is never finished," its peculiar and resourceful functioning comes from the ability to "swallow the world and [be] swallowed by the world" (317). Not only do the Arturans submit to radical bodily alteration in order to model themselves upon the masthead of the freak, but the body undergoes all kinds of novelistic permutations in order to expand the coordinates of our current cultural mythology of the freak. When Olympia tracks down Miss Lick, an independent philanthropist who finances the education of "physically ruined" women, she becomes acquainted with examples of the productive possibilities of physical aberrancy that go beyond the spectacular gimmickry of the sideshow. As she sits in Miss Lick's apartment watching videotapes of "traumatically scarred women" who have gone on to intellectual and professional careers, Olympia's ideas of femininity as a biologically pathological condition connect up with her brother's earlier freakish exploits. Lick gives an account of Linda, a woman who saved her child from burning to death but caught fire herself:

> Different girl entirely from what she had been. Old pursuits, interests, wiped out entirely. Friends tried to be polite but she made them nervous. Boys all gone west as far as she was concerned. Interesting to see the change. She seemed to have taken in the situation completely while she was still in the hospital. Turned her head around. She studied. All that old energy of hers turned to books. . . . She's a chemical engineer. (157–58)

This rendition parallels Arty's earlier speech about the utility of the freak. The fact of such a "deforming" accident jettisons Lick's subject from the community of the norms and completely reroutes the traditional feminine story of marriage and children into one of "all brain stuff" (Dunn 158).

Linda's expulsion from a life based upon physical coordinates—"she couldn't rely on being cute and catching a man" (Dunn 158)—leads Lick to conclude that a more desirable life of the mind results. Rather than follow the modernist linkage of physical deformity and interior pathology, Dunn strategically distorts the "physical material" of femininity into a lineage of intellectualism and professional accomplishment. As Lick explains to Olympia, "It's not that surprising when you think about the precedents . . . Crippled painters and whatnot" (158).

Because the physical surface acts as the evaluative criteria for femininity, as it does disability, an alteration in the exterior presentation also redefines avenues of individual opportunity and Bakhtinian "possibility." As "the grotesque" surfaces in the guise of third-degree burns and Linda (at the prodding of Miss Lick) turns down "numerous cosmetic options" that could provide a way back into the society of the norms, Olympia registers an increasing alarm as she recognizes a disturbing determinism at work in the realm of the biological. While she is uncertain about the openly "defor- mative" projects of Miss Lick and Dr. Phyllis (who performs the Franken- stein-like surgery for the Arturans), she also understands that the alternative proves to be equally violent and basely ideological. If the "materials" of belief are predominantly bound to physical appearances, and thus the body, then her earlier maxim that "the true freak must be born, not made" may be alarmingly "truthful." Since bodily markers such as femininity and disabil- ity seem to "explain" the incapacities of entire populations as well as indi- viduals, the physical surface functions as a guide to the truth of individual potential. In this way, the body serves as a particularly effective metaphor for the operations of cultural belief, since its constitutive compounds are *simultaneously* historically malleable and biologically absolute.

Despite the physical basis of Olympia's own annexation from an able-ist culture, she begins to more fully comprehend the nature of sedimented bio- logical mythologies only in the wake of her associations with Dr. Phyllis and Miss Lick. As her associative repertoire of public myths that connect biol- ogy and pathology increases—she also links the "deformations" of race and poverty with those of disability and femininity—Olympia acts as a conduit for the reader's alternatives. At one point she realizes that her own life has negotiated a parallel "mobility" in the face of a seemingly "immobilizing" physical condition:

> A hunchback is not agile enough for efficient skulking. But my voice can take
> me anywhere. I can be a manicured silk receptionist, a bureaucrat of impen-
> etrable authority, or an old college chum named Beth. I can be a pollster

> doing a survey of management techniques or a reporter for the daily paper
> doing a feature on how employees view their bosses. Anonymous, of
> course—no real names used and all businesses disguised. (150)

Such a catalog of professional substitutions provides the narrator with a
variety of personas for the taking. In an age where the "voice" can act as the
medium of public intercourse, Olympia realizes—like her brother before
her—that being and identity are themselves devices for technological manipulation. As Avital Ronell has argued, technology has always grounded its
value in the ability to resuscitate and revitalize an imperfect body: "The
prosthesis . . . to a certain extent enjoys the status of the fetish, covering a
missing or inadequate body part, amplifying the potentiality of a constitu-
tively fragile organ" (88). While Arty re-creates his physical inadequacies as
the ideal instruments of a new philosophy through various special effects,
Olympia seeks to "escape" the social limitations of her physical presence
through an electronic "disguise." Rather than electing the hyperbolic and
artificially augmented visage of the freak, disability in this guise effaces itself
in the more ephemeral simulations of audio equipment.

In opposing the mythic freak to prosthetic assimilation Dunn determines
her narrator's disabling identity as perpetually oscillating between these two
unsatisfactory choices. Caught between the theatrical extravagance available to her siblings and the "annoyance" she represents to the intolerant
world of the "norms," Olympia's physical deviancy leaves her alienated
from a usable tradition and a communal identification. The narrator's intimacy with the market machinations of the freak show and her own marginal position within the family hierarchy of physical anomalies leaves her
to mediate between the conflictual meanings of physical difference in the
public and private realms. As the inheritor of the sordid family genealogy of
the Fabulon, Olympia strategically casts herself as the orphan of an extinct
economic tradition and as the idiosyncratic product of a genetic (and literary) experiment gone awry.

The critical quandary for Dunn's narrator is that the physical "fact" of
disability inevitably overrides the personal coordinates of the autobiographical subject. Threatened with the usurpation of the unique coordinates of
her story, Olympia's predicament alludes to a "transitional moment" in the
public meaning of disability. Rather than acting as the vehicle symbolizing
cultural collapse and fragmentation, as in the modernist tradition, Olympia
"naturalizes" the disabled body as the site of its own subjectivity and narrative interest. Once the distance of the third-person perspective of the
grotesque is challenged and interrupted by the now speaking subject of its
own metaphor, *Geek Love* establishes its own material metaphorics of the

body in cathedral-like fashion as that which houses the incomplete forces of history and species:

> I was full-grown before I ever set foot in a house without wheels. Of course I had been in stores, offices, fuel stations, barns, and warehouses. But I had never walked through the door of a place where people slept and ate and bathed and picked their noses, and, as the saying goes, "lived," unless that place was three times longer than it was wide and came equipped with road shocks and tires.
>
> When I had first stood in such a house I was struck by its terrible solidity. The thing had concrete tentacles sunk into the earth, and a sprawling inefficiency. . . . That building wasn't going anywhere despite an itchy sense that it was not entirely comfortable where it was. (321)

The "itchy sense" to which Dunn refers in this final sentence represents Olympia's understanding that an absolute "solidity" contains its own terror. While her own personal history in the traveling Fabulon provides her with a more fleeting sense of herself and others in time and space, Olympia's sense of discomfort arrives as she experiences a feeling of "unnatural" concreteness in the meaning of her physical being. Given the flaunted and exposed variations on themes of bodily conditions and appearances in *Geek Love*, this observation by the narrator formulates a final tragic philosophy that underpins the entire novel. Because the body "houses" the unique differences that compose the details of an individual subject, the "terrible solidity" of an immovable structure parallels Olympia's experience of her own "grounded" bodily identity. As the possibilities of her later adult life become increasingly circumscribed by social attitudes and perceptions of her person as a bald, albino hunchback, she encounters a terrifying fixity that cannot be undone. Like a house whose tentacles seem to be sunk deep into the earth, Olympia's multiple disabilities entrench her in the identity of inflexible narrative prosthesis. Cultural responses that have been programmed from the inscrutable depths of history and moored upon antiquated mythic lineages of titillation and revulsion leave her flailing to refute their power over the ways that she can imagine a suitable and more fluid self-definition.

This final project of Dunn's novel crystallizes around her attempt to unmoor disability from the "terrifying solidity" of its own history. By representing the "crux" of disabled subjectivity as existing in the prosthetic nexus of the mythic freak and the isolation of physical difference, Dunn's postmodern gambit is to flaunt the titillation of her absurdist fiction as a product of the historical baggage that we all carry. Rather than ostracize the invaluable contents of the literary grotesque, *Geek Love* demonstrates that we still experience the allure of the grotesque by participating in its perpetual rein-vention. In this sense the novel's "cultish" capital depends upon a readership still bound to the seduction of physical aberrancy as an inexhaustible "resource," while also demonstrating that the residue of this fetishistic inter-est nonetheless informs our current understanding of disability.

In the final chapter of *Freaks* Fiedler argues that a 1960s literary moment was founded upon the writing of a parasitic grouping of writers who are "pretenders" to the throne of the freak. In fact, despite the visible disap-pearance of the spectacular dimensions of the freak show there has been a mutation of its carnival presence in contemporary literature. To character-ize such a literary "revitalization" and return to the altar of freakishness, Fiedler disdainfully dredges up the term *geek,* as a way of simultaneously delineating and undermining this "newly" acquired literary taste for the grotesque. By way of explaining such a phenomenon he resuscitates the fol-lowing historical formula:

> The Geek, on the other hand, seems these days to be coming into his own, precisely because he is a fictional Freak, not merely perceived through a pre-existent mythological grid like Giants and Dwarfs and the Lion-faced Man, but invented to satisfy psychic needs bred by infantile traumas or unquiet ancestral memories. . . . What he eats raw [are] . . . repulsive forms of lower animal life, chiefly chickens and rats—biting off their heads before they are dead and slobbering his chin with their fetid blood. (342)

As an act, the geek played upon its own performative artificiality to seduce audiences. In comparison to the "real" deformities sported by the sideshow's human oddities, the geek was a "behavior" that paid homage to the physical specimens cataloged just beyond the flap of the circus tent. The "performer" whetted the appetites of its audience for increasingly out-landish spectacles promised by the freak show itself. The geek constructed its own status as a "living anomaly" out of the malleable tissue of behav-ior—biting off the heads of chickens and rats and "animalistically acting out" to entertain spectators before they imbibed the real thing. In doing so, the geek demonstrated that "freakishness" was a state of mind: packaged to appeal to its audiences' yearning for the unusual. The brash "acting out" of artistic perversity in Dunn's postmodern novel appeals to an appetite much like that of the geek and, in turn, self-consciously provides a space within which to interrogate the mythic packaging that designs our desires.

Afterword

"The first child born into the world was born deformed": Disability Representations in These Times

We began *Narrative Prosthesis* with an intent to analyze the shifting coordinates of disability representation in literature. Our central thesis situated itself around a belief that our stories come replete with images of disability and yet we lack a coherent methodology for recognizing and reckoning with that fact. Our effort has been to provide a series of analyses of key moments in a literary tradition of disability narrative.

Likewise, we have sought to comprehend literature as a medium of significance to our contemporary thinking about disability. Stories may be the preserve of stereotypical portrayals and reductive metaphors, but our emphasis stresses interpretive approach over retrograde imagery. What we "see" in these texts is often dependent on our own orientation or demeanor toward disability. "Out" and politicized scholars encourage the development of reading practices that embrace, transform, and reckon with our inherited disability story lines—much as Byron, in *The Deformed Transformed*, refashioned disability in Shakespeare—as a matter of Renaissance "ploy" and "stratagem"—into a matter of cosmic, social, and personal identity.[1]

Since the act of signification involves an entrance into an ambiguous field of meaning-making, our challenge here is to articulate some possibilities for the analysis of disability as an historically bequeathed subjectivity. The hereditary code that structures this history is neither complete nor inherently malfunctioning. Up to this point, our readings have set out to establish the terms of a more varied position from which we may approach our own contemporary moment's discursive understanding of disability. Consequently, we would like to conclude with the disability figuration that infuses recent U.S. writing as a prelude to an argument for the politics of close-reading strategies in the materialist tradition of Walter Benjamin.[2] Along the way we hope to identify an array of writers who provide a usable future map for the representation of disability.

At the foundation of our disability politics lies the contention that disability scholars and activists should not cede the literary field, or conceptions of traditional literary study, to the dismissive critical stance that narrative merely replays retrograde politics of disability. For instance, Lennard Davis has argued that the novel has historically cast disability as a sign of abnormality in need of a narrative correction. Such an approach places literature within a post-Marxist framework as a tool of dominant ideology and an organ of oppressive politics. Frank Kermode comes at the issue of novel form in a similar, yet more generic way, by arguing that all narrative seeks "a sense of an ending." In this we may understand that disability in narrative is inherently correctable and thus in need of fixing—the end of the abnormal is always located in its restitution within the fold of the normal. From this critical angle, narrative approaches disability as a wound in need of a dressing, and thus the narrative act is completed only to the extent that the breach is healed and a disruptive anomaly is concealed beneath a more modest covering.

We would argue that an effective approach to the politics of disability narrative needs to be localized culturally and historically. There is no universal narrative that can do justice to the variegated historical patterning of its material meanings. The "sense of an ending" that Kermode and Davis warn against can indeed result in oppressive characterizations of disability; however, many fictions, particularly modernist and postmodernist antinarratives, seek out means for disrupting the popular disability expectations that accrue around normalcy narratives. Because the "normalcy narrative" line of argumentation can be convincingly established for "dominant" golden-age Hollywood cinemas and popular stories of overcoming, what we will term *disability counternarratives* frequently contest this manner of storytelling. Indeed, Paul Longmore has effectively demonstrated the "kill or cure" imperative that infuses popular film and television plots that introduce disabled characters only to "solve" their "problems." We are contending that many literary works, and even later film practices, precisely because they openly challenge the dominant narrative trends Longmore identifies, offer up disability counternarratives—poetical and narrative efforts that expand options for depicting disability experiences.

In this afterword we would like to trace out a tradition of disability counternarrative from modernist symbolic experiments already broached in our earlier chapter on Sherwood Anderson to the more reform-minded disability politics of postmodern U.S. literature and poetry as evidenced in the writing of Dunn. In tracing this tradition, earlier critiques within disability studies of the inherently "flawed" narrative of "cure or kill" formulas can be complicated. We also delve into contemporary approaches to disability developed in previous readings of postmodernism.

Foundational to modernism is the idea that any narration is impinged upon by the subjective and partial nature of the individual perspective that controls the story. The distinction of a partial perspective in modernist literary innovations, thus, will also end up producing characters individuated by reference to "wounds" or wounded identities and their corresponding frailties. Jake Barnes in Ernest Hemingway's *The Sun Also Rises* presents a case in point. The novel deviates from the prototypical modernist equation of disability with social collapse. In this way, Hemingway accomplishes a full-fledged disability critique of contemporary society when his protagonist openly refuses to "work up" his disability into a metaphor for the lost generation at the suggestion of his fishing buddy. This critique on Hemingway's part comes on the heels of his own experience as a wounded war veteran and his lifelong struggles with depression; they would also prefigure his further disablement after two plane crashes in the 1950s and his suicide, a response to an unbearable personal debility.[3]

Building on the modernist dependency upon apocalyptic symbology of disability, outlined in our discussion of Anderson's *Winesburg, Ohio,* postmodern narrative does not seek to fully repair or resolve a character's impairment, but rather delves into the social, personal, political, and psychological implications of impairment as bequeathing a social awareness. This yields a literature teeming with disability as a matter of identity, perspective, and subjectivity. As a result, we will contend that disability studies bears responsibility for recognizing and assessing the productive possibility in our era's approaches to figuration and narrative of disability.

Literary Curiosity Closets

More than a matter of purely literary and artistic concerns, an engaged struggle with the implications of disability policies and attitudes infuses American literature of the last century. In fact, when cataloged, the most influential works of the contemporary period become a curiosity closet of physical and cognitive "deviance" in our time: Sylvia Plath narrates the violence of her own institutional experiences in *The Bell Jar;* Jean Stafford tells of eating disorders and the utility of performing feminine inability in her celebrated short story "Bad Characters"; Robert Lowell's "mind is not right" in his groundbreaking collection of poetry *Life Studies;* and in Thomas Pynchon's *The Crying of Lot 49,* Oedipa Maas can recognize the process of U.S. historical "amnesia" only by referencing the experience of an epileptic seizure. In *The Bluest Eye,* Toni Morrison structures Polly Breedlove's identity around a limp that forces her to leave school and keeps her permanently disenfranchised from mythologies of racial beauty and belonging. Wallace Stegner's Pulitzer-winning *Angle of Repose* tells the story of a wheelchaired family archivist who offsets his own immobility by imaginatively existing in the Victorian record of his grandparents' lives. Even one of Joan Didion's more acclaimed new journalist essays, "The White Album," finds resolution for the tumultuous sixties in the arrival at the fact of her own diagnosis with multiple sclerosis: "The startling fact was this: my body was offering a precise physiological equivalent to what had been going on in my mind," and, by extension, the culture (47).[4] This catalog provides a glimpse into a voluminous closet of literary curiosities. However, rather than referencing social disorder by recourse to a disabled body—as did previous generations—contemporary American literature references the disabled body through an exposé of the social discord that produces it as aberrant.

This list of an influential series of "contemporary classics" reminds us that Americans learn perspectives on disability from books and films more than from policies or personal interactions. The list includes some of the most popular, discussed, and studied "stories" in the country. It also underscores, in contrast to the claims of many scholars of disability, the insurrectional drive in art toward an interrogation of repressive norms. By definition, literature makes disability a socially lived, rather than a purely medical, phenomenon. Disabled characters fill the pages of literary narrative even as disabled people in society are locked away or sequestered from view. This characteristic intimacy with disabled characters in literature makes our stories a rare exception to the exclusions encountered by disabled people in their lives. Even given the penchant for metaphorizing disability along the lines of cultural collapse, literature provides us with a unique space for contemplating the complexity of physical and cognitive differences that is absent from nearly every other discursive space.

As we have argued, beginning in late modernism, U.S. literary work will *critique* the politics of a false "transcendence" wrought by disability plotlines that circulate within conventional story lines and popular Hollywood film. This critique will result in innovative disability plots that refuse transcendence into "cures" or tragedy in "death." While many factors contribute to this narrative project in U.S. literary traditions, two stand out: (1)

the practice of medical murder and eugenics policies by the Nazis that realized, on a mass scale, many of the "mercy death" solutions for disabled infants initially propagated in the United States; and (2) the legacy of a modernist poetics that embodied an accord between historical crisis and rhetorical form. In the ambiguous "play" of modernist poetical forms, postmodern writers inherit the terms for a critique of residual oppression of disability within traditional plotlines and story structures.

Take, for example, four novels that bring us to the threshold of a direct encounter with disability identities and social attitudes: William Faulkner's *The Sound and the Fury* parallels the violence enacted upon the body of a person with Down's syndrome with the South's corruption at the hands of the North; J. D. Salinger's *Catcher in the Rye* critiques entertainment mediums for perpetuating a pervasive logic of eugenics toward people with disabilities; Harper Lee's *To Kill a Mockingbird* critiques the segregation of disabled people and the attendant mythmaking that results; Ken Kesey's *One Flew Over the Cuckoo's Nest* interrogates the damaging ethos of charity as well as the institutional incarceration that reduces disabled people's lives. Yet of these, only *Cuckoo's Nest* has been recognized for its disability perspective, and that largely on antimedical grounds. Of the four novels, it is also the one least taught in American schools. If we add Hemingway's *The Sun Also Rises* (1926), Steinbeck's *Of Mice and Men* (1937), and Keyes's *Flowers for Algernon* (1966), we sense the disability "lessons" that infuse U.S. educational curricula, the contemporary literary canon, and film history. In this manner we would argue for the need in disability studies to recognize media as one of the domains within which we encounter disability most often and most viscerally.

The many representations of disability in the aforementioned catalog largely build upon a U.S. modernist project that had found an accord between historical "breakdown" and rhetorical form. In the modern classic *The Sound and the Fury,* William Faulkner begins his story of a fallen Southern aristocracy through the point of view of Benjy, a thirty-three-year-old character with a cognitive impairment. While nearly all of the criticism of the novel "promotes" Benjy to the status of a symbolic representative of human tragedy, on closer reading the chapter provides an important sustained reading of the social circumstances surrounding the reception of cognitive disability. All of the Compson family members are explicitly judged in relation to their ability to imagine Benjy's humanity. His father, Jason Sr., his sister, Caddy, and the black maid, Dilsey, all provide examples of those who are capable of recognizing the value of Benjy's contribution to the family. However their perspectives are violently contrasted with those of other family members who advocate Benjy's incarceration within the household (a common violence committed against disabled people), enforced sterilization (38,000 cognitively disabled people were sterilized during the period of the novel), or institutionalization in the state insane asylum at Jackson, Mississippi (Braddock, forthcoming). Although it has gone critically unrecognized that the novel provides a scathing critique of this dehumanizing environment within which disabled people function, the novel holds out Benjy's experience not as a sign of wider cultural collapse but as the barometer for just how far the social fabric has unraveled around him.

By the middle of World War II, Americans were becoming familiar with the fact that "mercy death" solutions for disabled people, a subject of much public discussion in the United States during the 1920s and 1930s, had been enacted systematically, and on a mass scale, during the Third Reich. Such awareness had consequences for writing practices. For example, disabled author Flannery O'Connor maintained in the 1950s that sentiments on disability breed murderous attitudes toward children with disabilities:

> sentimental attitudes toward handicapped children, which encourage the habit of hiding their pain from human eyes, are of a piece with the kind of thinking that sent smoke billowing from the chimneys of Auschwitz. I would venture to guess, in fact, that many parents of handicapped children would hesitate to dismiss this comparison as a grotesque exaggeration. (Cited in Oë 94)

O'Connor connects the erasure of disabled lives as a matter of their depiction within a sentimental frame. The "sentiment" evoked by stories creates a "habit" of "hiding their pain from human eyes"—a dangerous convention that contributes to the enactment of further social violence. We can recognize in O'Connor's critique of sentiment the serious political undercurrents of disability narrative resistance that inform postwar depictions of disability. Sentiment epitomizes the act of narrative closure itself, in that a problem is repaired and the story ends with the uplift of a successful repair. An audience would be reassured of the reintegration of the disabled body and thus leave the story scene confirmed in a knowledge that the breach has been healed. Barring the reality of this "quick fix" in the lives of disabled people, O'Connor's premise is that their erasure or obliteration in fine sentiment denies the fact that the quick fix is not available. To move this observation into a literary context, social violence toward disabled people would be predicated on their obliteration in the wake of their noncompliance with the rehabilitating mission of narrative.

Many writers of O'Connor's generation, in theorizing their own narrative methods, decry the dangers of traditional story structures based upon various formulas of closure. Yet, in the wake of global carnage against non-militarized citizens in general, and the murder of disabled people in Nazi hospitals in particular, post–World War II novels address narrative resolutions and disability narration as dynamically intertwined. As a result, "sentimentality" in stories seeking an easy fix in the miraculous repair of disability comes under increasing scrutiny by writers who demonstrate the gap between the fantasy life of film depictions and the legacy of "euthanasia" deaths.

For example, disability-based critiques of trite formulas of narrative resolution can be found at numerous junctures in Salinger's *Catcher in the Rye,* with a literary critique of early-twentieth-century eugenics also a significant strand of the novel's narrative politics. The main character and narrator, Holden Caulfield, "hates the goddamn movies" largely because they perpetuate insipid myths about certain rehabilitation and easy cures for disability. Holden tunes into these vapid media rituals performed on the bodies of disabled characters in the wake of modern medicine's inability to rescue his own brother from leukemia. Most notably, *Catcher* contains an extensive critique of the "fake" disability setups in the popular 1941 film *Random Harvest,* the unnamed movie that is showing throughout the Christmas season at Radio City Music Hall. This section of the novel merits recognition in its own right for its cogent analysis of representations of disability: because stories drive toward "solving" disabilities, audiences experience a facile alleviation of any need to ascribe social complexity to the experience of disability. Sentimental plotlines, like that of *Random Harvest,* offer impossible solutions by situating disability as an either/or condition forever hovering somewhere between tragic death or sudden cure, "the only two acceptable states" (Finger 4). Conventional narrative for Salinger signifies a dangerous determinism in that, like medical diagnoses, it forecasts an inevitable "end" for those caught within its prophetic trajectory.

In order to combat this narrative determinism, the novel seeks an alternative structure for comprehending the nuances of disabled experience. In a later chapter on "Verbal Expression," Salinger will locate a feasible alternative in the concept of "digressive" narratives that refuse the erasure sought by cure-or-kill endings. The chapter contends that if one digresses enough from socially acceptable topics, one inevitably arrives at an interesting disability conundrum. Holden tells of a boy in his Verbal Expression class whose speeches Holden likes best.

> [T]hey kept yelling Digression! at him the whole time . . . he'd start telling you about that stuff—then all of a sudden he'd start telling you about this letter his mother got from his uncle, and how his uncle got polio and all when

he was forty-two years old, and how he wouldn't let anybody come to see him in the hospital because he didn't want anybody to see him with a brace on . . . It's *nice* when somebody tells you about their uncle. Especially when they start telling you about their father's farm and then all of a sudden get more interested in their uncle['s polio]. (183–84)

That the would-be writer loses credit for digressing into the topic of his uncle's disability experience indicts a logic that would negate any direct apprehension of devalued biological conditions. Whereas disability as narrative "problem" provides the opportunity for a quick fix in mainstream media, digressive arrivals at the social difficulties presented by disabling conditions foreshadow the development of a postmodern ethics of reading.[5]

Salinger's strategies parallel those of theorists such as Walter Benjamin who proffer a plodding reading style as a necessary antidote to the rapid soundbites and predigested formulas of electronic communications. In this way postmodern fiction will go on to revise traditional plotlines as an inescapable diagnostic death-sentence for those labeled as "incurables." A new narrative take on disability casts the traditionally passive object of medical definitions and able-ist story lines in the role of active subject who willfully deviates from culturally prescribed treatments.

In opposition to the lethal sense-making of movie stories, Holden develops his own extended fantasy of founding a commune for deaf-mutes in the Rocky Mountains. Holden delights in having arrived at a scandalous plot to exempt himself from participation in mainstream culture by purposely adopting a multiply disabled existence. His scheme ironically capitalizes upon the social exclusion of people with disabilities in order to inoculate himself from further cultural contamination. He pursues this vision of cultural "hold-out" in deadly earnest: "I got excited as hell thinking about it. I really did. I knew the part about pretending I was a deaf-mute was crazy, but I liked thinking about it anyway" (199). Holden's fantasy includes marrying a deaf-mute girl, having a lot of children, buying them books, and "teaching them to read and write" amid the solitude available beyond the reach of telephone or antenna. His screenwriter brother, D.B., who has sold his soul to Hollywood, will be allowed to visit as long as he doesn't write any movies in the cabin. Rather than able-bodied opportunism, Salinger's narrator seeks an almost Nietzschean "transvaluation of all values" by artfully championing that which is socially devalued as the most worthy of emulation.

O'Connor's link between "sentimentality" and mass murder erupts in *Catcher* around the discussion of Phoebe's afternoon trip to see the eugenics propaganda film, *The Doctor,* at New York's Lister Foundation.[6] Phoebe's claim to admire the film's doctor who has been jailed for his "mercy deaths" of disabled infants evidences her own cultural brainwashing in the same way that she is excited over getting to play traitorous Benedict Arnold at her school's Christmas pageant: "It's a special movie they had at the Lister Foundation. Just this one day they had it—today was the only day. It was all about this doctor in Kentucky and everything that sticks a blanket over this child's face that's a cripple and can't walk. Then they send him to jail and everything. It was excellent" (163). Phoebe goes onto recall that *The Doctor* portrays a child angel visiting the "mercy killer" in his jail cell in order to thank him for his act of physician-assisted suicide, reassuring audience members that pediatric euthanasia perfectly accords with nature and narrative.

For Holden, Phoebe's misplaced sympathy for the film's doctor, who is willing to go to jail in order to defend his right to "assist" crippled infants to die, evidences his sister's brainwashing by an adult world that is not only indifferent, but lethal, to disabled children. In *Catcher,* films portray disabling predicaments only to assuage public repulsion *and* immerse audiences in fantasies of resolution—producing and removing the threat of disabled misfits from the world altogether. In Holden's search for a story line that can dignify the memory of his brother, yet avoid the lethal sentimentality of film, in particular, and narrative in general, *Catcher in the Rye* enacts the digressive narrative politics it extols.

Narrative Cohabitation

Faulkner's equation of the segregated South with the infantilization of disabled people, and even the eugenics logic interrogated in *Catcher,* will all be picked up as themes in Harper Lee's novel of 1960, *To Kill a Mockingbird. Mockingbird* creates an accord between Atticus Finch's defense of an accused disabled black man and his children's fascination with a man "whose mind was bad." Whereas a local African American church supplied Faulkner's Benjy with the sole space for disabled entry into a public domain, no such sanctuary exists for Arthur "Boo" Radley in 1930s Maycomb, Alabama. Indeed, the novel opens with a discussion of the limited institutions available to mentally disabled children and adults in depression-era America: the state mental asylum, the county jail, or one's family home ("chained to a bed," as the children imagine). While the entire story line drives toward "the day Boo came out" of his house, an earlier event pervades community mythology: at the moment Arthur reached adulthood, his mother ran into the street screaming that her mad son had stabbed her in the thigh with a pair of scissors. The scissor incident results in his incarceration in a makeshift cell in the county jail's basement, a solution that protects his family from the insult of having him serve time with the other prisoners in town—black men. Later that year, the sheriff insists that the family take him home before he perishes from the wretched conditions.

Arthur Radley will eventually satisfy Scout's desire and "come out" of his isolation when he knifes the lower-class white man, Tom Ewell, who has attacked her brother, Jem. The novel concludes with their law-abiding father concurring with the local sheriff that Arthur's role in protecting his children should be concealed rather than brought before a jury. The context for Atticus's decision is supplied by the recent jury decision to convict an innocent Negro of rape. Given the local jury's willingness to sentence on the basis of racism rather than reality, the idea of bringing "Boo" Radley to trial, even in an effort to claim him as a hero, would be tantamount to holding a public forum on another "myth" of criminality: disabled monstrosity.[7] Boo's incarceration within the very center of town results in a pervasive public mythmaking about mental impairment—his threat is the one "horror" upon which segregated black and white communities concur. Thus the day Boo "comes out" will also signify the day the child-narrator, Scout, grows up, and parallel, if not fully secure, the lesson in race relations she has recently acquired. In other words, she learns that the real "horror" in town is not black folks or disabled neighbors, but the violence wrought by projected fantasies onto their figures by white able-ist America itself. These lessons may seem basic; however, *Mockingbird* continues to hold sway four decades later as one of the most purchased and taught novels in U.S. history. Clearly, many of us crave these lessons in humanity taught to us by Scout's liberal white father, Atticus Finch—a character frequently compared to Lincoln himself as the embodiment "of a sermon."

Disability studies will find that *Mockingbird* bears much the same weight for disability issues as it does for race relations. In the latter tradition, *Mockingbird* is much like Harriet Beecher Stowe's *Uncle Tom's Cabin;* it represents a powerful reflection of dangerous beliefs back to the dominant culture. Both its African American and disabled characters present us with noble victims, more than any kind of delineated perspective upon culture. This lack of intimacy with the lives of its social victims is quite clear in the book: in traveling back with Boo Radley to his porch at the story's conclusion, Scout undertakes a journey that leads us to the *threshold* of a disabled perspective upon the community. However, Scout's epiphany of seeing the world through Boo's eyes simply by standing next to him on his porch never gets translated into a delineated vision for the reader. Thus the novel instructs us in a lack of information and will not venture to characterize Boo Radley's point of view beyond his caring attention to the lives of Atticus's children (as evidenced by all the gifts he leaves for them in the hollow of a tree). We find that whereas he has succeeded in narrating the details of their lives, their own counternarration of him consists of "monster" myths, games, and mockery. In this, *Mockingbird* attempts to bring readers face-to-face with "Boo"—a name imposed upon him in the first place—but it does not take us beyond the threshold and into his residence. Indeed, it must enshrine respectful distance as a form of charitable cohabitation—safely returning him to his isolated status in the neighborhood.

Nonetheless, *Mockingbird* is *directly about* making the terrain of disability and disabled people less alien. Disability issues proliferate in the novel: Jem's "deformed" arm provides pretext for the story; Atticus is blind in one eye; Tom Robinson's "useless" right arm proves his innocence during the rape trial and is the reason for his death; Mrs. DuBose taunts neighbors from a wheelchair perch on her front porch. The novel's aesthetic landscape provides a glimpse into a multiply differentiated physical universe. "Boo," however, represents the full nonparticipant sequestered within the community, the "mockingbird" of the book's title. Atticus tells his children that it's a "sin to kill a mockingbird" because they are harmless creatures—he would replace any violent result of "horror stories" with a more charitable impulse.

Yet even this demand for charity becomes insufficient to the obligation the Finch family will ultimately incur to "Boo" for his physical defense of them. As a result, *Mockingbird* situates cognitive disability as the most inaccessible perspective on a hierarchy of human value. "Boo" represents the noncontributing life in a town itself largely unemployed during the depression. Whereas the disability literary tradition works to locate (and sometimes salvage) some single exemplar of the "nonhuman" among the human, our state disability social policies continue to enact rehabilitation practices that remain firmly linked to selecting out a group of disabled people that remain "noncurable" and hence "nonintegratable." It is from just such distinctions between disabled social participants and disabled nonparticipants that a contemporary disability universe emerges.

This very hierarchy between those marked for eventual "cure" and those consigned to perpetual incarceration undergirds a novel published just two years later, Ken Kesey's *One Flew Over the Cuckoo's Nest* (1962). It is the mental institution's division of "chronics" and "acutes" that Randall P. MacMurphy will dispute in his contest to Nurse Ratched's rules of order and in his befriending of a schizophrenic "acute," Chief Broom. Like *Mock-*

ingbird, Cuckoo's Nest will merge racial violence and disability identity, largely through the fact that all events are told from the perspective of an institutionalized Native American. Ken Kesey, the twenty-three-year-old author, claimed little familiarity with the Native traditions he depicts, yet wrote the novel during his graveyard shift as an orderly at the Menlo Park Veteran's Hospital. The ensemble cast of "crazies" he depicts—Harding, Ellis, Cheswick, Martini, Tabor—were all based on the personalities of actual mental patients whom Kesey had befriended.

In 1974, the film production would follow a similar route: filming at the Oregon State Mental Institution, putting nearly eighty actual patients on the payroll, befriending patients as an acting strategy, including patients as extras and walk-ons.[8] This employment of disabled people on the set serves as one of the few examples of integration in film history. Kesey disputed the adaptation of Chief Bromden to film, claiming that the film lost the true illness of the characters by making mental impairment too much a matter of social adjustment. This distinction does not intend to yoke the asylum patients to their disorders as much as it gestures at Kesey's effort to recognize cognitive disability as the organic basis for a discernible disabled subjectivity. *Cuckoo's Nest* infiltrates the mind-sets of its characters by theorizing the relationship between conditions such as schizophrenia and obsessive-compulsive behavior as comprehensible reactions to deadening social forces and institutional violence. Kesey terms this apparatus of the asylum institution "the combine." The novel argues that many of the patients' behaviors have been exacerbated by the very institutional apparatus set up to treat them. The inmates held in thrall to "the combine" have developed their behaviors, at least in part, as a rote performance that mimics the mind-numbing routines of institutional life. This mutually reinforcing dehumanization of patient and laborer alike produces a dependency that inhibits understanding the interests of those incarcerated. Both novel and film retain a powerful critique of institutions for producing and maintaining a population of inmates. Even today, historians credit the novel with initiating a reevaluation of state hospitals in the United States and the film with securing many states' bans on electroshock therapy.

Although we could critique the "impersonation" of disability in literature by able-bodied authors, as in the case of Faulkner's version of Down's syndrome as obsessive immediacy or Kesey's diagnostic differentiations between "chronics" and "acutes," or in film, as in the case of the domesticated adaptations of disabled experience in *Mockingbird* and *Cuckoo's Nest*, these works provide glimpses of artists who parallel Katherine Dunn in her attempt to cross the threshold of disabled subjectivity. Rather than leave us on the porch only to gesture at Boo's *alien* point of view, a willing-ness to imagine disability proves tantamount to a literary revolution within the cultural imaginary. Importantly, these works violate the conventions of intimacy and distance that have largely characterized our approaches to rep-resentations of disability in literary history to this point. The constructed cultural estrangement from disabled people's perspectives that have been shrouded in mystery must fall away. Our writers and filmmakers possess the unique opportunity to dismantle our alienating mythologies by risking entry into this seemingly unimaginable or uninhabitable universe.

Narrative Immobility

Not only do these disability stories exist, but they comprise a substantive portion of our literary canon. It is up to disability studies to recognize them, interpret them, claim them. We need to provide the critical lens that refracts the social realities and artistic goals informing the deployment of disability. In this book, we have termed this pervasiveness of disability characteriza-tion *narrative prosthesis,* in order to get at the primacy of representations of disability in our national literature and to theorize its productive value for writers and artists alike. The study of disability in the humanities must per-form a sustained archeological operation upon the country's narrative archive. In many ways we might read the literature of disability as trying to supply us with this very recognition. Even in our own immediate moment we can look for ways in which writers provide readers with a more earnest encounter with disability.

For example, Richard Powers's novel *Operation Wandering Soul* por-trays children throughout history as taking leave of the home front in order to seek out uncertain destinations as a narrative equivalent to the process of maturation. In contrast to the "holding pattern" that defines stable "adult" identity in the novel, children throughout history appear to be perpetually unfinished and "on their way." Their harrowing journeys trace pathways ranging from St. Stephen's Children's Crusade of 1212 to "boat children" making their way across the Pacific to the shores of California. Powers's his-torical retrieval of myths about childhood exodus explores the terrifying irony of adult narratives of childhood innocence that lead directly to ritual violence enacted upon their figures.[9]

However, the journey in Powers's *Wandering Soul* is unique in that its child protagonists populate a forgotten pediatrics ward bereft of adequate stories to explain their existence. Because of their various disabilities, they

have been "exiled" from the mythological paradigm of mobility traditionally viewed as the most human of activities. Relegated to a hospital in the
center of Los Angeles, these children serve no adult dreams. In this way,
Powers dramatizes a definition of disability as that which unmoors populations from the "human" materials of storytelling itself. Consequently, the
promise of direction and arrival bound up in a journey are more accurately
represented in the novel by a more uncertain aimlessness or "wandering."
The options provided by the adult stories that ensnare the children present
a dangerous venture into the absolutes of belief systems and the attendant
devaluation of "broken" children. Rather than locating an acceptable universal story for its diverse characters, the novel delves into a postmodern
project of metanarrative that would shift and multiply mythic possibilities
for reimagining alternative trajectories for disabled lives.

In the pediatric unit, story time kicks off with a reading of "The first child
in the world was born deformed," a common origin myth for cultures as
diverse as the Shinto and the Mycenean. During its narration, the adult vol-
unteer storyteller, Linda, realizes that the myth rationalizes the eradication
of disabled children: first man and woman make a reed boat for the "mal-
formed" child (whom they bitterly name "The Leech") and abandon him to
the whims of the ocean. Even as the storyteller moves onto other stories, the
listening children intercede with questions about the Leech's fate. This leads
the storyteller to renarrate a life for the deformed first child: Leech sails
around the world (no need to walk in a boat), picks up bottled messages,
and eventually runs into the famed historical journeyman, Henry the Navigator, whose global exploits the disabled child's arrival precipitates. On the
boat, Leech dreams of other creatures like himself and avoids the "hard
places" that will not accommodate his vessel. Catching sight of Henry, he
sees "another abused, deformed child," but one who has built "a lookout
tower" from which he can stare across the sea, "looking for a way to
escape" (88). In turn, the Navigator sees a "kid" in the boat who is "dark,
shrunken, deformed," one whose face is that "of an old friend of his, from
school days. The Navigator has known the face for so long that he can't
place it" (88). The two characters identify with each other instantaneously,
and this very recognition of the need for an escape spawns the age of exploration. Thus, Powers ironically inaugurates the age of mobility with this
encounter between two disabled personages. As the story tells of Leech and
Henry waving at each other in an ecstasy of disability awareness, a child lis-
tener interrupts to dispute the accuracy of the refugee fantasy with the terms
of her own life. Disability identity as it pilots across cultural boundaries still
runs aground on the straits of distinct racial and cultural histories.

This resignification of standard myths and legends continues as the children take their own reenactment of the Pied Piper of Hamelin on the road to local schools—entertaining nondisabled schoolchildren with an all-crippled rendition. Their performance emphasizes the ironical exclusion of three disabled children from the host of others who disappear while following the Piper's ill-fated performance into the mountainside.

Indeed, *Wandering Soul* merits attention for its rendition of a complex interplay of disabled subjectivities; in the performance, the excluded trio of disabled children form a union partially *out* of their awareness that each one fails to comprehend the different physical limitations and experiences of the other. The exclusionary awareness constitutes a further glimpse into a complexly wrought disabled identity in the novel. It also comprises an element of the fully inclusive nature of the renegade culture the children develop among themselves—every "outcast" holds interest and value among the others. The children fashion their connections on the pediatric ward into an alternative family circuit that embraces its members and contests their attendant devaluation by the able-ist adult world beyond the hospital walls. Ultimately, the integrity of Powers's highly experimental novel becomes most clear in the self-questioning of the pediatric surgeon who worries that the children are pointing to his own status as a medical Pied Piper. The adults bequeath the children stories, and the children, empowered by a group alliance, revise them for their utility to interpret the nuances of disabled lives.

The choice of the Pied Piper that the troupe reenacts proves no accident. The original poem was penned by Robert Browning as an instructive tale for the crippled son of a close friend. The same resignification of Browning's poem also transpires for the character of a newly paralyzed teenager in Atom Egoyan's film adaptation of Russell Banks's 1992 novel, *The Sweet Hereafter*. The story depicts the girl's struggles after surviving a bus accident that steals the lives of her classmates. Rather than a tale of survivor's guilt or a journey to the local surgeon's office for a quick fix to her paraplegia, the story engages its character as one who comes to terms with her life as a disabled person. Without romanticizing her portrayal, she evolves into a complex character who makes a conscious decision to stop a community of vengeful parents from pursuing the material gain of a lawsuit against the bus company on behalf of the "killed and maimed." Rather than seeking retribution for her disablement, she refuses to comply with an economic motive that will ultimately fail to "return" her to a semblance of her original wholeness.

In a deviation from the original novel, Egoyan returns us to Browning as a poetic disability predecessor in order to retrieve a more useful model for lessons on her life. All of these works result in complex characterizations of disability experiences; their portraits show disability creativity spawned by defiance of normative expectations. This historical retrieval provides more than just a personal vision for the contemporary situation of disabled people; disability in the literary archive provides evidence of disabled others before us who sought to artfully negotiate a fraught and violent cultural terrain. There is an historical alliance supplied by such recognitions that relieves the isolation of many disabled lives.

The Last Frontier

In 1962 the literary critic Leslie Fiedler declared that disabled people represented a "last frontier" that American fiction was intent on conquering. Why does disability erupt at every turn in our national literature? Because, like race, disability represents a powerful, yet culturally un-interrogated conflict within the national psyche. It is the site where the conflictual nature of our beliefs about "viable lives" gets acted out.

In *A History of Disability,* Henri-Jacques Stiker argues that the query about disabled people's *integration* is not enough—we must press instead for the recognition of disability as *integral* to cultural understanding. While disability occupies a less integrated position within mainstream culture, it commands an integral location in our literature. There is an honesty to the literary portrayals discussed in this volume in that they do not profess to "solve" disability as a problem, but rather they seek to manifest the depths of doubt which reside in the recesses of the cultural imaginary.

As Kenzaburo Oë explains, we cannot know a culture until we ask its disabled citizens to assess it. Disabled perspectives reflect back an image of a culture that too easily assures itself of its own humanity. The achievement of humanity must be reevaluated in each social epoch and between generations. Like equality, our relationship to disability is neither finished nor absolute. This disability studies methodology situates itself closely to the literary practices we have discussed here. Our best literature seeks to articulate the vantage point of the socially devalued. This is the politics of reading, or re-reading, that the humanities approach to disability studies must render sensible.

Notes

Introduction

1. We take our understanding of literature as a parasitic or "antidisciplinary discipline" from John Limon's intellectual history *The Place of Fiction in the Time of Science*. Limon describes literature's refusal to professionalize as a result of its rejection of the formal rules and disciplinary proofs that govern the hard sciences. In this way, fiction situates itself as a reactive discourse seeking to debunk the authority of scientific disciplines by destabilizing their various historical claims to truth-telling.

2. In *The Body and Physical Difference* we argue that minority studies have traditionally positioned disability as the "real" of deviance from which they must distance themselves (5–6).

3. In her radio program *Beyond Affliction: The Disability History Project*, Laurie Block supplies a history of disability activism that led to the passage of section 504 of the Rehabilitation Act. Much of this history details efforts to mainstream people with physical disabilities out of the special-education classroom while often leaving those with cognitive disabilities behind (see also Richard Scotch's *From Good Will to Civil Rights*). Henry Friedlander discusses the insidious differentiations that individuals, families, and institutions were forced to make between physical and intellectual disabilities to avoid extermination in the Nazi asylums. His book, *The Origins of Nazi Genocide*, situates the genocide of people with disabilities as integral to the later murders carried out against Jews, gays, and Gypsies.

4. The work of Slavoj Žižek has sought to complicate the "textual" solutions offered up by deconstructionism. Instead of reducing discourse to ideological manipulation, Žižek uses Lacanian theory to argue that there is always a material residue left behind that proves recalcitrant to the efforts of deconstructivists. We follow out this stubborn recalcitrance of materiality from a parallel, yet slightly different perspective. Rather than deny physical or cognitive limitations (or chalk them up to a purely ideological prescription of dominant ideology), we grapple with the social meanings assigned to physical and intellectual disabilities while not denying the literality of impairment. British disability studies has offered up the important distinction between "impairment" and "disability" in order to differentiate between material and ideological experiences. Yet in this study we want to try and avoid this theoretical partitioning off of the physical and textual realms by contemplating their inevitable intersections more specifically across literary texts.

5. There are several studies of cripples that resemble the drawings on the cover of *Narrative Prosthesis*. Many art historians have argued over their authorship by attributing them to Brueghel or Bosch. We have decided to side with those who attribute them to Brueghel because the studies appear more mimetic than allegorical. Unlike Bosch's paintings, which have a decidedly more fantastical effect, Brueghel's works use his direct observation of cripples as the basis for his political satires. While Bosch sought to create figures that suggest an other-worldly quality, Brueghel delineated his cripples as studies drawn from life that secondarily serve a political commentary.

6. We make a more extended argument about the perfected bodily aesthetic of classicism in our essay, Snyder and Mitchell, "Infinities of Forms." As part of that analysis we also argue that Raphael's last painting, *The Transfiguration,* uses the disabled body of the demoniac to deviate from the increasingly static conventions of physical symmetry.

7. In his groundbreaking essay, "Screening Stereotypes," Paul Longmore makes a similar point about television's need to alleviate an audience's sense of concern for people with disabilities by miraculously curing their deviances by the end of the production. In accomplishing this ruse of special effects, media participates in the elimination of disability through an evasion of its social meanings.

Chapter 1

1. The earliest interpretations of disability in literature involved sociological research that tended to use films and stories as briefly exemplary of contemporary concerns with cultural attitudes. The sociological approach to literature provided some of the earliest categories of disability types such as: the supercrip, tragic innocence, beggarly imposters, and limping villains. The paradigm tended to reduce literary and filmic texts to the purely exemplary by rendering representation as merely indicative of public response.

2. We discuss this important distinction between disability and other areas of minority studies in literature in our introduction to *The Body and Physical Difference.* See particularly our comments on pages 4–9.

3. We use the phrase "social realism" in this chapter to identify a group of critical arguments that demonstrated the measurable gap that existed between the reality of contemporary lives lived with disabilities and the images of those lives in film and literature. We borrow the term from Marxist criticism that forwards artistic efforts as valuable in so far as they attempt to correct the historical record by representing the lives and material conditions of the "real" working classes. While the phrase has been used somewhat pejoratively in some critical circles, we mean to employ it here as descriptive of an influential approach to disability studies in the humanities.

4. As a result, disability literary critics can scan Medical Humanities: Literature, Arts, and Medicine database <http://www.medwebplus.com/obj/652> for books that feature issues of importance for disability scholarship. An example of this tendency includes rebuke of the film version of *One Flew Over the Cuckoo's Nest* as an

"anti-psychiatric" film. Developing on a parallel arc to the negative-image school, the medical diagnostic school of criticism sought to accomplish corrective surgery upon misbegotten disabled characters. In chapter 4 we discuss the comments of Donald S. Miller and Ethel H. Davis, who published essays in medical journals during the late 1960s and early 1970s that located fictional literary characters with orthopedic disabilities. Their approach assumes that the less advanced medical knowledge of previous cultures is evident in the naive arguments put forward by amateur authors. Rather than analyze disability portrayals, Miller and Davis offer up diagnostic advice about possible corrective techniques that might be performed upon these literary disabilities today.

Chapter 2

1. Many critics have designated a distinctive space for "the literary" by identifying those works whose meaning is inherently elastic and multiple. Maurice Blanchot identifies literary narrative as that which refuses closure and readerly mastery—"to write [literature] is to surrender to the interminable" (27). In his study of Balzac's *Sarrasine,* Roland Barthes characterizes the "plural text" as that which is allied with a literary value whose "networks are many and interact, without any one of them being able to surpass the rest; the text is a galaxy of signifiers, not a structure of signifieds; it has no beginning; it is reversible; we gain access to it by several entrances, none of which can be authoritatively declared to be the main one" (5). Ross Chambers's analysis of oppositionality argues that literature strategically deploys the "play" or "leeway" in discursive systems as a means of disturbing the restrictive prescriptions of authoritative regimes (iv). As our study develops, we demonstrate that the strategic "open-endedness" of literary narrative is paralleled by the multiplicity of meanings bequeathed to people with disabilities in history. In doing so, we argue not only that the open-endedness of literature challenges sedimented historical truths, but that disability has been one of the primary weapons in literature's disruptive agenda.

2. In his important study *Enforcing Normalcy,* Lennard Davis theorizes the "normal" body as an ideological construct that tyrannizes over those bodies that fail to conform. Accordingly, while all bodies feel insubstantial when compared to our abstract ideals of the body, disabled people experience a form of subjugation or oppression as a result of this phenomenon. Within such a system, we will argue in tandem with Davis that disability provides the contrastive term against which the concepts of health, beauty, and ability are determined: "Just as the conceptualization of race, class, and gender shapes the lives of those who are not black, poor, or female, so the concept of disability regulates the bodies of those who are 'normal.' In fact, the very concept of normalcy by which most people (by definition) shape their existence is in fact tied inexorably to the concept of disability, or rather, the concept of disability is a function of a concept of normalcy. Normalcy and disability are part of the same system" (2).

3. Following the theories of Lacan, Slavoj Žižek in *The Sublime Object of Ide-*

ology extracts the notion of the "hard kernel" of ideology. For Žižek, it represents the underlying core of belief that refuses to be deconstructed away by even the most radical operations of political critique. More than merely a rational component of ideological identification, the "hard kernel" represents the irrationality behind belief that secures the interpellated subject's "illogical" participation in a linguistically permeable system.

4. There is an equivalent problem to the representation of disability in literary narratives within our own critical rubrics of the body. The disabled body continues to fall outside of critical categories that identify bodies as the product of cultural constructions. While challenging a generic notion of white, male body as ideological proves desirable in our own moment within the realms of race, gender, sexuality, and class, there has been a more pernicious history of literary and critical approaches to the disabled body. In our introduction to *The Body and Physical Difference,* we argue that minority discourses in the humanities tend to deploy the evidence of "corporeal aberrancy" as a means of identifying the invention of an ideologically encoded body: "While physical aberrancy is often recognized as constructed and historically variable it is rarely remarked upon as its own legitimized or politically fraught identity" (5).

5. For Naomi Schor the phrase "bad objects" implies a discursive object that has been ruled out of bounds by the prevailing academic politics of the day, or one that represents a "critical perversion" (xv). Our use of the phrase implies both of these definitions in relation to disability. The literary object of disability has been almost entirely neglected by literary criticism in general until the past few years, when disability studies in the humanities have developed; and "disability" as a topic of investigation still strikes many as a "perverse" interest for academic contemplation. To these two definitions we would also add that the labeling of disability as a "bad object" nonetheless overlooks the fact that disabilities fill the pages of literary interest. The reasons for this overabundance of images of disability in literature is the subject of this book.

6. The title of Thomson's *Extraordinary Bodies: Figuring Disability in American Culture and Literature* forwards the term *extraordinary* in order to play off of its multiple nuances. It can suggest the powerful sentimentality of overcoming narratives so often attached to stories about disabled people. It can also suggest those whose bodies are the products of overdetermined social meanings that exaggerate physical differences or perform them as a way of enhancing their exoticness. In addition, we share with Thomson the belief that disabled bodies prove extraordinary in the ways in which they expose the variety and mutable nature of physicality itself.

Chapter 3

1. Robert Garland cites Dionysios on the establishment of an official Roman council that determined which children were too weak or deformed to live. Rather than dictate the murder of these children, Garland argues, the council "merely

released parents from the otherwise binding obligation to raise them" (16). Garland goes on to point out that in the middle of the fifth century B.C., the less severe "release" of parents from responsibility turned into the mandated drowning of "weak and monstrous" children by the paterfamilias (17).

2. During the narration of the capture of Jerusalem in II Samuel 5:6–10, King David is reported to have directed his soldiers to smite all Jebusites and the lame and the blind with a fatal blow to the windpipe. Old Testament scholars have puzzled over the appropriate way of contextualizing the follow-up statement that "David hates the lame and the blind." Some have argued that the segment's meaning suggests that the blind and lame incited the Jebusites to war against David's troops; others have argued that the phrase suggests the superstition that if one comes in contact with the blind and lame, one will become blind and lame oneself (McCarter 137, 138); still others have interpreted the passage to mean that killing is preferable to maiming the opposing army, "for otherwise the city will be filled with mutilated men whom we have wounded but not slain, and I find such men intolerable" (McCarter 140). Nevertheless, each of these interpretations attempts to extricate King David from seeming to hold uncharitable sentiments toward cripples.

The removal of the "physically unsightly" is central in Leviticus, where those with physical blemishes are denied access to the temple and priests with deformities are barred from practicing sacred rites at the altar. Issuing from a series of injunctions against preparing animals with blemishes or open wounds for eating, the deformed and crippled are associated with contagions and malignant spirits that are visited upon sinners by a disapproving God.

3. In contradistinction to the advocacy of murder and ostracization of cripples in the Old Testament, the New Testament sets up its alternative value of acceptance and tolerance by curing cripples. Rather than barring the deformed or incapacitated from religious practice, Jesus Christ heals the infirm, deformed, and possessed and opens up the temples to them. Nonetheless, the cure of cripples still predicates their inclusion upon the erasure of their physical differences prior to their admittance to the new religious order. Examples of this story abound: Matthew 4:23, 8:7–16, 9:35, 10:1–8, 11:5, 12:10–22, 15:30–31, 21:14; Luke 5:15–17, 6:7–19, 7:22, 22:51; Apostles 4:14, 8:8; John 12:40.

4. In the essay "Of Cripples," discussed later in this chapter, Montaigne explains that a deformed body was often used as the revelation of one's criminality and guilt in the late Middle Ages. Since the punishment for offenses such as witchcraft—an accusation that was often solidified with the evidence of physical scars, deformities, and differences—was death by a draught of hemlock, Montaigne argued that external appearances proved too superficial a method for determining such a drastic sentence. He claims that those who would believe they can reasonably condemn others to death must, by definition, overvalue the purity and virtue of their own lives.

5. Barbara Maria Stafford argues that the Enlightenment's emphasis upon the symbolic nature of the visible surface compensated for a lack of access to the body's interior. She cites Lavater as the "master physiognomist" whose premise was that

the exterior served as a symptomatic mirror of the interior and could be used as a means of exposing the truth of a less tangible realm (84). Cureau argued that physiognomy was an "infallible means for exposing [the] feigning" of internal deceit and moral corruption (cited in Stafford 85). The dangerous associations of this tool of early empiricism for cripples is evident in the developed critiques forwarded by the eighteenth-century hunchbacked German philosopher Georg Cristoff Lichtenberg, who disparaged physiognomy as an art of prophecy that proved no more "reliable than weather forecasts" (*Hogarth* 126).

6. Lennard Davis argues that definitions of bodily norms developed simultaneously with the rise of medical models of pathology and the quantitative analysis espoused by Bisset Hawkins, Adolphe Quetelet, and others. Quantitative catalogs and measurement of bodies in terms of "averages" and deviation made statistics an important tool in the hands of medical scientists and researchers. Statistical study was applied to the body as a means of enshrining "middle-class man" as "placed in the mean position of the great order of things" (*Enforcing Normalcy* 27). Davis demonstrates that this collusion between medicine and quantitative analysis promoted disabled individuals as the contrastive tool that allowed the concept of normalization to gain an empirical foothold in institutional and social perceptions of deviancy.

7. In his important study *Racial Hygiene*, Robert Proctor argues that the Nazis murderously perverted the original meaning of the term *euthanasia* from a more humanistic conception of "an easy or gentle death" to a recommendation "as a means of cutting costs or ridding society of 'useless eaters'" (178). As evidence of the influence and righteousness of the social utility of euthanasia as eugenics and genocide, the Nazis cited their practices as spilling over into the United States and Britain. The Nazi proponents of euthanasia also made reference to the "elimination of the unfit" by the ancient Spartans (180). Upwards of seventy thousand sick, physically disabled, and cognitively disabled people had been killed by 1941 as a "stage rehearsal for the subsequent destruction of Jews, homosexuals, communists, Gypsies, Slavs, and prisoners of war" (177).

8. Most recently, arguments over the ethical conundrums posed by the scientific mapping of human genes has reinstated historical arguments over the possibility of eradicating life with genetic "flaws." The human-genome project "promises" an ability to potentially identify, correct, and/or obliterate defective genetic material as the latest step toward a "cure" of physical and cognitive disabilities. Such hopes have been resuscitated (particularly since the 1950s) as a corrective intervention in the mutational principles that persist in the blueprints of life itself. Richard Powers's novel *Operation Wandering Soul* suggests that medicine seeks to overcome the "irrational" and dynamic principle of the body by denying its inherently mutational characteristics. Such a utopian premise situates medical rhetoric as dangerously paving the way for apocalyptic rationales of extermination.

9. In this chapter we will retain the term *cripple* in order to keep the term's traditional denotative and connotative meanings available for scrutiny. The contemporary term *disabled* groups people with physical and cognitive differences as a

politicized identity that critiques medical and pathological terminology and protests our lack of access to powerful cultural institutions. In spite of this self-naming tactic, *cripple* still resonates for many disability activists as a term of negation that must be resignified to resist denigrating cultural narratives. See the remarks of Cheryl Marie Wade on the rhetorical power of the term's reappropriation in the documentary video *Vital Signs: Crip Culture Talks Back*. Disabled communities embrace discomforting social vocabulary to simultaneously refute the shame and stigma of biology and reflect back able-ist images upon those who perpetuate them. This political tactic is much like the reclaiming of the term *queer* in the gay and lesbian community.

We use the term *cripple* to stress its historical associations with essentialist notions of malignancy and incapacity. The term constructs individuals and groups violating social fictions of symmetry, health, and normalcy, as embodying a marked deviance. Buried in the term is much more than a descriptive designation of individual limitation; it is an evaluative term that qualitatively differentiates between bodies in terms of aesthetics and abilities. Cripples are those who inspire pity and pathos while also evoking fears of divine retribution and an illogic in nature. They are often believed to be the bearers of secret revelations about the inner workings of the universe. As early as 1374, Chaucer playfully portrays cripples as exposing the ruse of performed physical conditions: "It is ful hard to halten unespied Bifor a crupul, for he kan the craft."

10. All quotations in the English are from Donald Frame's 1943 translation. We will also include the citations for the French immediately following the English translation.

11. In the introduction to her translation of Paré's *Des Monstres*, Janis L. Pallister explains that "by the end of the sixteenth century treatises on monsters had become a veritable genre" (xxii).

12. We are using a literary conception of Zarathustra, as a flawed character rather than a realization or literal expression of Nietzsche's philosophical ideal. Peter Berkowitz argues that many of Nietzsche's contemporary critics misread his work as confusing the intention to "overcome morality with its actual overcoming, [Nietzsche] mistakes the desire to discover or invent new modes and orders of thought for their discovery or invention, and mixes up ambition to found new forms of life with their successful establishment" (5). By placing Nietzsche's work in this more speculative vein, Berkowitz demonstrates that characters such as Zarathustra espouse grandiose theories that the author often parodies and lampoons.

13. Classicist Robert Garland links together hunchbacks and dwarves; both figures of satiric excess were kept on hand at Roman courts. Holinshed's *History of England* reiterated Sir Thomas More's reporting of Richard III's hunchbacked stature, but Shakespeare's version gave substance to the premise that scoliosis, interpreted as a sign of nature's disgust, provides sufficient motive on which to hang a drama. In *Wild Swans at Coole* (1919) Yeats places a symbolic hunchback in an esoteric triad of figures anchoring a tradition of poetic questing. In the "Hunchback and the Saint," Yeats's "Hunchback" declares:

STAND up and lift your hand and bless
A man that finds great bitterness
In thinking of his lost renown.
A Roman Caesar is held down
Under this hump.

Georg Lichtenberg's biographers celebrate the eighteenth-century Hogarthian interpreter's improbably cheerful demeanor as further evidence of his exceptional defiance of natural expectations. Disability studies could help us interpret Lichtenberg's brilliant elucidations of a democratic deformity among lower-class grotesques in the streets of London in *Hogarth's World* as the disabled critic's own identification with Hogarth's general dispersal of featural anomalies.

14. For Jung and his students, the ugliest man, the clown, the dwarf, the mad, the foolish, all denote an "inferior function" within the archetypal paradigm. Recognizing this "problem," they make their own redemptive and superstitious inversion of cripples by exclaiming that they not only represent obvious misfortune, but can also designate good luck (mana) for primitive peoples: "All crippled people, people marked by an obvious misfortune, are considered uncanny and they have magic prestige. Either they are avoided carefully, as unlucky people are avoided by primitives because they spread bad luck, or they are supposed to contain mana, having obviously been chosen as particular and peculiar vessels" (Jung 1235).

Such a thought, ventriloquized by Jung, into the cultures and minds of "primitive peoples," allows Jung to give voice to a superstition even as he maintains the scientific framework of the discussion. Absented from the audience of the Jungian exchange over their meanings, the cripples become distanced, archetypal, and denotative "spirits or ghosts" of the principle of the unconscious. They pose the symptom of a riddle that can be solved and shelved—a task that Zarathustra himself could not accomplish. In posing an impossible either/or—superstition or mana—as the definition of disabled people, Jung's thought epitomizes what Lennard Davis diagnoses as the construction of the fiction of normalcy: "When we think of bodies, in a society where the concept of the norm is operative, then people with disabilities will be thought of as deviants" (*Normalcy* 29). Jung would rectify the social discomfort that disabled people present to the psyche by requesting the perceiver to look more deeply into the source of his or her own discomfort. Such psychological correctives reorient the problem away from the social situation of cripples into a narcissistic encounter with the self.

15. The textual quotations are taken from Walter Kaufman's translation. We will also include citations from the German text, *Also Sprach Zarathustra: Ein Buch für Alle und Keinen.*

16. We would like to thank our colleague James Porter for pointing us toward this important historical connection between Emerson and Nietzsche made by Stanley Cavell.

17. Heidegger points out that Nietzsche first intimates his "most profound thought of eternal return of the same" near the conclusion of *The Gay Science.* Orig-

inally citing the arrival of this insight during a walk in Oberengadin during 1881, Nietzsche would communicate the idea three times in his published career—*The Gay Science* (1881), *Thus Spoke Zarathustra* (1884), and *Beyond Good and Evil* (1886). For Heidegger the thought is expressed incompletely and even surreptitiously, and thus he concludes that one must infer the true nature of its "terrible meaning": "If our knowledge were limited to what Nietzsche himself published, we could never learn what Nietzsche knew perfectly well, what he carefully prepared and continually thought through, yet withheld" (Heidegger 15).

Chapter 4

1. The late Irving Zola compiled lists of films with disabled characters that are available in his papers. Paul Longmore's "Screening Stereotypes" theorizes the "isolated" presentation of disabled characters that are rendered without social identity. Martin Norden's *Cinema of Isolation: A History of Physical Disability in the Movies* provides a thorough catalog of representations of disability in U.S. cinema. This chapter concerns the function of disability within a cinema intent on developing narrative modes of visual expression. Many films and international film movements represent disability in compelling and provocative ways. A recent website (<www.caravan.freeserve.co.uk>) lists over two thousand titles that represent and explore disability themes.

Noteworthy is the fact that many writers, finding themselves in contention with Hollywood's increasing monopoly on storytelling, took issue with the genre repetitions of film stories. In our afterword we discuss *The Catcher in the Rye* as an example.

2. Barton's definition of physiognomy follows Martine Dumont's work on the diagnostic system developed by Johann Casper Lavater.

3. Publicity for the technological accomplishments that render disability "real" on screen accompany acclaim for performances of disability. Much recent work in film studies has sought to analyze the spate of Oscars awarded to actors who impersonate disabled people on screen. A "special effects" analysis, as well, extends to an assessment of the effects of disability portrayals by actors such as Jon Voigt, John Savage, Tom Hanks, Gary Sinese, and Willem DaFoe, who exert tremendous star appeal. The "able" physical character of the actors remains to reassure an audience, even in the performance of impairments. Moreover, as the severe critical disapproval that met Tod Browning's use of real disabled actors for "freaks" demonstrates, audiences and critics like to reassure themselves about the artifice and manufacture behind the appearance of "real" impairment.

The development of still photographic practices reveals a similar history of physiognomic investments. For example, turn-of-the-century photographer August Sanders set out on a project to record and collect the variety of human "types" as evidenced by feature, gesture, and anomaly. That his efforts resulted in a collection that exceeded the boundaries of physiognomy and demonstrated instead the infinite multiplicities in human features may help to explain why the Third Reich burned all his negatives: his photographs no longer confirmed a fascist project that depended upon delineating racial and biological "types." For an example of the documentary ambition behind filming disabled "freaks," see David Lynch's *Elephant Man* (1980).

4. The convention of visibly "marking" lead characters has been picked up and adopted by diverse genres, often without the presumption that corporeal aberration yields a vengeful mission. These include, for example, gangster films such as Howard Hawks's influential *Scarface* (1932), which is notorious for making a game of the gangster's facial scar as a patterned motif and commentary upon brutal erasure—X marks the man, remarks upon the man, and stands as the signature for corporate murders.

Even documentary "stories" cannot refrain from these flourishes: in the recent acclaimed Imax film *Africa's Elephant Kingdom* an ancient bull with his broken tusk serves as narrator and guide into a drama of the elephant kingdom that takes as focus the matriarch named "Torn Ear." Physical losses seize the storyteller's regard and key us into the idiosyncrasy that consecrates individuals from out of the ranks of a herd. These ruptures in the field of vision instruct viewers to identify lead figures by means of their physical anomalies. That these anomalies are meant for the purpose of narrative convention, and not character identification, becomes obvious in the gift shops outside, where one finds shelves full of restored and nonblemished elephant figures.

5. We should remember that even today medical researchers seek the source for birth anomalies in locations as diverse as the gene pool, environmental disasters, and prenatal behavior.

6. In *The Year of the King*, Antony Sher recounts that his director, Bill Alexander, argued that Richard III represents the first sophisticated character in Shakespeare's oeuvre. Not only does Richard represent the blossoming of the Renaissance's critique of the Middle Ages as a barbarous period in England's history, but he was the prototype for the singular individual hero that Shakespeare would successfully deploy in his mature plays.

7. Historical and literary notoriety for "hunchback" figures is readily available as among those more visible and socially managed disabilities. In his study *The Eye of the Beholder* Robert Garland associates hunchback figures with sinister dwarves who are kept on hand for festive mockery at court. Velázquez commemorates this practice in a series of royal portraits that include their companion dwarves. In a recent talk, Henri-Jacques Stiker interprets Velázquez's method as a matter of interrogatory disruption.

As we discuss in chapter 3, Nietzsche's hunchback poses unanswerable metaphysical points that send Zarathustra into a dark era of aloof self-questioning. More recently, Bernardo Bertolucci's film *The Conformist* (1971) depicts a hunchback as emblematic of a tradition of humanistic freedom. As with *Thus Spake Zarathustra*, Bertolucci's protagonist is so mystified by the hunchback professor's commitments that he suffers his own crisis of conscience. *The Conformist*'s "hunchback scholar" is sacrificed in a horrific scapegoat ritual that demonstrates a reprehensible and superficial loyalty among fascists.

Katherine Butler Hathaway's *The Little Locksmith* depicts the torture of rehabilitative machinery she endured as a child. In chapter 6 we discuss elements of a counterdiscursive female tradition in hunchback representation, such as that invoked by Katherine Dunn's *Geek Love*. Study of femininity and "deformity" continues the tradition of finding social implications for the apparently indiscernible origins of a curved spine. In these narratives, a "hunch" represents postural laxness that must be guarded against by proper decorum and posture training. When women with scoliosis are made to serve as sign and warning against postural laxness, there would appear to be even more cultural "fixing" of one's embodiment as threat.

8. The pamphlet was titled *The Hump Conference*. It begins with Homer's characterization of the humpbacked Thersites, who "was the ugliest man who came to Troy: bow-legged, lame in one foot, his humped shoulders stooping over his chest" (cited in Mack 277).

9. In contrast, Laurence Olivier, who performed Richard in one of the most widely distributed films of the late 1950s, found the element of caricature as a powerful aspect of the play, claiming to perform the character as a cross between Hitler and Disney's Big Bad Wolf (Colley 172). That Olivier saw fit to perform Richard for film helps to explain his ready enthusiasm for the visual properties of the role.

10. Many performances in history have freely adapted the play to suit their predilection. As early as 1700, Colley Cibber constructed a Richard saga out of Shakespeare's three "War of the Roses" history plays and apparently authored some of the current version's more notorious lines. The case of Cibber also reveals an earlier example of a "stunted" artist innovating upon Shakespeare's formulas; he is said to have declared that his own physical limitations made the adaptation of *Richard III* an obvious choice.

11. The issue of "on-site" research into the behaviors of incarcerated disabled people by able-bodied actors impersonating them is also taken up in our afterword in a discussion of the documentary on the making of *One Flew Over the Cuckoo's Nest* (1975). Actors Danny DeVito and Christopher Lloyd explain that the unique "characters" they come to impersonate evolved from mimicking a selected patient's own idiosyncratic and repeated gestures.

12. A critic explains Sher's method: "For the hunchback to mesmerize and repulse us simultaneously, he had to exhibit an animal power born of his deformity, absolutely and without question. It was a matter of being 'severely deformed, not just politely deformed'" (Cerasano 620).

13. In *Creativity and Disease*, Phillip Sandblom *applies* this idea of Bacon's in order to theorize the effects of congenital anomalies on artists—namely Byron.

14. That disability offers a social predicament more than a personal limitation in this reading of the play explains why many critics in disability studies have taken a certain appalled delight, rather than offense, in new stagings of it.

15. Metaphor closes down the interpretive field opened up by physical differences. One example: the release of *Edward Scissorhands* was accompanied by widespread press commentary that his hands were intended to metaphorize adolescent

immaturity, a comment that foreclosed on director Tim Burton's fairly entrenched and developed social analysis of disability.

Chapter 5

Portions of this chapter first appeared as "Too Much of a Cripple: Ahab, Dire Bodies, and the Language of Prosthesis in *Moby Dick*." *Leviathan: A Journal of Melville Studies*. 1 (March 1999): 5–22.

1. For a further discussion of critical elisions of disability in literature, see the introduction to our edited collection of essays, *The Body and Physical Difference*.

2. In this chapter we provide page citations for the Norton critical edition, first, and then the Northwestern/Newbury volume, second.

3. The history of disability's linkage to the text of revenge in literature and philosophy is suggested in our discussions of Shakespeare's *Richard III* and Bacon's "Of Deformity" in chapter 4 and of Nietzsche's cripples in *Thus Spoke Zarathustra* in chapter 3.

4. Many scholars have pointed out the pervasive perception that accommodation of disability changes the environment for too few people and, thus, appears as an adamantine request for "special accommodations." Ahab is faulted in a similar manner in *Moby-Dick* for his attempts to make the ship conform to his own abilities and body are interpreted as willfully singular and superfluous to all but himself. This observation becomes the original onus for Ishmael's reading of Ahab as "monomaniacal" and "obsessive."

5. We explore this reading in more depth in chapter 1. Suffice it to say here that Melville's purpose in having Ahab personally confirm his own malignant motivations and desires parallels those of Shakespeare and Dryden, by staging the confessional monologues of disabled characters in such a way that they confirm the suspicions of other characters. This nullifies any ambiguity that might persist in an audience's interpretation.

6. There have been lengthy critical discussions of Ishmael's uneven or inconsistent narrative perspective. We want to argue that Ahab must be described by a limited omniscient narrator largely in order to reveal that Ishmael's and the crew's suspicions about the captain's motivations are accurate, as opposed to another instance of projection on their parts. Thus, Ishmael's perspective gradually gives way to a less "embodied" narrative perspective that can more easily shuttle between Ahab's interior and exterior being.

7. While instances of the novel's use of Ahab's disability as the explanatory source of his character abound, the following quote can act as a pointed example of this tendency in the novel:

> It is not probable that this monomania in him took its instant rise at the precise time of his bodily dismemberment. Then, in darting at the monster, knife in hand, he had but given loose to a sudden, passionate, corporal animosity; and when he received the stroke that tore him, he probably but felt the agonizing bodily laceration, but nothing more. Yet, when by this collision forced to turn towards home,

and for long months of days and weeks, Ahab and anguish lay stretched together in one hammock, rounding in mid winter that dreary, howling Patagonian Cape; then it was, that his torn body and gashed soul bled into one another; and so interfusing made him mad. (184–85)

8. In her groundbreaking work *Primate Visions: Gender, Race, and Nature in the World of Modern Science,* Donna Haraway contends that "nature" is always constructed by ideological and historical perspectives disguised as factual and organic: "neither sex nor nature is the truth underlying gender and culture, any more than the 'East' is really the origin and distorting mirror of the 'West.' Nature and sex are as crafted as their dominant 'others' " (12).

9. The emphasis that Ishmael places upon the futility of his interpretive gesture resonates with Montaigne's own commentaries that recognize the limits of human knowledge. For example, the idiosyncratic narrator in "Of Cannibals" comments wryly upon our pursuit of understanding in the midst of pervasive ignorance: "We grasp at all, but catch nothing but wind." Placing Ishmael in the tradition of Montaigne further emphasizes Melville's commitment to an ethics of the limits of knowing the Other that we develop in chapter 3.

10. In *Body Criticism: Imaging the Unseen in Enlightenment Medicine and Art,* Barbara Maria Stafford argues that the science of physiognomy was part of a general attempt to exaggerate the significance of physical surfaces in order to provide a reliable corollary to the relatively inaccessible internal body. In this sense Melville and many of his artistic counterparts followed the lead of medicine by privileging bodily surface (particularly physical disability) as a mirror of psychological ill health and moral contamination.

11. All emphasis in these extracts is added.

12. Hawthorne's "Rappacini's Daughter" and Crane's "The Monster" situate their stories around a tale of a blemished character who attempts to be resurrected to an illusory state of biological wholeness and perfection by a medical doctor.

13. Diane Price Herndl demonstrates that the bedridden feminine figure exposed ideological patriarchal associations about female impotence and passivity. Maria Frawley argues that Harriet Martineau's *Life in the Sickroom* demonstrates the fascination of Victorian writers and audiences with the function of convalescence. Frawley argues that Martineau and other writers used the trope of convalescence as a means to argue for a period of physical rest that allowed one to perform the "work" of exercising the mind upon the meaning of one's existence. Cindy LaCom lays out a significant body of work in nineteenth-century Britain that deploys disabled female characters. Her analysis argues that disability often precluded female characters from "healthy" heterosexual courtship rituals. As a consequence, works by canonical male writers such as Anthony Trollope tend to use disabled female characters as sexual sycophants. As an alternative, writing by women such as Charlotte Yonge employs disabled female figures as powerful novelistic presences who resist the sexualized objectifications of their male counterparts. In a book that applies disability studies paradigms to American literature and culture (*Extraordi-*

nary Bodies), Rosemarie Garland Thomson traces out the pervasive presence of disabled female figures in women's sentimental fiction. In order to establish the graceful, self-effacing presence of the angel in the house, nineteenth-century American women writers use disabled female foils who are domestically awkward and non-self-sufficient to artificially augment the virtues of their female protagonists. Thomson traces this trope across the work of influential writers such as Harriet Beecher Stowe, Rebecca Harding Davis, and Elizabeth Stuart Phelps.

Chapter 6

This chapter first appeared in *The Disability Studies Reader,* edited by Lennard Davis (New York: Routledge, 1998).

1. Brian McHale endeavors to elude the critique of assigning a definition to postmodernism by explaining that the conundrum of the critic is to "insist[ ] on the discursive and constructed character of Postmodernism . . . while at the same time preserving a sense of the provisionality, the 'as if' character, of all such constructions" (1). In this chapter we want to argue that while Dunn's *Geek Love* is not synonymous with a definition of postmodernism, it does share some important characteristics with other works that have come to be associated with the critical rubric itself.

2. We are using Mikhail Bakhtin's notion of the grotesque here as a way of gesturing toward literary conventions that have dominated the deployment of the body as a fantastical landscape that can be distorted for social, aesthetic, and political ends. While Bakhtin's arguments refer to an utterly constructed "body" in the literature of folklore and, in particular, the work of Rabelais, we use it in this chapter to represent a critical tradition that discusses the body as a "tool" available to art. Although the concept of the "literary grotesque" is distinct from representations of disability in literature, the two share cultural coordinates and, thus, inform one another.

3. Bakhtin makes this connection between exterior and interior lives when he argues that the grotesque performs a critical task of mediation for its audience: "As we suggest, the grotesque ignores the impenetrable surface that closes and limits the body as a completed phenomenon. The grotesque image displays not only the outward but also the inner features of the body: blood, bowels, heart and other organs. The outward and inward features are often merged into one" (Bakhtin 318).

4. Ironically, it is Anderson's theory of "static" truths that parallels the complaints against "fixing" the meaning of postmodernism that we cited in note 1. To construct a definition of self or a literary category echoes with alarms of a less dynamic existence that "perverts" Anderson's characters and reverberates into our current critical climate.

5. Many scholars have analyzed the disturbing intersections between early-twentieth-century art, literary modernism, and the ascendancy of the eugenics movement. See, for example, Norden; Trombley; Pernick; and Gilman, *Difference and Pathology.*

6. Part of Fiedler's grouping of artists wallowing in an age of the "explicit" are John Barth, Brian DePalma, Craig Nova, James Joyce, Ursula LeGuin, Alan Fried-mann, and Lindsay Gresham.

7. The mid–nineteenth century charged that "in theories of monstrosity the maternal element repressed the legitimate father. The maternal imagination erased the legitimate father's image from his offspring and thus created a monster" (Huet 8). Thus, Dunn involves herself in an inversion or revision of this paradigm in explaining that Aloysius gives birth to the idea of conceiving his own carnival of birth defects, thus reestablishing the father's hand in the tetratogenic process.

Afterword

1. One can find Lord Byron's recasting of Shakespeare's villainous hunchback Richard III in his own Faustian drama *The Deformed Transformed*. Byron, who had a club foot, claimed that the source of his dramatic effort stemmed from an incident in his childhood when his mother called him "a lame brat" in a moment of rage. According to the dramatist, the outburst plunged him into a life of self-consciousness over the visibility of his "deformity" (Byron 477).

Importantly, *The Deformed Transformed* centers upon the yearnings of a dis-abled protagonist named Arnold, who believes his "hunchback" deprives him of love from family and women alike. While Arnold is contemplating thoughts of sui-cide as a drastic alleviation of his social predicament, Satan materializes and offers to take Arnold's soul in exchange for the aesthetically perfect body of Achilles. Iron-ically, after Arnold takes on the body of Achilles and Satan perversely dons Arnold's sloughed-off disabled exterior, the protagonist discovers that his conquered lover, Olimpia, spurns him for the misshapen visage of his hellish counterpart. Such an outcome underscores Byron's interest in distancing disability from its too singular association with the despair that he believed characterized the essence of "the human condition."

Byron believed that *The Deformed Transformed* would prove to be his magnum opus. Yet when Shelley read an early draft and told him that he thought the work uninspired and derivative of Goethe, Byron threw the entire manuscript into the fire. Despite the melodramatic gesture of disgust with Shelley's response, Byron had secretly kept another copy of the manuscript hidden. The drama was never finished and Act III only exists in an incomplete, albeit evocative, state.

2. For a lucid interpretation of the effects of Walter Benjamin's concepts of rev-olutionary interpretive and literary practices see Eagleton's *Walter Benjamin*, 112–13, in particular, which spells out useful conjunctures between representational analyses, close-reading habits, and political praxis. Roland Barthes, during his Marxist-deconstructivist phase, contends in *Le plaisir du texte* that slower reading practices yield an interrogative vantage. Jacques Derrida, of course, stakes much of the politics of deconstruction on this point. See in particular, his defense of the pol-itics of deconstructive reading as yielding a deliberative politics in "But Beyond."

3. Joan Didion discusses the centrality of Hemingway's bouts with depression and disability in "Last Words."

4. Didion picks up the antinarrative necessities inaugurated by disability recognitions directly. "The White Album" begins at a time "when I began to doubt the premises of all the stories I had ever told myself"—a time when the public image of Didion as an accomplished writer conflicts with the inaccurate psychiatric reports that find her symptoms to be a product of delusion. Didion's version of multiple sclerosis as a diagnosis without meaning only applies because this essay will not offer up the day-to-day life of negotiating MS. Though, in reflection, we get exactly that in an essay where "all connections were equally meaningful and equally senseless." The periodic remissions and exacerbations of the disorder's course follow the narrative "rerouting" that Didion works at achieving: "the nervous system gradually changes its circuitry, and finds other, unaffected nerves to carry the same messages" (44).

5. Caulfield's admiration for Richard Kinsella's "digressions" into disability narration is made to correspond to Salinger's own narrative methods. Holden's younger brother's death from leukemia, the incident that precipitates the narrative, is included as an afterthought to an in-depth description of the baseball glove Holden inherits from him. Only through indirection and digression, upon his roommate's pleading for a plagiarized essay no less, does Holden Caulfield divulge his brother Allie's death from leukemia. Looking for a descriptive essay topic, Holden unearths a left-handed baseball glove, inscribed with poems in green ink. After protracted detailing of the glove's appearance, he explains, "It belonged to my brother Allie. He's dead now." In this, Holden duplicates the method of digression he admires in his fellow student's oral reports.

Like Montaigne's description of Socrates' shoes (discussed in chapter 2), Allie's glove signifies the absence of Allie in its own tangible preservation of his body. Unlike Socrates' shoes, the glove bears little evidence of the wearer's unique physical imprint. Rather, Allie's immersion in poetical traditions, his inscription of other poets' words upon every available square inch of leather, becomes his defining uniqueness—a literary commitment that has been lost. Allie's glove evokes its wearer—and his now haunting absence—as a crossroads of poetical countertexts. Baseball gloves don't easily assume the shape of their wearer, but like the participatory life that gives Holden so much trouble, they provide a substitute shape that is vaguely modeled on a human original. Perfect prosthetics, baseball mitts extend the capacity of hands for the single act of catching balls. This glove embodies Allie's outfielder strategy; while he dons the shape of participation, poetry enables him to stay in the game. With green ink camouflaging the words, Allie appeared a member of the team. Allie's ability to blend team sport and literary commitment evades his older brother; Holden views Allie's "pretense" of involvement in both worlds as a lost art.

6. The narrative of eradication that undergirds eugenics finds forceful expression in a popular 1904 textbook: "Physical, mental, and moral degenerates are increasing out of proportion to the increase of normal classes . . . we will never empty the jails, reformatories, penitentiaries, and insane asylums by legislation

alone" (*Eugenics* i). In its detailing of a "Black Stork" documentary film, such as that shown for educational purposes by the Lister Foundation, *Catcher* notifies readers that a U.S.-based euthanasia movement precedes the Nazi social policy of murdering disabled people. In opposing movieland's plot-driven resolutions and the dangerous "realism" of medical murder, literary antinarrative will seek a means for pursuing "incurables" by positing a moral high ground in digression. See Martin Pernick's *The Black Stork* for analyses of the many popular "bio-pic" films that sought to validate euthanasia of disabled infants in 1910s and 1920s America.

7. Jem said, "He goes out, all right, when it's pitch dark. Miss Stephanie Crawford said she woke up in the middle of the night one time and saw him looking straight through the window at her . . . said his head was like a skull lookin' at her . . . Boo was about six-and-a-half feet tall, judging from his tracks; he dined on raw squirrels and any cats he could catch, that's why his hands were bloodstained—if you ate an animal raw, you could never wash the blood off. There was a long jagged scar that ran across his face; what teeth he had were yellow and rotten; his eyes popped, and he drooled most of the time. 'Let's try to make him come out,' said Dill, 'I'd like to see what he looks like' " (13).

8. Only a small number of other films have utilized disabled actors in film roles. Most notorious is the 1932 film *Freaks* by Tod Browning, which depicts the revenge of freak-show performers upon their able-bodied fellows. The 1946 film drama *The Best Years of Our Lives* employs a double amputee (Harold Russell) to portray the struggles of a vet returning from World War II. During a discussion in our video *Vital Signs* of the special effects used to "disable" actor Gary Sinese in the movie, *Forrest Gump,* the writer Kenny Fries points out that unlike other minority portrayals, disabled people are not allowed to play themselves even when the script calls for a disabled character. Special effects could as easily "make" a disabled actor a "walkie" for early, predisability scenes.

9. In a critical study of children's fiction, Jacqueline Rose argues that the classification, children's fiction, is a misnomer. Adults who write and read stories to children emphasize the separate "worlds" of adults and children. "Children's fiction" embodies the instructional objectives and moral imperatives of an adult world. In Rose's view, childhood as a separate region emerges as an invention of adults. Consequently "Children are no threat to [adult] identity because they are, so to speak, 'on their way.' . . . Their difference stands purely as the sign of just how far [adults] have progressed" (13).

Works Cited

Albrecht, Gary. *The Disability Business*. Newbury Park, CA: Sage, 1994.

American Film Institute's 1912 Richard III. 2800 West Olive Avenue. Burbank, CA 91505.

Anderson, Sherwood. *Winesburg, Ohio*. 1919. New York: Penguin, 1982.

Aristotle. *Aristotle on the Athenian Constitution*. Trans. F. G. Kenyon. London: George Bell and Sons, 1904.

Bacon, Francis. *Francis Bacon: A Selection of His Works*. Ed. S. Warhaft. Toronto: Macmillan, 1965.

Bakhtin, Mikhail. *Rabelais and His World*. Trans. Helene Iswolski. Bloomington: Indiana UP, 1984.

Barbauld, Anna Laetitia. *The Works of Anna Laetitia Barbauld With a Memoir*. Vol. 2. London: Paternoster-Row, 1825.

Barthes, Roland. *Le Plaisir du Texte*. Paris: Éditions du Seuil, 1973.

———. *S/Z: An Essay*. 1970. Trans. R. Miller. New York: Hill and Wang, 1974.

Barton, Tamsyn S. *Power and Knowledge: Astrology, Physiognomics, and Medicine under the Roman Empire*. Ann Arbor: U of Michigan P, 1994.

Berkowitz, Peter. *The Ethics of an Immoralist*. Cambridge: Harvard UP, 1995.

Berry, Ralph. "Richard III: Bonding the Audience." In *Mirror Up to Shakespeare: Essays in Honour of G. R. Hibbard*. Ed. J. C. Gray. Toronto: U of Toronto P, 1984: 114–27.

Blanchot, Maurice. *The Space of Literature*. 1955. Trans. Ann Smock. Lincoln: U of Nebraska P, 1982.

Bladerunner. Dir. Ridley Scott. Perf. Rutger Hauer. 1982.

Blau, Herbert. "Responses to Leslie Fiedler: I. Herbert Blau." International Center for the Disabled in Collaboration with the United Nations. *Pity and Fear: Myths and Images of the Disabled in Literature, Old and New*. Proceedings of a Literary Symposium, 1985: 14–20.

Block, Laurie, with Jay Allison. *Beyond Affliction: The Disability History Project*. National Public Radio, 1998.

Bogdan, Robert. *Freak Show: Presenting Human Oddities for Amusement and Profit*. Chicago: U of Chicago P, 1990.

Bordo, Susan. *Unbearable Weight: Feminism, Western Culture, and the Body*. Berkeley: U of California P, 1993.

Braddock, David, and Susan Parish. "An Institutional History of Cognitive Disability." In *The Disability Studies Handbook*. Ed. G. Albrecht, M. Bury, and K. Selman. Newbury Park, CA: Sage, 2000 (forthcoming).

Bragg, Lois. "From the Mute God to the Lesser God: Disability in Medieval Celtic and Old Norse Literature." *Disability and Society* 12 (2) (1997): 165–77.

Brown, Constance. "Olivier's *Richard III*: A Re-evaluation." *Film Quarterly* 20 (1967): 23–32.

Brown, Eleanor Gertrude. *Milton's Blindness*. 1934. New York: Columbia UP, 1974.

Brueggemann, Brenda, Sharon Snyder, and Rosemarie Garland Thomson, eds. *Enabling the Humanities: A Disability Studies Sourcebook*. New York: Modern Languages Association, 2001 (forthcoming).

———. *Lend Me Your Ears: Rhetorical Constructions of Deafness*. Washington, D.C.: Gallaudet U P, 1999.

Byron, Lord. *The Works of Lord Byron*. Ed. E. Coleridge. Vol. 5. New York: Charles Scribner's Sons, 1901.

Campbell, Katie. *The Steadfast Tin Soldier*. Morris Plains, New Jersey: Unicorn, 1990.

Canguilhem, Georges. *The Normal and Pathological*. Intro. M. Foucault. Trans. C. Fawcett and R. Cohen. New York: Zone, 1991.

Cavell, Stanley. *A Pitch of Philosophy: Autobiographical Exercises*. Cambridge: Harvard UP, 1994.

Cerasano, S. P. "Churls Just Wanna Have Fun: Reviewing *Richard III*." *Shakespeare Quarterly* 36 (5) (1985): 618–29.

Chambers, Ross. *Room for Maneuver: Reading the Oppositional in Narrative*. Chicago: U of Chicago P, 1991.

Colley, Scott. *Richard's Himself Again: A Stage History of Richard III*. New York: Greenwood, 1992.

Couser, G. Thomas. *Recovering Bodies: Illness, Disability, and Life Writing*. Madison: U of Wisconsin P, 1997.

Darke, Paul Anthony. "*The Elephant Man* (David Lynch, EMI Films, 1980): An Analysis from a Disabled Perspective." *Disability and Society* 9 (3) (1997): 327–42.

Davidson, Iain F. W. K., Gary Woodill, and Elizabeth Bredberg. "Images of Disability in Nineteenth Century Children's Literature." *Disability and Society* 9 (1) (1994): 33–46.

Davies, Anthony. *Filming Shakespeare's Plays: The Adaptations of Laurence Olivier, Orson Welles, Peter Brook, and Akira Kurosawa*. Cambridge: Cambridge UP, 1988.

Davis, Lennard. *The Disability Studies Reader*. New York: Routledge, 1997.

———. *Enforcing Normalcy: Disability, Deafness, and the Body*. New York: Verso, 1995.

———. "Normalcy and the Novel." *The Disability Studies Handbook*. Ed. G. Albrecht, M. Bury, and K. Seelman. Newbury Park, CA: Sage, 2000 (forthcoming).

de Baecque, Antoine. *The Body Politic: Corporeal Metaphor in Revolutionary France, 1770–1800*. 1993. Trans. Charlotte Mandell. Stanford: Stanford UP, 1997.

de Certeau, Michel. *Heterologies: Discourse on the Other*. Trans. Brian Massumi. Manchester: Manchester UP, 1986.

Derrida, Jacques. "But, Beyond . . . (An Open Letter to Anne McClintock and Rob Nixon)." In *"Race," Writing, and Difference*. Ed. H. Louis Gates Jr. Chicago: U of Chicago P, 1985.

Deutsch, Helen. "The Exemplary Case of Dr. Johnson." In *Enabling the Humanities: A Disability Studies Sourcebook*, ed. B. Brueggemann, R. Garland-Thomson, and S. Snyder. New York: Modern Languages Association, 2001 (forthcoming).

———. *Resemblance and Disgrace: Alexander Pope and the Deformation of Culture*. Cambridge: Harvard UP, 1996.

Deutsch, Helen, and Felicity Nussbaum, eds. *"Defects": Engendering the Modern Body*. Arbor: U of Michigan P, 1999.

Didion, Joan. "Last Words." *New Yorker*, November 1998, 74–80.

———. "The White Album." *The White Album*. New York: Simon and Schuster, 1970: 11–48.

Dimock, Wai-chee. *Empire for Liberty: Melville and the Poetics of Individualism*. Princeton: Princeton UP, 1989.

Dodd, William. *The Beauties of Shakespeare*. London: T. Waller, 1757.

Dryden, John. *The Dramatic Works*. New York: Gordian, 1968.

Dubus, Andre. "An Interview with Andre Dubus." *AWP Chronicle* 29 (1) (1996): 1–6.

Dunn, Katherine. *Geek Love*. New York: Warner, 1989.

Eagleton, Terry. *Walter Benjamin; or, Towards a Revolutionary Criticism*. 1981. London: Verso, 1985.

Eberly, Susan Schoon. "Fairies and the Folklore of Disability: Changelings, Hybrids, and the Solitary Fairy." *Folklore* 99 (1) (1988): 58–77.

Ellmann, Richard, and Charles Feidelson Jr., eds. *The Modern Tradition: Backgrounds of Modern Literature*. New York: Oxford University Press, 1965.

Emerson, Ralph Waldo. *Essays and Journals*. Intro. Lewis Mumford. Garden City, NY: International Collectors Library, 1968.

The English Patient. Dir. Anthony Minghella. 1996.

Evans, Elizabeth Cornelia. *Physiognomics in the Ancient World*. Philadelphia: American Philosophical Society, 1969.

Faulkner, William. *The Sound and the Fury*. 1927. New York: Vintage International, 1990.

Fiedler, Leslie A. *Freaks: Myths and Images of the Secret Self*. New York: Simon and Schuster, 1978.

———. "The Higher Sentimentality." *One Flew Over the Cuckoo's Nest*. 1962. New York: Viking/Penguin, 1996: 386–95.

———. "Pity and Fear: Myths and Images of the Disabled in Literature and the Popular Arts." International Center for the Disabled in Collaboration with the United Nations. *Pity and Fear: Myths and Images of the Disabled in Literature, Old and New.* Proceedings of a Literary Symposium, 1981: 1–13.

Finger, Ann. "Helen and Frida." *Kenyon Review* 16 (summer 1994): 1–7.

Frame, Donald. *Montaigne's "Essais": A Study.* Englewood Cliffs, NJ: Prentice-Hall, 1969.

Frantic. Dir. Roman Polanski, 1987.

Frawley, Maria. "'A Prisoner to the Couch': Harriet Martineau, Invalidism, and Self-Representation." *The Body and Physical Difference: Discourses of Disability.* Ed. David T. Mitchell and Sharon L. Snyder. Ann Arbor: U of Michigan P, 1997: 174–88.

Freaks. Dir. Tod Browning, 1932.

Friedlander, Henry. *The Origins of Nazi Genocide: From Euthanasia to the Final Solution.* Chapel Hill: U of North Carolina P, 1995.

Frow, John. *Cultural Studies and Cultural Values.* Oxford: Clarendon Press, 1995.

Garland, Robert. *The Eye of the Beholder: Deformity and Disability in the Graeco-Roman World.* Ithaca, NY: Cornell UP, 1995.

Gartner, Alan, and Tom Joe. *Images of the Disabled, Disabling Images.* Praeger, 1987.

Gilman, Sander. *Difference and Pathology.* Ithaca: Cornell UP, 1985.

———. *The Jew's Body.* New York: Routledge, 1991.

Girard, René. *Violence and the Sacred.* 1972. Trans. Patrick Gregory. Baltimore: Johns Hopkins UP, 1977.

Gleeson, B. J. "Disability Studies: A Historical Materialist View." *Disability and Society* 12 (2) (1997): 179–202.

Greenblatt, Stephen. *Renaissance Self-Fashioning from More to Shakespeare.* Chicago: U of Chicago P, 1980.

Griffith, Mrs. Elizabeth. *The Morality of Shakespeare's Dramas.* London: T. Cadell, 1775.

Grosz, Elizabeth. *Volatile Bodies: Toward a Corporeal Feminism.* Bloomington: Indiana UP, 1994.

Hafferty, Frederic W. and Susan Foster. "Decontextualizing Disability in the Crime Mystery Genre: The Case of the Invisible Handicap." *Disability and Society* 9 (2) (1994): 185–206.

Halberstam, Judith. *Skin Shows: Gothic Horror and the Technology of Monsters.* Durham, NC: Duke University P, 1995.

Hankey, Julie. *Richard III: Plays in Performance.* Totowa, NJ: Barnes and Noble, 1981.

Haraway, Donna. *Primate Visions: Gender, Race, and Nature in the World of Modern Science.* New York: Routledge, 1989.

Hayles, N. Katherine. "Postmodern Parataxis: Embodied Texts, Weightless Information." *American Literary History* 2 (3) (1990): 394–421.

Heidegger, Martin. *Nietzsche.* Vol. 2: *The Eternal Recurrence of the Same.* Trans. David F. Krell. New York: Harper and Row, 1984.

Hemingway, Ernest. *The Sun Also Rises*. 1926. New York: Collier, 1986.

Herndl, Diane Price. *Invalid Women: Figuring Feminine Illness in American Fiction and Culture, 1840–1940*. Chapel Hill: U of North Carolina P, 1994.

Hevey, David. *The Creatures That Time Forgot: Photography and Disability Imagery*. New York: Routledge, 1992.

Holmes, Martha Stoddard. *Fictions of Affliction: Physical Disabilities in Victorian Culture*. Ann Arbor: U of Michigan P, 2000.

Huet, Marie-Helene. *Monstrous Imagination*. Cambridge: Harvard UP, 1993.

Hughes, Bill, and Kevin Paterson. "The Social Model of Disability and the Disappearing Body: Towards a Sociology of Impairment." *Disability and Society* 12 (3) (1997): 325–40.

I Know What You Did Last Summer. Dir. Jim Gillespie. 1997.

Jeffreys, Mark. "The Visible Cripple (Scars and Other Disfiguring Displays Included)." *Enabling the Humanities: A Disability Studies Sourcebook*. Ed. B. Brueggemann, R. Garland-Thomson, and S. Snyder. New York: Modern Lanaguages Asssociation, 2001 (forthcoming).

Jung, C. G. *Nietzsche's "Zarathustra": Notes of the Seminar Given in 1934–1939*. Ed. James L. Jarret. Vol. 2. Princeton: Princeton UP, 1988.

Kant, Immanuel. *Lectures on Ethics*. Trans. J. B. Schneewind. 1930. New York: Harper and Row, 1963.

Kent, Deborah. "Disabled Women: Portraits in Fiction and Drama." *Images of the Disabled, Disabling Images*. Ed. A. Gartner and T. Joe. New York: Praeger, 1987: 47–63.

Kermode, Frank. *The Sense of an Ending: Studies in the Theory of Fiction*. London: Oxford UP, 1968.

Kesey, Ken. *One Flew Over the Cuckoo's Nest*. 1962. New York: Viking/Penguin, 1996.

Krell, David Farrell. *Infectious Nietzsche*. Bloomington: Indiana UP, 1996.

Kriegel, Leonard. "Disability as Metaphor in Literature." *Images of the Disabled, Disabling Images*. Ed. A. Gartner and T. Joe. New York: Praeger, 1987: 31–46.

Kuhse, Helga, and Peter Singer. *Should the Baby Live? The Problem of Handicapped Infants*. Oxford: Oxford UP, 1985.

LaCom, Cindy. "'It Is More Than Lame': Female Disability, Sexuality, and the Maternal in the 19th-Century Novel." *The Body and Physical Difference: Discourses of Disability*. Ed. D. Mitchell and S. Snyder. Ann Arbor: U of Michigan P, 1997: 189–201.

Lee, Harper. *To Kill a Mockingbird*. 1960. New York: Warner, 1982.

L'Estrange, Roger. *A History of the Life of Aesop*. London: Thomas and Tappan, 1808.

Lichtenberg, Georg Christoph. *Hogarth on High Life: The Marriage à la Mode Series from . . . Commentaries*. Trans. and ed. Arthur S. Wensinger with W. B. Coley. Middletown, CT: Wesleyan UP, 1970.

———. *Über Physiognomik, wider die Physiognomen. Zu Beförderung der Men-*

schenliebe und Menschenkenntniss. Steinbach: Anabas Verlag Günter Kämpf, 1970.

Limon, John. *The Place of Fiction in the Time of Science: A Disciplinary History of American Writing.* Cambridge: Cambridge UP, 1990.

Longmore, Paul. "Screening Stereotypes: Images of Disabled People in Television and Motion Pictures." *Social Policy* (summer 1985): 31–38. Rpt. in *Images of the Disabled, Disabling Images.* Ed. A. Gartner and T. Joe. New York: Praeger, 1997: 65–78.

Looking for Richard. Dir. Al Pacino. 1996.

Lowell, Robert. *Life Studies.* New York: Farrar, Strauss, and Cudahy, 1959.

Mack, Maynard. *Alexander Pope: A Life.* 1985. New York: Norton, 1988.

Markels, Julian. *Melville and the Politics of Identity: From "King Lear" to "Moby-Dick."* Urbana: U of Illinois P, 1993.

Martin, Terence. "The Romance." *The Columbia History of the American Novel.* Ed. Emory Elliott. New York: Columbia UP, 1991.

McCarter, P. Kyle, Jr. *II Samuel: A New Translation with Introduction, Notes, and Commentary.* Garden City, NY: Doubleday, 1984.

McHale, Brian. *Constructing Postmodernism.* New York: Routledge, 1992.

McKellen, Ian, and Richard Loncraine. *William Shakespeare's "Richard III": A Screenplay.* Woodstock, NY: Overlook, 1996.

Meijer, Marianne S. "Guesswork or Facts: Connections between Montaigne's Last Three Chapters (III: 11, 12 and 13). *Yale French Studies* 64 (1983): 167–79.

Melville, Herman. *Moby-Dick.* Ed. H. Hayford and H. Parker. New York: Norton, 1967.

———. *Moby-Dick; or, The Whale.* Ed. Harrison Hayford, Hershel Parker, and G. Thomas Tanselle. Evanston: Northwestern UP, Chicago: Newberry Library, 1988.

Miller, Donald S., and Ethel H. Davis. "Disabled Authors and Fictional Counterparts." *Clinical Orthopedics and Related Research* 89 (Nov.–Dec. 1972): 76–93.

———. "Shakespeare and Orthopedics." *Surgery, Gynecology, and Obstetrics,* February 1969, 358–66.

Mitchell, David T., and Sharon L. Snyder. "Exploring Foundations: Languages of Disability, Identity, and Culture." *Disability Studies Quarterly* 17 (4) (1997): 241–47.

———. *Vital Signs: Crip Culture Talks Back.* Brace Yourselves Productions. Marquette, MI. 48 mins. Beta SP, 1996.

Mitchell, David T., and Sharon L. Snyder, eds. *The Body and Physical Difference: Discourses of Disability.* Ann Arbor: U of Michigan P, 1997.

Montaigne, Michel de. *The Complete Works of Montaigne: Essays, Travel Journal, Letters.* Trans. Donald Frame. Stanford: Stanford UP, 1948.

———. *Les Essais de Michel de Montaigne.* Ed. Pierre Villey. Paris: Librairie Félix Alcan, 1931.

Morris, Meaghan. *The Pirate's Fiancee: Feminism, Reading, Postmodernism.* London: Verso, 1988.

Murphy, Robert. "Encounters: The Body Silent in America." *Disability and Culture.* Ed. Benedicte Ingstad and Susan Reynolds White. Berkeley: U of California P, 1995: 140–58.

Nietzsche, Förster. *The Life of Nietzsche: The Lonely Nietzsche.* Trans. Paul V. Cohn. Vol. 2. New York: Sturgis and Walton, 1915.

Nietzsche, Friedrich. *Also Sprach Zarathustra: Ein Buch alle und keinen.* Stuttgart: Alfred Kröner Verlag, 1964.

———. *Götzendämmerung.* Stuttgart: Alfred Kröner Verlag, 1964.

———. *Thus Spoke Zarathustra.* Trans. Walter Kaufman. 1954. New York: Viking Penguin, 1966.

———. *Twilight of the Idols/The Anti-Christ.* Trans. R. J. Hollingdale. New York: Penguin Classics, 1990.

Norden, Martin. *The Cinema of Isolation: A History of Physical Disability in the Movies.* New Brunswick, NJ: Rutgers UP, 1994.

Oe, Kenzaburo. *A Healing Family: A Candid Account of Life with a Handicapped Son.* New York: Kodansha, 1996.

Ondaatje, Michael. *The English Patient.* New York: Knopf, 1982.

One Flew Over the Cuckoo's Nest. Dir. Milos Forman. 1975.

Paré, Ambroise. *Oeuvres Complètes.* Vol. 3. Paris: J. F. Malgaigne, 1841. Microprint, History of Science Collections, U of Oklahoma, 1970.

Paré, Ambroise. *On Monsters and Marvels.* Trans. Janis L. Pallister. Chicago: U of Chicago P, 1982.

Pernick, Martin. *The Black Stork: Eugenics and the Death of "Defective" Babies in American Medicine and Motion Pictures since 1915.* New York: Oxford UP, 1996.

Phillips, James E. "The Tempest and the Renaissance Idea of Man." *Shakespeare Quarterly* 15 (2), 1964: 147–59.

Plato. *The Symposium.* Trans. Alexander Nehamas and Paul Woodruff. Indianapolis: Hackett, 1989.

Pointon, Ann, and Chris Davies, eds. *Framed: Interrogating Disability in the Media.* London: British Film Institute, 1997.

Powers, Richard. *The Goldbug Variations.* New York: Harper-Collins, 1991.

———. *Operation Wandering Soul.* New York: William Morrow, 1993.

Plath, Sylvia. *The Bell Jar.* New York: Bantam, 1972.

Proctor, Robert. *Racial Hygiene: Medicine under the Nazis.* Cambridge: Harvard UP, 1988.

Pynchon, Thomas. *The Crying of Lot 49.* 1965. New York: Harper and Row, 1990.

Richard III. Dir. James Keane. Perf. Frederick Warde. 1912.

Richard III. Dir. Laurence Olivier. 1955.

Richard III. Dir. Richard Loncraine. Perf. Ian McKellen. 1995.

Richard III Society. "Was Richard III a Hunchback?" *Richard III and Yorkist History Server.* <www.richardiii.net/deformity.htm>.

Riding, Alan. "To Be, or Not to. . . , O.K., Cut!" *New York Times,* September 17, 1995, 17–18.

Robertson, John M. *Montaigne and Shakespeare: And Other Essays on Cognate Questions*. 1897. New York: Haskell House, 1968.

Rogin, Michael Paul. *Subversive Genealogy: The Politics and Art of Herman Melville*. New York: Knopf, 1983.

Ronell, Avital. *The Telephone Book: Technology, Schizophrenia, and Electric Speech*. Indianapolis: Indiana UP, 1990.

Rose, Jacqueline. *The Case of Peter Pan; or, The Impossibility of Children's Fiction*. London: Macmillan, 1984.

Salinger, J. D. *The Catcher in the Rye*. 1945. Boston: Little, Brown, 1991.

Sandblom, Philip. *Creativity and Disease: How Illness Affects Literature, Art, and Music*. 1982. New York: Marion Boyars, 1997.

Scarry, Elaine. *The Body in Pain: The Making and Unmaking of the World*. Oxford: Oxford UP, 1985.

Schor, Naomi. *Bad Objects: Essays Popular and Unpopular*. Durham, NC: Duke UP, 1995.

Scotch, Richard. *From Good Will to Civil Rights: Transforming Federal Disability Policy*. Philadelphia: Temple UP, 1984.

Shakespeare, Tom. "Cultural Representations of Disabled People: Dustbins for Disavowal." *Disability and Society* 9 (3) (1994): 283–99.

Shelley, Mary Wollstonecraft. *Frankenstein; or, The Modern Prometheus*. New York: Portland House Illustrated Classics, 1988.

Sher, Antony. *The Year of the King: An Actor's Diary and Sketchbook*. New York: Limelight Editions, 1994.

Snyder, Sharon, and David T. Mitchell. "Infinities of Forms." *Enabling the Humanities: A Sourcebook in Disability Studies*. Ed. B. Brueggemann, R. Garland-Thomson, and S. Snyder. New York: Modern Languages Association, 2001 (forthcoming).

Sophocles. *Oedipus the King*. Trans. F. Storr. New York: Washington Square, 1994.

Stafford, Barbara Maria. *Body Criticism: Imaging the Unseen in Enlightenment Art and Medicine*. Cambridge: MIT P, 1994.

Stafford, Jean. "Bad Characters." *Bad Characters*. New York: Farrar, Strauss, 1964: 3–30.

Starobinski, Jean. *Montaigne in Motion*. Trans. Arthur Goldhammer. 1982. Chicago: U of Chicago P, 1985.

Stechow, Wolfgang. *Bruegel*. 1940. New York: Henry N. Abrams, 1968.

Stegner, Wallace. *Angle of Repose*. 1971. New York: Penguin, 1992.

Stewart, Susan. "Of Ghosts and Prime Numbers." *Textual Analysis: Some Readers Reading*. Ed. M. A. Caws. New York: Modern Languages Association, 1986.

Stiker, Henri-Jacques. *A History of Disability*. Trans. William Sayers. Ann Arbor: U of Michigan P, 1999.

Stone, Deborah A. *The Disabled State*. Philadelphia: Temple UP, 1984.

Thiher, Allen. *Revels in Madness: Insanity in Medicine and Literature*. Ann Arbor: U of Michigan P, 1999.

Thomson, Rosemarie Garland. *Extraordinary Bodies: Figuring Physical Disability in American Culture and Literature.* New York: Columbia UP, 1997.

———. *Freakery: Cultural Spectacles of the Extraordinary Body.* New York: New York UP, 1996.

Thurber, Shari. "Disability and Monstrosity: A Look at Literary Distortions of Handicapping Conditions." *Rehabilitation Literature* 41 (1–2) (1980): 12–15.

Trombley, Stephen. *The Right to Reproduce: A History of Coercive Sterilization.* London: Weidenfeld and Nicolson, 1988.

Truitt, W. J. *Eugenics: The Science of Human Life.* Marietta, OH: S. A. Mullikin, 1916.

Vick, Marsha C. "'Defamiliarization' and the Ideology of Race in *Moby-Dick.*" *CLA Journal* 35 (March 1992): 325–38.

Wahl, Otto F. *Media Madness: Public Images of Mental Illness.* New Brunswick, NJ: Rutgers UP, 1995.

Wilson, Edwin, ed. *Shaw on Shakespeare: An Anthology of Bernard Shaw's Writings on the Plays and Production of Shakespeare.* New York: E. P. Dutton, 1961.

Wills, David. *Prosthesis.* Stanford: Stanford UP, 1995.

Winn, James Anderson. *John Dryden and His World.* New Haven: Yale UP, 1987.

Woolf, Virginia. *A Room of One's Own.* 1921. New York: Harcourt, Brace, 1981.

Ziarek, Ewa. "'Surface Stratified on Surface': A Reading of Ahab's Allegory." *Criticism* 31 (summer 1989): 271–86.

Žižek, Slavoj. *The Sublime Object of Ideology.* New York: Verso, 1989.

Zola, Irving. "'Any Distinguishing Features?'—the Portrayal of Disability in the Crime-Mystery Genre." *Policy Studies Journal* 15 (3) (1987): 487–513.

Index

abnormalcy, 38. *See also* normalcy
Addison, Joseph, 110
Aesop, 30, 109
Albrecht, Gary, xi
American Renaissance, 133
American Sign Language, 33
Americans with Disabilities Act, x
Anderson, Sherwood. See *Winesburg, Ohio*
Aristotle, 60
artists, disabled, 110. *See also* disability
Augustine, Saint, 71
Austin, Mary, 33
authors, disabled, 30–35, 163. *See also* disability
Awkward, Michael, ix

Bacon, Sir Francis, 32, 103, 106–7, 109, 114
Bakhtin, Mikhail, 142, 157–59
Banks, Russell, 13, 177
Barbauld, Laetitia, 133–34
Barthes, Roland, 48
Beauties of Shakespeare, The. See Dodd, William
Benjamin, Walter, 164, 170
Blackenstein, 100
Bladerunner, 100
Blanchot, Maurice, 48
Blau, Herbert, 16
Bodin, Jean, 71
body, as idealized norm, 7, 29, 38, 49–50, 121, 125, 138. *See also* disability; normalcy; physiognomy
Bordo, Susan, 49
Borges, Jorge Luis, 16
Bosch, Hieronymus, 4

Braddock, David, and Susan Parish, 168
Bragg, Lois, 42
Bredberg, Elizabeth. *See* Davidson, Iain F. W. K., Gary Woodill, and Elizabeth Bredberg
Brontë, Charlotte, 16
Brown, Constance A., 113
Brown, Eleanor Gertrude, 31
Browning, Robert, 177
Brueghel, Pieter, 4–5
Byron, Lord, 30, 32, 111, 163

Canguilhem, George, 29, 64, 121
Catcher in the Rye, The, 13, 50, 167, 169–71
Cavell, Stanley, 82–83
Certeau, Michel de, 53, 56, 70–71
Chambers, Ross, ix, xii, 48
changelings, 25–26
Christ, Jesus, 81, 83
Cibber, Colley, 112
cognitive disabilities, 27, 33, 39, 167, 173–75
counternarratives, 164, 173. *See also* disability
Couser, G. Thomas, 22
Crane, Stephen, 30
cripple, 4, 34–35; as erotic object, 74–75; of Montaigne and Nietzsche, 65–93

Darke, Paul, 23
Davidson, Iain F. W. K., Gary Woodill, and Elizabeth Bredberg, 26
Davies, Chris. *See* Pointon, Ann, and Chris Davies

Davis, Ethel H. *See* Miller, Donald S., and Ethel H. Davis
Davis, Lennard, 7, 28–30, 125, 164
deafness, 22–23, 33
de Baecque, Antoine, 62–63
de Beauvoir, Simone, 150
Defoe, Daniel, 32
Derrida, Jacques, 124
Descartes, René, 49, 137
determinism, 2, 159, 169
Deutsch, Helen, 31, 38
Dickens, Charles, 17, 36
Didion, Joan, 166
Dimock, Wai-chee, 119, 127–28
dire bodies, 135–36
disability: as deviance (stigma), x, 1–3, 5, 8, 17, 19, 35, 39–40, 48, 50, 53, 74–75, 85, 132, 152, 165; as device, of characterization, 1, 6, 10, 12, 17–18, 47–50, 55, 64, 135; in film, 95–101; hierarchies of, 3, 68, 121, 173; in identity politics, 35, 44, 165, 176; isolated (isolating), 20, 23, 29–30, 51, 135, 166, 173, 178; psychology of, reductive, 106, 113, 116, 123, 163; rights, movement for, 27, 35, 88, 109; as signifier, 3, 43, 47–48, 103–4, 106–7, 123; as social critique, 1, 12, 28, 34, 50, 104; and subjectivity, 1, 10, 13, 32, 42, 57–58, 93, 142, 149–52, 163–65, 174, 177–78
disability, historical perspective on: Enlightenment attitude toward, 11, 31, 66, 103, 106, 137; history of, 1, 40–45, 65, 161; literary history of, 48, 52–64; medieval attitude toward, 103; modern attitude toward, 12, 142–45, 160, 164–67; postmodern attitude toward, ix, 12, 142, 146–62, 164–67, 170, 176; Renaissance attitude toward, 4–5, 100–105, 108, 111, 113, 115; Restoration attitude toward, 107, 110; Romantic attitude toward, 129, 132–33, 163; Victorian attitude toward, 2, 12, 26–27, 42, 112, 121, 128, 131, 133–39
disability studies, ix, xiii–xiv, 40–45,

59, 114, 165–78; biographical criticism, 30–35; methodologies of representation, 10, 15–16; negative imagery, 16, 17–21, 23, 25, 37, 40; new historicism, 24–30; social realism, 21–25; transgressive reappropriation, 8, 21, 35–40
Dodd, William, 109, 113
Dryden, John, 107–9, 122
DuBois, W. E. B., 21
Dubus, Andre, 22
Dunn, Katherine. See *Geek Love*

Eberly, Susan Schoon, 25–26, 41
Edwards, Martha, 27
Egoyan, Atom, 13, 50, 177
Elephant Man, 23
Ellmann, Richard, and Charles Feidelson, 145
Ely, Bishop, 102
Emerson, Ralph Waldo, 82–83
English Patient, The, 95, 98
eugenics (euthanasia), 13, 28–29, 65, 167, 169–71
Evans, Elizabeth Cornelia, 60

Faulkner, William, 13, 50, 167–68, 174
Feidelson, Charles. *See* Ellmann, Richard, and Charles Feidelson
femininity, ix, 27–28, 158–59
Fiedler, Leslie, 13, 36, 39, 146–47, 152–53, 162
Foster, Susan. *See* Hafferty, Frederic W., and Susan Foster
Foucault, Michel, xi, 6
Frame, Donald, 67–69
Frankenstein, 16, 56, 100, 132, 136
Frantic, 100
Frawley, Maria, 27, 133
freak(s), 36, 150–62; freak show, 20, 37–38, 146–49
Freaks, 100
Freud, Sigmund, 125
Frow, John, 44

Gartner, Alan, and Tom Joe, 17
geek, 162

Geek Love, 12–13, 48, 50, 142, 146–62, 174
gender, ix, 33
Gerber, David, 29
Gilman, Charlotte Perkins, 27
gimp, 35
Glenville, Peter, 112
Goldfinger, 98
Gordon, Jan, 28
Greenblatt, Stephen, 105
Griffith, D. W., 97
Griffith, Mrs., 109–10
Grosz, Elizabeth, 57–58
grotesque(s), 34, 67, 69, 102, 142–49, 157, 160–62

Hafferty, Frederic W., and Susan Foster, 19–20, 22
Halberstam, Judith, 33
Hamilton, Elizabeth, 28
Hawthorne, Nathaniel, 27
Hayles, N. Katherine, 149
Hegel, Georg Wilhelm Friedrich, x
Heidegger, Martin, 83
Hemingway, Ernest, ix, 16, 165, 167
Hephaestus, 16, 42, 53
Herndl, Diane Price, 26–27, 133
Hevey, David, 23–24
Hitchcock, Alfred, 24, 98
Hitler, Adolf, 116
Holmes, Martha Stoddard, 42
Holocaust, 9, 13, 41
Hopper, Dennis, 98
Huet, Marie-Helene, 69
Hugo, Victor, 99

I Know What You Did Last Summer, 99
Iliad, 110

James, Henry, 111
Jeffrey, Mark, 97
Joe, Tom. *See* Gartner, Alan, and Tom Joe
Johnson, Samuel, 30–31
Jung, C. G., 80–81

Keats, John, 30

Kent, Deborah, 17, 21
Kermode, Frank, 164
Kesey, Ken. *See One Flew Over the Cuckoo's Nest*
Keyes, Daniel, 167
Krell, David Farrell, 134
Kriegel, Leonard, 17–19, 21

Lacan, Jacques, 50
LaCom, Cindy, 27, 133
Lavater, J. C., 58, 128
Lawrence, D. H., 28
Lee, Harper. *See To Kill a Mockingbird*
Lee, Nathaniel, 107
Longmore, Paul, 17–20, 29, 51, 164
Looking for Richard, 101, 116–17
Lowell, Robert, 166
Lukács, Georges, 21
Lumière, Auguste, 97

Mack, Maynard, 31, 110
madness, 39–40
Manet, Édouard, 4
Mansfield, Katherine, 30
Man with the Golden Arm, The, 98
"marked bodies," ix–xii, 54–55, 61, 133
Martineau, Harriet, 27
Marxism, 21; post-Marxism, 164
materiality of metaphor, 48–51, 57, 63
McHale, Brian, 141
McKellen, Ian, 115–16
Meijer, Marianne S., 67–69, 74
Melville, Herman. *See Moby-Dick*
Mesopotamia, 60
Miller, Donald S., and Ethel H. Davis, 112
Milton, John, 30–31
Miner, Madonna, 29
Mitchell, David, and Sharon Snyder, 27–28, 30, 43, 51
Moby-Dick, 11–12, 16, 17, 48, 50, 99, 119–39
modernism, 141. *See also* disability, historical perspective on
Molina, Caroline, 28
monstrosity (monsters), 38, 70–71, 77, 132, 152, 158, 172–73

Montaigne, Michel de, 16, 48, 50, 84, 89, 91–93, 95, 103, 106; and canni-balization of the Other, 70; "Infinities of Formes," 10–11, 66–78
More, Sir Thomas, 102
Morris, Meaghan, 9
Morrison, Toni, 16, 32, 167, 178
Murphy, Robert, xi

Narrative prosthesis, 1, 15, 17, 29, 41–43, 47–64, 66, 92, 98, 142–43, 161, 175–78; definition of, 4–10
Nature, 71–72, 105–6, 110, 131; nature, 145
Nazis, 3, 13, 41, 89, 95, 167, 169
Nietzsche, Friedrich, 9, 16, 34–35, 41, 48, 50, 66–68, 92–93, 95, 134, 170; and eternal return, 83, 85; and "higher men," 10–11, 87–89; and inverse cripples, 82–83, 155; *Thus Spoke Zarathustra*, 77–89; *Twilight of the Idols*, 34, 89–91; and Uber-mensch, 79–80, 84
Norden, Martin, 20
normalcy, 29, 37, 40, 48; anonymity of, 55, 154–57; narrative of, 164; normativity (normalizing), 8, 44, 51, 59, 70, 124, 156; "norms," 155–60
Novalis, 134
Nussbaum, Felicity, 27, 38

O'Connor, Flannery, 33, 168, 170
Oë, Kenzaburo, 16, 33, 51, 178
Oedipus the King, 10, 48, 61–62, 107
Olivier, Laurence, 112–13, 116
Ondaatje, Michael. See *English Patient, The*
One Flew Over the Cuckoo's Nest, 13, 50, 167, 173–74
Overbeck, Franz, 91

Pacino, Al, 101, 116–17
Paré, Ambroise, 71–73
Parish, Susan. See Braddock, David, and Susan Parish,
Passion Fish, 22

performing deformity, 103–17. *See also* disability
Pernick, Martin, 28
phrenology, 12, 128–29
physiognomy, 12, 58–61, 76–77, 96–97, 100, 111–12, 117, 128–31
Piano, The, 28
Plath, Sylvia, 165
Pointon, Ann, and Chris Davies, 20
Pope, Alexander, 30–32, 38, 110
postmodernism, 141. *See also* disability, historical perspective on
Powers, Richard, 13, 41, 50, 175–77
Pride of the Marines, The, 29
Prometheus, 131–32
prosthesis, xiii, 6–8, 123, 160; in *Geek Love*, 154; language of, 12, 124–27, 139; and prosthetic alteration, of Ahab, 120–39. *See also* narrative prosthesis
Proust, Marcel, 30
Pynchon, Thomas, 166

queer studies, 3

Rabelais, 157
race, ix, 2, 33, 159, 172, 176, 179
Random Harvest, The, 169. See also *Catcher in the Rye, The*
Raphael, 4
Reeves, Christopher, 24
Renaissance. *See* disability, historical perspective on
Restoration. *See* disability, historical perspective on
Richard III, 11, 16–18, 21, 32, 36, 48, 50, 55, 93, 101–17, 122, 163; film adaptations of, 95– 101. *See also* Warde, Frederick
Richard III Society, 102
Richard's Himself Again: A Stage History of "Richard III," 102–3
Rogin, Michael Paul, 119
Ronell, Avital, 160
Rousseau, Jean Jacques, 39

Salinger, J. D. See *Catcher in the Rye, The*

Sandblom, Philip, 32
Scarry, Elaine, x, 64
Schor, Naomi, 52
Scott, Sarah, 27, 38
Shaftesbury, earl of, 107
Shakespeare, Tom, 23
Shakespeare, William. See *Richard III*
Shaw, George Bernard, 111
Shelley, Mary Wollstonecraft. See *Frankenstein*
Sher, Anthony, 113–15
Snyder, Sharon. *See* Mitchell, David, and Sharon Snyder
Socrates, 30, 34, 76, 89–91, 109
Sophocles. See *Oedipus the King*
Stafford, Barbara Maria, 54, 58–60, 96, 108
Stafford, Jean, 165
Starobinski, Jean, 103
Steadfast Tin Soldier, The, 47, 54–56, 143
Stechow, Wolfgang, 4
Stegner, Wallace, 166
Steinbeck, John, 167
Stewart, Susan, 29
Stiker, Henri-Jacques, 44, 178
Stowe, Harriet Beecher, 172
subjectivity. *See* disability, and subjectivity
Sweet Hereafter, The, 13, 50, 177

Tacitus, 69
Thiher, Allen, 39–40
Thomson, Rosemarie Garland, 28, 37–39, 82, 120, 133

Thurber, Shari, 18
To Kill a Mockingbird, 13, 50, 167, 171–75
Touch of Evil, 100
Twain, Mark, ix, 33

Venus de Milo, 28
Vick, Marsha C., 119
Victorians. *See* disability, historical perspective on
Virgil, 106, 132

Wahl, Otto, 39
Walpole, Horace, 102
Warde, Frederick, 11, 97, 99–101, 114
War of the Roses, 104
Waterdance, 22
Whitman, Walt, 33
Wills, David, 7–8, 53, 124
Winesburg, Ohio, 12, 48, 50, 142–49, 164–65
Woodill, Gary. *See* Davidson, Iain F. W. K., Gary Woodill, and Elizabeth Bredberg
Woolf, Virginia, 21, 30, 33
World War II, 168–69

Year of the King, The, 113–15
York, House of, 102, 106
Yuan, David, 28

Ziarek, Ewa, 125
Žižek, Slavoj, x
Zola, Irving, 21–22

Printed and bound by CPI Group (UK) Ltd, Croydon, CR0 4YY

09/06/2025

14685670-0001